TUBOB

Two Years in West Africa with the Peace Corps

By

Mary E. Trimble

To Rachel
So good talking to you!
Mary E Trimble

Tubob
Two Years in West Africa with the Peace Corps

Tubob: Two Years in West Africa with the Peace Corps is a memoir. The author has made every effort to remain true to her experience. In some instances, names have been changed, and in the interest of clarity, some characters are combined.

Printed in the United States of America

Cover design and photography by Bruce Trimble

Published by ShelterGraphics
155 Woodgrove Lane
Camano Island, WA 98282

OTHER BOOKS BY MARY E. TRIMBLE

Tenderfoot

McClellan's Bluff

Rosemount

In loving memory of my parents,

Clinton and Elsie Fowler,

who primed me for adventure.

stuffed them into boxes kept under the desk. Within seconds he crawled back under the desk, cramming himself in front of the boxes. He was good. I was so proud of him.

Bruce's and my eyes locked. As we had joked many times in the past two years, we silently asked, "Whose idea was this anyway?"

Tom Mosier, head of United States Agency for International Development (USAID) in The Gambia, and George Scharffenberger came out from their safety places to greet our visitor. "Stay right where you are, folks," Tom said, his voice tight.

The door opened and a man strode in. He was probably an officer in charge; he reeked of authority. We couldn't tell if he was a nationalist or a rebel from the local security force, Field Force they called it, which, together with disgruntled leftists, had started the coup several days earlier. He was a big man and to me he looked sinister. My stomach clenched. His black face glistened with sweat. He carried a rifle and wore a hand gun at his side. His eyes darted around the room. "This is good. Stay under cover. I have ordered that this house is not to be hit, but you never know..."

He nodded to Tom and George, and left. No one spoke until we heard a soft knock on the door. He was gone. Bruce sprang up and reassembled the radios just as a signal was coming through. He brought the mic with him back under the desk.

"Candyland, Lollypop. Candyland, come in. You guys okay?"

Bruce responded, his rich voice calm. "Lollypop, Candyland. Yes, we're okay. One of the local officers just paid us a visit and..." An explosion, even closer this time, drowned out his voice.

Downtown Banjul

Chapter 2

*M*y long-held dream was coming true. Since I was a kid and read everything I could get my hands on about Africa, I'd longed to see it, hear it, smell it. Now that we were here, how would I react? What could I possibly say that would equal the elation I felt, finally realizing my dream? Africa!

The big Pan American 747 touched down. I'll never forget the day–July 20, 1979. As soon as we landed, the air conditioner stopped working. After an interminable delay, the plane lumbered to a stop. We'd arrived, I was in Africa! I turned to my husband Bruce, "If I don't get this bra off, it's going to melt right into my skin."

We stepped off the plane onto the hot, muggy tarmac, carrying our hand luggage. We filed into Senegal's Dakar airport, hot, thirsty and weary after nearly 24 hours of travel from our staging area in Philadelphia. I found a restroom and took off my bra, never to wear one again for the next two years.

Mingling with people in the airport, I noticed how dark they were with almost blue-black skin. Rarely had I seen such black people. Among the trainees, we had one African American, Al, and he was light by comparison. Al said to me, "Wow, I don't even feel like a black man here."

Our piles of luggage came to us on wheeled carts, luggage for a two-year stay for the nine of us trainees. Uniformed luggage handlers began shouting, pulling and shoving to get at the luggage. A tall fellow, white, maybe six feet six inches, stepped in and spoke in what we later learned was Wolof. The luggage handlers stepped back. George Scharffenberger introduced himself. He was the Assistant Director of Peace Corps, The Gambia, and he would accompany us the rest of the way to our assigned country.

We stepped forward in an orderly fashion to claim our luggage, two medium-sized trunks for the two of us, each weighing exactly forty pounds, the maximum allowed. After going through customs with George helping us through every step of the way, we loaded our luggage into a truck parked outside and we all climbed into a van bound for our hotel.

On the way George briefed us on what to expect, such as people trying to sell us things or wanting to take us places. He suggested we decline. The Dakar water wasn't safe to drink. "Drink only bottled water, even to brush your teeth." Keep your mouth closed when taking a shower. Travel in pairs, etc.

The van was relatively comfortable, but once we stepped out, it was like opening an oven door. We were ushered into the cool hotel. George's parting words were to the effect that we should enjoy the hotel's air conditioning, implying we wouldn't have it for the next two years.

* * *

We were staying only one night, so we didn't unpack more than what we needed for the next day. We had a few hours before George would pick up the group to take us to dinner.

Although it was tempting to stay in the cool room, perhaps take a nap, we wanted to see all that we could of Dakar, the capital of Senegal. And we needed bottled water. The small bottles furnished in our hotel room were drained dry the moment we stepped into our room.

About a half block from the hotel, a man approached and spoke to us first in French. Drawing blanks from us, he tried in English. "I want to be your friend. I am Mondou."

We smiled at the man and told him our first names. He was delighted. "Mr. Bruce, Miss Mary, let me show you what I will give to you, my new friends." He pulled out a heavy silver bracelet. Alarmed that we'd fallen into a trap so quickly, we put up our hands in rejection of the "gift."

"No, thank you," we said almost in unison.

We turned away, Bruce holding my arm firmly. We're long-time walkers, both tall with long strides, but we weren't a match for Mondou. He managed to get in front of us, blocking our way. "You don't like this one? Here, I have more." He opened his coat. Racks of jewelry hung from the inside of his coat. I wondered how, in that heat, it was even possible to wear a coat, let alone be burdened with all that heavy metal.

"No," Bruce said firmly. We turned away again.

"Here, let me give it to you as a gift."

"No, thank you," Bruce repeated.

Mondou stepped in front of us again, clearly irritated. "I am giving it to you as a gift," and slipped it into Bruce's shirt pocket.

"No, thank you, we...." Bruce began.

"You cannot refuse a gift." He had us there. We didn't know the culture well enough to know whether or not this was true.

"All right, thank you." We again turned. Mondou shouted at us. "When someone gives you a gift, then you must give him a gift!" People turned to look at the commotion.

Bruce sighed and pulled the bracelet out of his pocket. "Then, here, take it back." The man, angry now, shoved Bruce's hand away, acting offended to the core.

"Okay, have it your way. No deal, buddy." Bruce held my arm with a vice grip and we finally made distance between Mondou and us.

"Bruce, I need to get out of this heat." Between the temperature and the nasty scene with Mondou, it felt like my blood was beginning to boil. I noticed a little store. "Let's go in there and see if they have bottled water. Maybe air-conditioning."

In contrast to Mondou, the salesman in the store barely could be bothered to take our money. He had an item we wanted, needed, and he had all the time in the world to serve us. He didn't ask if there might be something more we needed, he just waited for us to make up our minds.

Armed with four liters of water, we made our way back to the hotel, assured that we'd seen all we needed to of Dakar.

A few minutes after seven, George picked up the nine of us in front of the hotel in the big white van. On the way he explained that he had been a Peace Corps volunteer in Senegal for four years. The home we were going to belonged to his African family. He gave us a few pointers on African etiquette. It was early evening and dark when we arrived and it had cooled down a bit. We stepped into a low concrete structure with a corrugated tin roof. The man of the house greeted George warmly, and as George introduced us, the man greeted us with a "hello" in English. George explained that was the only English our host knew.

One wooden chair graced the room, but, at George's example, we each folded ourselves down on one of several floor mats scattered around the room. Soon, the man's wife brought in a large shallow bowl of food. George suggested we all gather around. I looked for silverware, but then remembered they don't use eating implements. George helped himself first, using the first two fingers of his right hand as a scoop. The food went from the serving bowl into his mouth. The food was warm, but not hot, and served with a spicy meat sauce. It was good, at least the small portion I managed to get into my mouth. I noticed with dismay the amount of rice that sprinkled the front of my dress.

The host brought out bottles of soft drinks. "They don't usually drink anything with their food," George explained, "but they know you are new here and are very thirsty." I imagine that George actually paid for this meal, wanting us to have the experience of eating African food in an African home.

I heard voices nearby. "Won't the family be joining us?"

"No," George answered, "they eat separately from guests."

After dinner, George thanked the family in Wolof, said a few things that made them laugh, probably at our expense, and we left.

Our first meal in an African home was very special to me.

The next morning George again came for us. We packed our luggage into the pick-up truck and then piled into the van bound for the airport for the short flight to The Gambia.

Landing in The Gambia, our home for the next two years, was a huge milestone. We had been preparing for the Peace Corps for nearly a year by this time. From when we first investigated the possibility of joining the Peace Corps, to visiting their downtown Seattle offices, to choosing the country, and then wading through reams of paperwork to apply, it seemed surreal that we finally had reached our destination.

The Gambia, the smallest and westernmost country in Africa, is surrounded on three sides by Senegal with fifty miles of Atlantic Ocean coastline as its western border. At the western end, the country is not quite thirty miles wide on either side of the Gambia River and that belt of land narrows to about thirteen miles inland.

Again gathering our luggage, we piled into two smaller vehicles, Peugeot pickup trucks equipped to handle passengers in the truck bed, to be taken to a Catholic seminary now out for summer session. The Gambia was about ninety-seven percent Muslim, but there were a few Catholics and the Church had been trying for years to get a Gambian priest graduated from the seminary. So far it hadn't happened.

Our driver, who spoke no English, drove a long way before I noticed we appeared to be going in circles. He was lost! He finally got out of the truck to ask for directions. I could see his agitation and I felt my own anxiety. We finally arrived and joined the others who were inside waiting for us. The seminary, a two-story concrete building, was in Bakau, a suburb of the capital city, Banjul.

Yvonne Jackson, the Peace Corps Director for The Gambia, a pretty African American with relaxed curly hair worn in fashionable disarray, graciously greeted us and gave a little talk. George then briefed us on what we could expect for the next two days. In the meantime, we were wilted and ready to drop. It had been hours since we'd had anything to drink.

I finally spoke up. "George, is there a place we could get something to drink?" The others nodded.

"I'm so sorry, you all must be dying of thirst." He said something to a kitchen worker and they brought out pitchers of water, still warm from having been boiled, and glasses of assorted sizes and shapes. We all gulped water as fast as they could pour more into our glasses.

"Guys, I'm sorry," George apologized again. "It's dangerous for you to be this thirsty. Remember to always carry clean water with you." Clean water. That would be the theme of both our jobs for the next two years with the Peace Corps.

When we applied with the Peace Corps, we actually responded to a UNICEF (United Nations International Children's Emergency Fund) job at a well digging operation to be filled by a Peace Corps volunteer. The job description stated that the volunteer could be married, but the spouse must be willing to work in the health field. Bruce qualified to be mechanical advisor for a field office in a village at the far end of the country, "upriver," as they said. I was perfectly willing to be a health worker, though I couldn't imagine what that would entail.

We were the only married couple in our training group.

Our room at the seminary consisted of two metal-framed single beds of different heights, a chest of drawers, and a small table with two chairs. We pushed the beds together. Although there was no air conditioning in the seminary, a ceiling fan helped keep us relatively comfortable. We all shared a bathroom down the hall, men and women. Of course, it was a seminary, an all-boys' school. The house had a common room, what we would call a living room. A separate concrete building just a few steps away housed the dining hall, which would also be our classroom.

Our cook, Landing, and much of the kitchen staff would be with us for the duration of our ten weeks of training. We arrived mid-July and, if all went well, would be sworn in as Peace Corps volunteers at the end of September.

Meals seemed a little strange at first. Landing, a tall pleasant Gambian, tried very hard to please us with what he imagined was American food, served with silverware. Actually, he managed quite well with what was available, European canned goods and what fresh meat and vegetables he could find. All on a limited budget. The first meal of macaroni and cheese, ground beef patties and British canned green beans was tolerable. Having spent years cooking for a family, I could appreciate the effort he put into preparing our meals. Most of the others, freshly out of college, weren't so generous in their appraisal. Whenever Landing prepared a Gambian meal, however, it was superb. Bruce and I wished he would stick to what he did best. I was just thankful I didn't have to cook or do the dishes.

Another wonderful benefit during training was having our laundry done by women from a nearby village. We simply dumped it all in a pile—no name tags—and two or three times a week clean clothes appeared on sheets spread on the grass. Underwear in one section, dresses in another, pants in another. It's amazing how you recognize your own clothes. I don't recall losing even one article of clothing.

Many Africans at the seminary worked for the Peace Corps and made themselves available to help us. We soon learned which ones spoke English, who were the drivers, who had authority.

The first evening George outlined what our ten weeks of training would involve. Afterward our group of nine sat on a variety of chairs and stools placed around the wide hallway by our rooms, sharing observations. We were all excited with anticipation.

Settling into bed that first night, we marveled at the noise. Crickets chirped, traffic swept by with lots of honking, but almost drowning out everything else were men's noisy conversations. We couldn't understand a word, of course, but they were all talking very loud. Our room faced the front and they sat in the front yard of the seminary. It went on for hours. Of course, we were pretty keyed up, but both of us so tired, just dying to get some sleep. Finally, the group outside broke up, the traffic died down, then just the crickets chirped us to sleep. It was glorious. Hot, too, though the ceiling fan helped keep us comfortable.

We slept naked, with spare sheets close by in case we needed to cover ourselves. I dreamt I was being poked with needles. I kept pushing the needles away until I woke up enough to realize I really was being poked. Or bitten. I reached for my flashlight. Yikes! Ants marched across my body. I woke Bruce and he tracked down a trail of red ants. Bruce, who thinks of things like that, had brought a can of bug spray and he started at the origin of the organized march. We rid the bed of the little munchers, applied anti-itch (also Bruce's idea to bring) to my stomach and settled in again for a good night's sleep.

We were off to a bit of a rocky start, but things would smooth out, I was sure.

The Peace Corps office, Banjul

Chapter 3

*E*arly risers, Bruce and I didn't have to be awakened and had already been on an early morning walk, enjoying the relative coolness. We heard a cow bell being rung and figured it was our breakfast call. Edwaard, the bell ringer, took his job seriously and continued to ring the bell several minutes into the meal.

George, Assistant Peace Corps Director and in charge of our group, had returned to his own home for the night, but arrived by the time we finished our meal. This was Sunday, a day off for us. He suggested we try out the beach and told us how to get there, an easy ten-minute walk, through the American Chargé d'Affair's property and down the bluff to the beach. Or, we could go into Banjul and explore The Gambia's capital city. He told us where we could catch a bus and which bus to take back.

Among George's several warnings was one about wild dogs which were dangerous and rife with disease. They usually ran in packs and avoided people, but he warned us not to befriend them.

George gave each of us an envelope containing local currency, "walk-around money," he called it. "This is supposed to last until the end of the month, so use it carefully." It seemed a sufficient amount to me. After all, they were housing and feeding us.

Fellow volunteer Annie, in The Gambia to become a small business advisor, sat across the table. A recent college graduate, Annie was a pleasant, diminutive woman from Texas. "Would you guys like to go to Banjul with me?"

"Sure," I said, "let's go this morning and maybe we'll have time to check out the beach this afternoon." I glanced at Bruce and he nodded in agreement. We'd meet by the front door in a few minutes.

The half-hour bus ride allowed us to see a bit more of the countryside, though from the bus route we mostly saw industrial areas. Passengers shouted to one another as they boarded the bus. They often sat three to a seat, even though on a Sunday morning the bus wasn't crowded and there were empty seats. Several men carried heavy burlap bags; women carried basins of fresh produce, some had live chickens that they held upside down by their feet. The chickens didn't make a sound, but their eyes darted back and forth.

At what seemed like the center of town, people filed off the bus, most of them going into the market place. We followed.

Banjul, dirty, smelly and noisy, wasn't nearly as developed as Dakar, at least the parts we saw. True, we were new and didn't understand a lot of things, didn't know the language. No one approached us with something to sell, but the market seemed overwhelming. We'd left the seminary in a relatively cool morning, but by nine it was hot and made even more uncomfortable by crowds of people, ear-splitting noise of honking cars, shouting, and braying donkeys. More flies than I'd encountered in a lifetime buzzed at our sweaty faces.

Everywhere we went people called to us, "Tubob!" George had explained this meant "stranger," usually a white person. But they didn't say it in a mean way, or in a friendly way, either, just "Tubob" as a matter of fact. They didn't want anything from us, just to announce, apparently, that they knew we were strangers.

We had hoped to buy something at the market, but the experience was so cringy with the flies, noise, and crowds we lost interest. "Let's get out of here and just walk around," Bruce suggested.

It seemed cooler on the streets, but there was no safe place to walk without encountering honking cars, carts being pulled by donkeys and swarms of people. We walked to the outskirts of the downtown area, into more of a residential section, and again felt disappointment at what we saw. There were no huts with grass roofs like we'd seen in pictures, no tidy, swept compounds.

Annie observed that it looked like a shanty town and indeed it was. Pounded out tin corrugate used as walls, roofs and fences was the norm here. Row houses lined the streets, low, perhaps 10 feet wide, 50 feet long, concrete structures like the one we visited in Dakar, but not nearly as nice. Many of the houses looked like they had melted, perhaps worn away from rain, and many were blackened from years of cooking-fire smoke. It appeared many people cooked outside over open fires. Grimy strips of cloth covered doorways, probably for privacy but also to keep flies out.

Worst of all were the open sewers running along the street. The smell was awful. In places we found sidewalks made from blocks of concrete but occasionally a loose or uneven slab of concrete revealed flowing sewage underneath. Litter lined the streets and we witnessed many people throwing trash on the ground.

We decided we'd had enough and, following George's directions, found the bus stop to return to Bakau and the seminary. A single dog rushed up to us, a good-sized dog, maybe a German shepherd mix, waving his tail frantically. Remembering George's warning, we tried to shoo him away, but he insisted on staying near us, sitting close to our feet.

We'd move, so he wouldn't touch us, but he'd crowd closer. We willed the bus to come so we could rid ourselves of this latest threat.

A bus swayed toward us. The door swung open and the dog bounded in with Bruce. The bus driver glared at us. "No dog!"

"It isn't our dog," Bruce said.

"Get that dog off bus!" the driver commanded. Passengers gave us dirty looks and made efforts to avoid the dog.

"That is not my dog!" Bruce responded, but tried to make the dog get off the bus with no success. We found seats here and there on the crowded bus. None of us could sit together, but the dog stuck with Bruce and sat beneath his bare legs. Bruce visibly cringed, probably regretting wearing shorts. The bus driver shook his head in disgust and pulled out into the traffic, honking his way through town.

Finally reaching our destination, the three of us climbed off the bus, the dog at Bruce's heels. The driver shouted, "Next time you no take dog on bus!"

"At least the driver spoke English," Annie commented. I hadn't even thought about it, but it probably was unusual. On the other hand, The Gambia had been a British colony and the official language was English. We were told English was normally used with official business; otherwise, people spoke in tribal languages.

"What are we going to do about the dog?" I glanced at Bruce and could see he was about at the end of his patience.

He lunged at the dog. "Hey, get out of here!" The dog backed away, gave Bruce a sorrowful look and fell in behind us for the short distance to the seminary.

Arriving at the seminary, we hurried in and shut the door. A Catholic priest, an African from Senegal and teacher at the seminary, entered the room. We'd been introduced to him at breakfast. "Father," I began, "there's a dog that's been following..." and in bounded the dog through the open window, curtains parting on either side of him. The priest fled the room and slammed the door.

We stood looking at each other, wondering what to do. The dog, triumphant, sat next to Bruce, tail sweeping the floor.

Mr. DeCosta, one of the Gambians working for the Peace Corps as an instructor, entered the room and, seeing the dog, laughed. "That isn't a wild dog," he said. "He probably belonged to some tubob who had to leave. I'll take care of him."

He opened the door. "Come on, dog." The dog didn't move, apparently wanting to stay with us. Mr. DeCosta took him gently by the scruff of the neck. "Come on, boy." The dog reluctantly followed.

When Mr. DeCosta returned, I gathered my courage to find out what he'd done with the dog, fearing that he'd had the animal destroyed.

Mr. DeCosta nodded, apparently understanding my concern. "The Chargé d'Affair lives just down the street. I asked if the dog could live there and he said yes, he could be a part of the pack. That tubob has many dogs. The dog will be fine with him."

After lunch Bruce and I went to the beach. We invited Annie to join us but she decided to stay and read in her room. Covering our swim suits with regular clothes, we walked by many lovely homes. We later learned these homes housed mostly expatriates, people of different nationalities working for various Gambian agencies. Many of them had guards by their gates, as did the Chargé d'Affair. The guard saw our towels and waived us on. We followed the path through to the back leading to a high bank above a glorious beach.

Wide, sandy beaches graced the Atlantic Ocean. The ocean here was comfortably cool and refreshing. We both gave sighs of relief. How delightful to be comfortable and alone with each other. We saw two or three people from our group and waved, but we just spent the time together, in the water and with short bursts of lying in the sun.

At this point Bruce and I had been married for only one year. When staging in Philadelphia, Meri Aimes, who would later be my boss in The Gambia, took us aside. "The Peace

Corps experience can either make or break a marriage. If you guys feel your marriage is under strain, let us know. We'll make adjustments." She assured us we would be living and working in the same part of the country, though Bruce's job might require him to travel a bit in-country.

We went into this knowing that there would be challenges. To be alone, just the two of us, especially in training, would be rare, but very precious to us. We preferred each others' company, but tried, as with Annie, to be sociable.

We reluctantly left this beach paradise, fearing we'd be seriously sun-burned if we stayed longer. As we walked through the yard, we looked for the dog but didn't see him that day. They might have had him tied up until he got used to his new surroundings. But from time to time we'd see him at the Chargé d'Affair's residence as we walked through to go to the beach. He'd wag his tail at us, but never attempted to follow. He had a home and a good tubob to take care of him.

* * *

Monday morning, right after breakfast, training began. Gone were the days when trainees performed calisthenics. In the early Peace Corps days, training took place in the United States. For the last many years, training was usually held in-country. A big part of training is learning the cultural aspects of the country. The other, of course, is learning the local language. The two main languages spoken in The Gambia are Wolof and Mandinka, but there are seven languages commonly spoken in the country. The language we learned would depend on the type of work we'd be doing and where we'd be living. Volunteers living near Banjul, in the "downriver" part of the country, would learn Wolof. We would learn Mandinka, since we'd be living "upriver." With our group of nine, it was a five Wolof and four Mankinda split.

Mr. DeCosta briefed us on some of the cultural issues we needed to know. For instance, women never exposed their thighs and he suggested that we never wear shorts or short skirts. Bare breasts meant nothing here as women openly breast fed their children. But, he said, that would not be true of us. Tubob women should not show their breasts. Although this was a mostly Muslim country, women here did not totally cover their bodies like in some African countries. But modesty was important, for both men and women. Men, however, could wear walking shorts.

Mr. DeCosta, tall and stately, was an art teacher and an expert on local art, fabrics, wood, and ceramics. He radiated confidence and dignity, yet was always ready with a laugh. Having worked with Americans, Mr. DeCosta provided a wonderful bridge between cultures. One of his many jobs with Americans had involved working with Alex Haley's troop when he visited The Gambia to research his own Mandinka heritage and eventually publish his book *Roots*.

One of our projects that day involved going into Banjul for a briefing on health issues by the Peace Corps nurse, Ann Saar. A truck would take us there and the driver was ready to go. Bruce, however, had been asked to go to Yundum, near Banjul, so he could meet the people with whom he would be working. Since this was the rainy season, much of the shop business, such as equipment repair, was conducted at Yundum. Someone from the shop had come to the seminary to pick him up. Later, I could brief Bruce on the instructions from the nurse.

Then I remembered. Before we left our room that morning, one of the drivers had handed me a large envelope. He couldn't speak enough English to tell me what it was, but had said something that included the words "tubob" and "Banjul." I'd put it aside, thinking I'd figure it out later. Now it occurred to me that the envelope was something I needed to take. I ran up to our room to get it. When I returned, the truck was gone.

My heart thudded. Oh, no! What should I do? There were no other vehicles around. We were all too new to each other for anyone to realize I was missing.

Although we hadn't ridden in a taxi, I'd seen them on the streets. Coming from Seattle, I'd really never had the occasion to ride in a taxi. I'd seen them from time to time, mostly around the airport, but not as commonly as I knew they were, say, in New York. I went to the busy street in front of the seminary and hailed the first one I saw. Around Banjul, taxis are often regular cars, some with taxi markings, some not. A regular taxi stopped for me and I squeezed in, making four passengers in the back seat, two plus the driver in front. I tried to act confident, "Peace Corps building, please." No acknowledgment. Well, hopefully he heard me. I'd wait until we got into Banjul.

As we arrived everyone climbed out but me. "Peace Corps building," I repeated. The driver said something to one of the passengers, a nicely dressed African man with a briefcase, apparently a local businessman. The man leaned back into the taxi and in perfect English said, "This taxi only stops here. I will help you find this place."

Well, so much for not going places with a stranger. The man gestured for me to walk with him. "You are in the Peace Corps?"

"Yes, we just arrived and I got separated from my group."

"I think I know where this building is. I will take you there." He was a pleasant fellow and we chatted about the United States, where he had never been, but he had been to England. Our destination was a distance away and he took a wrong turn, asked for directions, and, to my immense relief, we finally arrived at the Peace Corps office, a rather drab yellow concrete building.

I shook his hand. "Thank you so much for your kindness. I never would have found this place without you."

He smiled at me and turned to leave. He stopped and turned back. "Thank you for coming to our country. I wish you well on your journey here." I appreciated his kind words.

Entering the air-conditioned building, I noticed many people talking and laughing, but no one looked familiar. Someone noticed me and said, "Your group is in Ann Saar's office," and pointed to a door down the hall.

When I joined my group, about six people asked, "How did you get here?" When I told them, many were surprised. Impressed even.

Ann Saar nodded and said, "You'll do fine here. Do you have something for me?" she asked.

"Yes, that's what I went back to my room for, then missed my ride." I handed her the envelope. It contained a briefing of all our medical histories.

Ann's talk was most informative, even a little scary. The country was rife with diseases developed countries no longer dealt with, such as tuberculosis, leprosy, and polio. People frequently died from tetanus, snake bite, malaria and many tropical diseases she named that would soon enough be familiar to me.

Ann gave us tips on how to care for ourselves, when to make every effort to see her so that she could determine the next step, such as see a local doctor or perhaps a doctor in Senegal or even the United States. The nurse requested that any significant illness or injury be reported to her, that she was responsible for our health care. If we couldn't get to her, she'd come to us.

Ann asked how we were doing with our anti-malarial medication, Aralen. "Any bad dreams?"

"Yes!" I answered. We'd started the medication two weeks before we left for Africa and were to take two tablets weekly, on Sunday. The reason they suggested the day was so that we could remind each other to take it since it was very dangerous not to take the prophylactic regularly. I had begun to notice that every Sunday night I had terrible nightmares. I seemed to be the only one affected this way.

"Take one on Sunday, one on Wednesday," she advised. That did the trick—no more nightmares.

Ann also spoke at length about dogs. "You Americans are crazy about dogs, but here the dogs are not to be tolerated. They run in packs and can be very dangerous if cornered. Never feed them. At certain times of the year the Field Force will have a campaign to shoot them and for awhile the situation will be better." At the words "shoot them," there were gasps in the room.

Ann nodded thoughtfully. "You will see many things here that will seem harsh. You'll get used to it. This is a very poor country without the agencies you're used to."

Fisherman carrying his catch to the Bakau market

Chapter 4

O n the second full day of training, we divided into Wolof or Mandinka language groups. We were fortunate to have professional school teachers, men who taught during the school year, but who were on summer break and available to the Peace Corps.

Our Mandinka teachers, Yaya and Sainey, were experienced in working with tubobs and understood the process of learning. Yaya, probably in his forties, was married with several kids. Sainey, in his early twenties, was still single. Neither voluntarily talked about his personal life, but politely answered questions. Some instructors preferred to be called Mister and their surnames; others requested we call them by their first names.

Each day we spent about four hours learning Mandinka. This was my first foreign language. Somehow I'd never gotten around to taking a language in school. One of the surprising things to me was that learning a language isn't just swapping one word for another. It involves new sentence structures and ways of expressing ideas.

Great importance is placed on greetings in The Gambia. One doesn't just rush up to someone to say or ask something. They must first greet the person, shake hands, inquire about the family and people of the village before stating their business. The greetings actually take a few minutes. A big cultural lesson here for westerners is to slow down. The direct approach doesn't work in Africa.

Our group sat at one end of the dining hall near the kitchen; the Wolof group sat at the other end. Between loud voices coming from the kitchen and the hot room, I found it hard to concentrate. Outside, a huge tree spread its branches between the seminary and the dining hall.

"Yaya," I asked, "could we hold our class outside in the shade of that tree?"

"Of course. Let's take our chairs outside."

"Great idea," Bruce muttered to me. "I wonder why people here always talk so loud," his head nodded in the direction of the kitchen.

We were constantly hot, still not acclimated, so we welcomed the shade of the big tree and a slight breeze.

As we gathered, Yaya told us about the tree, the baobob. This African tree has been around for many generations and is used for shade in village meeting places. During the blooming season, women make a drink from its blossoms, similar to lemonade. It wasn't a pretty tree, its trunk looked rough, like roots, but the baobob's dense shade made up for its lack of grace. Our group usually met outside after that while the Wolof group stayed inside. Flies, mosquitoes and other insects found us, but the breeze made up for it.

None of the tribal languages spoken in The Gambia were written languages, but we were given a spiral-bound book that the Peace Corps had assembled with lessons and a brief translation dictionary. According to Yaya, we would learn faster if we were just immersed into the Gambian culture, but "you Americans always need a book to look things up." I agreed. I needed the crutch of the book and I continued to use that book the entire time we spent in The Gambia.

On the third evening at the seminary, the staff and neighboring dignitaries held a naming ceremony for us. This is something done for Gambian babies one week after birth. Since we would be living and working here, we needed to have Gambian names. It helped break barriers and the local people could remember our Gambian names.

One at a time, we were assigned names. I loved mine, Mariama Manneh, because the first name was so close to my own. Bruce was named Dawda Kinteh. Afterward we partied with food, strong sweet tea called attiah, and African drumming and dancing. From that moment on, our instructors called us by our Gambian names.

On some afternoons during training we went on field trips and one of the first was to the market in Banjul. The instructors each took three of us and Annie joined Bruce and me with her Wolof instructor, Musa. We rode in the pickup truck, a 404 Peugeot equipped with wooden bench seats along the sides and front of the bed, forming a U. A canvas top covered the bed of the truck, sort of like a covered wagon. This truck belonged to Peace Corps, but Peugeots were also commonly used as bush taxies. Two kitchen helpers joined us to buy food at the market. Twelve of us crowded into the back with two of the instructors up front with the driver.

We enjoyed this trip to Banjul, unlike our previous visit. Musa encouraged us to take money so that we could have the experience of purchasing items. Musa asked the three of us what we wanted to buy. I wanted to buy a dress. The clothes I had brought with me were fine for Seattle summers, but most were synthetics and too hot for this climate. He explained that we would go to a place near the market for a ready-made dress, but the usual thing was to buy fabric and hire a tailor. "Ready-made clothes are very dear." Oh, expensive.

Bruce wanted to buy food to take back with us. He never seemed to get enough to eat. I think part of that was the strangeness of the food. My appetite wasn't up to par, so I wasn't eating well and rarely felt satisfied after a meal. As we wandered through the market Musa explained that for some items you haggle over the price. "Many Americans have to learn how to do that," he acknowledged.

Bruce bought a half dozen apples. We were used to eating lots of fresh fruit and vegetables, and our current diet contained virtually no fresh produce. Musa haggled a bit over the price, but explained apples are not grown in The Gambia, so it was expensive for the vendor to get them. He turned to Annie, who wanted to buy peanuts. "We won't haggle over the peanuts. They are always the same price for a container." She bought a nice supply of aromatic fresh roasted peanuts, The Gambia's national product, measured from a tomato paste can. We bought two containers of nuts, too. I wondered if I'd ever learn which things to barter over. Musa explained that anything controlled by the government had a set price. Things that are always over-priced and the vendor expects to haggle are "jewelry, live animals, things like that."

On our way to a clothing store, we passed another little store with a few items. Musa pointed out that this was a typical privately-owned store, with an inventory of five or six items, at the most. He nodded to Annie. "This is the kind of store you'll be working with as a small business advisor."

We stepped in and Bruce immediately saw more food to take back with us. He pointed to a box of crackers and a jar of jam, both from England. Ah, this was more like it. Once we cooked for ourselves, I would have lots to buy from a market, but since all our meals were prepared for us, we would just buy snacks.

A few larger stores looked more successful and were owned and operated by East Indians. We passed one that sold electrical items and another that sold fabrics.

Musa was right, dress prices were very dear. I hesitated, but Bruce encouraged me to buy something loose and long so I could be more comfortable. I loved the dress I chose. Bright with yellow and brown flowers, the dress gathered at the yoke and fell full length. No waist band to gather heat. The short sleeves were loose and comfortable. Breezes drifted in and out of this wonderful dress. I almost lived in that dress until we could afford another. Musa quibbled a bit in Wolof over the price of the dress, but I think he felt out of his element in a women's clothing store.

* * *

Most days, from mid-afternoon until dinner, we were on our own, but with language homework. It was the hottest time of day. Bruce spent a few minutes going over the language assignment, then turned to more interesting reading. Following my usual over-achievement habits, I poured over our textbook, practicing the day's lesson.

We enjoyed staying in our room, sitting under the ceiling fan, away from flying insects, reading and eating our snacks of crackers and jam. We carefully doled out our treats to last several days. This became our practice throughout training, unless we participated in some group activity, such as a field trip. We discovered a small store within walking distance of the seminary that carried crackers, jam, and tinned cheese, Tubob food. We found the English lemon curd preserves excellent, and over the course of time we bought many jars. Africans didn't eat desserts, at least we weren't served any, and I think that accounted for part of our craving for the sweetness of jam.

Other trainees handled their cravings differently. Near dinner time, we sometimes saw Don, an entomologist, Lynn the musicologist, and a couple of others leaving. They'd found a pizza place. Bruce and I agreed that we wanted to stay within our budget of Peace Corps "walk-around money." Besides that, we wanted to go through training as it was intended. I didn't mind the food, though at times it was a little different, even strange, but so what? This was a cultural experience.

It wasn't long before those who went out to dinner were complaining about not having enough money. Bruce and I had brought money from home, but we were determined not to use it unless we really had to; it was what we considered our emergency fund.

Thrift isn't difficult for Bruce and me, but I know for some people it is very hard. Beer tastes good with a pizza dinner, and it all adds up.

* * *

For the entire seminary, there was only one bathroom. It had been intended as a boys' school and in the one room were toilets and shower-heads to accommodate several boys at one time. If someone went to the bathroom, it tied up the entire room. As a result, there was often a waiting line.

Bruce thought we could alleviate the congestion a bit by taking our showers at the same time. We really thought nothing of it. It freed us up to do other things and we were in and out quicker for the convenience of the others.

I don't know how it happened, but apparently one of the instructors told George about our arrangement in rather shocked tones. Gambians would never do such a thing. In a proper Gambian marriage, the husband never sees his wife naked. George very diplomatically approached Bruce with the problem.

"Well," Bruce said, "that can be their cross-cultural experience with us."

Surprised, George nodded. "Yes, I guess it can. You guys are married and this is what you do. I know you don't flaunt it. Okay, let's not worry about it."

* * *

One afternoon we went on another field trip to Abuko, about five miles southwest of Banjul. A Peace Corps volunteer met us as we climbed out of the truck. Catherine had the enviable Peace Corps job of working here. A naturalist, she was in her element and it was a pleasure to share her enthusiasm.

Abuko is neither a zoo nor game preserve, but an area of 180 acres for which equal emphasis is placed on protection and conservation of nature as a whole, a little bit of jungle in the middle of a savannah.

The Gambia is a world-class bird-watchers' paradise and, according to Catherine, more than 250 species had been identified at Abuko. We followed along after our guide, impressed by her vast knowledge. She stopped and pointed to the ground. "Be careful, step over this." At first I thought it was a rope or thin root, but then I detected undulating motion. Ants!

"Their bite is terrible. Don't let them crawl on you," she warned.

I knew all about these ants from our first night in The Gambia. She explained that these nomadic ants travel closely together to keep themselves warm and to protect their queen, who would be someplace in the center of the group.

Shade from giant scrub and huge trees--mahogany, kapok, acacia and palm--helped shelter us from the sun, but this was a hot time of day and sometimes the closeness of the vegetation seemed to capture the heat in pockets. A morning visit really would have been more ideal, but language training was first priority now with other activities worked around that main goal.

We arrived at a pond surrounded on three sides by thick vegetation, a perfect place to view birds without frightening them away. Catherine rattled off names of birds in impressive numbers: white egrets, giant kingfisher, hornbills, and woodhoopoes that darted to their young with food. I was enthralled with long-legged jacanas as they picked their way across the pond, stepping on huge lily pads as though they were stepping stones on a path. What a sight!

We trekked a distance to the Rescue Centre, the heart of Abuko. Red patas monkeys abounded and Catherine warned us to hang on to our purses. The monkeys loved to grab them and take them high up into the trees, sometimes dumping the contents. I slipped my cloth bag across my shoulder and clamped my arm across it. A monkey did pay me a fleeting visit, flinging its little arms around my legs. I was startled and concerned about my purse, but thrilled, too.

Two graceful antelope with white markings on sleek chocolate-brown hair stared back at us as we rounded a bend in the brush. Bruce thought they must be used to people to be so bold around us. Their ears swiveled in all directions, listening to the sounds our group made.

A huge tortoise hunkered down in a hole she'd dug to protect herself from the heat. As I mopped my sweaty brow, I thought she certainly had the right idea.

A keeper flung meat, still on bones, over a fence and the pursuant crunching convinced me to never cross paths with a hyena. As we walked on, we heard the human-sounding hyenas' "laugh." Very spooky. It was hard to believe the sound came from an animal.

We hoped to return another time, preferably in the cool of morning, when we would see more active birds and animals. Catherine said in the early hours we'd be more likely to see crocodiles and the giant monitor lizards. The walk back to our truck seemed endless in that heat. We were all drenched with sweat as we crowded into the back of the truck, stifling hot from sitting in the sun.

On our way back, we stopped at a lime-pressing plant, blissfully air-conditioned. The process is simple as explained by the Englishman who ran the plant. They crush the limes and sell the juice. Lime trees can be found throughout The Gambia and are easy to grow in that they don't attract bugs, don't require a lot of water and are fast growing. Once we were on our own, it would be good to buy limes to make our own limeade.

We were anxious to get back to the seminary to see if mail had arrived. No one from our group had received mail yet. We wrote home regularly, sending our letters to the Peace Corps office with one of the drivers and hoping they were mailed. We were eager to receive mail, especially from the kids, but again, no mail. It was probably too soon to expect any.

On the next Saturday, Mr. DeCosta asked if anyone would like to go to a Catholic church on Sunday and I spoke up. He offered to take me to his church, Star of the Sea, in Bakau. I was so pleased with the invitation and impressed with the Mass, especially the music. Singing a cappella, the choir's spectacular harmony had a broad sound with less vibrato than American music. I sat with Mr. DeCosta and his wife. After Mass, the Peace Corps nurse Ann Saar offered to take me back to the seminary since it would be on her way home.

Ann, an Australian, met her Gambian husband Mohammad at college in England. They married and eventually had four little girls. When her first daughter was born, Ann still had more than a year of college to finish. They visited The Gambia and left their daughter with Mohammad's parents. It wasn't ideal, Ann said, but better than having to find babysitters while she attended school and managed her nursing residency.

After graduation, they returned to The Gambia. Their little daughter spoke only Wolof! Ann had to take drastic measures to learn Wolof so she could speak to her own child and her in-laws. They hired household help with instructions to speak only Wolof. When I met Ann, she spoke like a native.

I asked her if she and Mohammad spoke to one another in Wolof. "Oh, no. Tribal languages cannot express heart-felt or intellectual concepts. It's very limiting. We'll say an occasional word in Wolof, a joke or something, but our discussions are in English."

"How about your daughters? Do they speak to one another in Wolof?"

"Sometimes and sometimes with their friends, but mostly it's English."

We remained friends with Ann and later had the pleasure of her company at our compound in Mansajang.

One evening, an excellent kora player, Jali Bakary Konteh, entertained us. Our musicologist, Lynn, had met Konteh previously when he visited the University of Washington. The musicians in The Gambia are really the historians, genealogists, and storytellers who pass their musical skills and stories on to their descendants. The name "Jali" actually referred to his musical status as a respected musician.

The kora, made from a large gourd and covered with cow hide, traditionally features 21 strings, but Jali Bakary Konteh's had 52. The tone of the kora resembled a harp, I thought, but was played more like the classical guitar. The jali's rich voice sang in Mandinka, and Yaya, our Mandinka instructor, translated. We found the concert thrilling.

Another evening a married couple who worked at the country's archives discussed The Gambia's family structure. They shared a concern of the elders that the family compounds were being influenced by western ways, compromising family unity. This was particularly true, they said, of areas surrounding the capital city, not so much in mid- and upriver communities. Evidence of this was seen in Banjul where people lived in temporary houses and were not surrounded by the safety of their families. "People are apt to get 'lost' in a big city, losing their sense of belonging and responsibility," the husband lamented. Having visited Banjul, I understood what he meant.

Some village elders tried to control this problem by limiting children to only the elementary years of schooling, so they wouldn't be tempted to leave the villages to pursue careers. This resulted in a very low literacy rate in The Gambia.

Yvonne Jackson, Peace Corps Director, also attended this meeting and added to the discussion. She reminded us that our western ways were not the best for everyone, even though they might work for us. What we could do as guests in this country was share our ways as an option Gambians might want to consider. But, she said, don't be surprised if they are unimpressed. "You women," she added, "will rebel with what you see women here endure. Try not to judge or show disapproval."

We visited a fishing village near Bakau on another Sunday. Bruce didn't go. His stomach was acting up and he had pretty serious cramps and diarrhea. It was a fun trip and

my first real glimpse of a traditional village, more like what I
expected to see in Africa. Huge racks held fish in different
stages of drying. The dead-fish smell was overpowering and
the hundreds of flies around the fish disgusting. People here
didn't seem to realize the danger of flies on food and made
no effort to cover the fish with netting. The villagers were
friendly and many knew Mr. DeCosta and greeted him as an
old friend.

There were no restrooms in any of the public places
we'd been so far. I finally had to ask Mr. DeCosta where I
could find a restroom.

"A what?"

"Ah, a bathroom."

"Oh, yes, a latrine." He went to the closest hut and
stepped up to the door and called out, "Konk konk."

People don't knock, probably because doors are rarely
closed in the daytime, and the doorways are covered with
cloth. Most construction was mud-brick covered with
concrete, so knocking wasn't effective. A woman stepped
out and greeted Mr. DeCosta in Wolof. She signaled me to
follow her. We traipsed through her hut into the back yard
and behind a woven-fenced partition. She handed me a
small brass tea-kettle which contained water. I took it from
her, not knowing why I'd need it.

As soon as I got into the enclosure I realized what the
teakettle was for. They didn't use toilet paper. To clean
yourself, you use the water from the kettle with your left
hand. Thus, food is eaten only with the right hand.

When I again joined Mr. DeCosta he chuckled and
asked if I figured out what to do with the teakettle.

"Oh, yes, but I don't know if it's a custom I'll embrace."

He laughed out loud.

Toward the end of the three weeks spent at the
seminary, we took a three-day trip to what would be our
assigned village, Mansajang, near the small town of Basse.
Our three volunteer entomologists (Sally, Don and Alan)
each traveled with their Gambian counterpart, as were our
three small business advisors (Annie, Nathaniel and
Norman). The others went with their assigned counterparts.

Bruce and I traveled together, since we were both assigned to the same village.

A word here about how the Peace Corps operates. Before sending a volunteer to a village, the Peace Corps first talks to the village chief, the Alkala. They determine the need and discuss the work expected of the volunteer and where he or she will live. In Bruce's case, the UN had determined they would continue the UNICEF well-digging project; in my case the Health Department said they could use another health worker in the Basse area, the closest town to the village of Mansajang. So our visit at this time was expected and many of the details worked out beforehand.

Bruce and I would report to George once we began our real work, so we traveled with him to Basse. The first 120 miles were paved, but on the next 125 miles we bumped along on deeply rutted roads with potholes that could easily break a truck's axle.

Along the way, we stopped at several volunteer homes so George could deliver their mail. It was interesting to see how they lived. Some lived in round grass-thatched roof huts, but most lived in row houses. These row houses, much nicer than those we saw in Banjul, normally housed two to four families, commonly an extended family. In most, each apartment had two rooms, but some only one. I found the row houses much hotter than huts with thatched roofs. Without a ceiling, heat radiates from the corrugated roofs. Some row houses, and huts too, had dirt floors; others had concrete.

We visited the working places of two volunteers, one at a clinic and one at a hospital. As it happened, the volunteers we visited were health workers.

At one point we gave two women volunteers a ride to the next village. We three took up the truck's cab, so they sat in the back of the small pickup. The weather had been very dry and clouds of red road dust shrouded the truck. When the two women in back climbed out, they were covered with red dust. They just laughed and brushed off themselves, and each other, and went on their way.

We were thrilled with the trip. Finally, we saw African living more like what we imagined it would be: family compounds, peaceful village scenes and friendly people. Chickens, goats, sheep, cattle, horses and donkeys grazed near family compounds. Amazingly, the sheep, bred for meat, didn't have wool coats like in America. It took us awhile to tell the difference between sheep and goats since their coats were so similar. On the road we saw monkeys in trees, swinging from branch to branch and scampering around on the ground, and even saw a troop of baboons.

We passed many people walking along the road with loads on their heads, the women often with babies slung on their backs. The men often stopped and waved. Hitching for a ride isn't done with a thumb, but rather the whole arm extended with a limp hand waving up and down. We picked up two men and gave them rides to the next village.

We had fun traveling with George. His quick sense of humor and his vast knowledge of West African culture impressed us and helped put us at ease. At one point he pulled off the road and pointed to a cone-shaped mound. "Do you know what that is?"

The mound looked solid, was about eight feet tall and about five feet across at its base. We hadn't a clue.

"A termite hill. They're as hard as concrete. I knew a fellow who died when his car plowed into one."

After George pointed them out, we continued to see them in rural areas.

During the three-month rainy season, the main roads allowed traffic, but many of the smaller connecting tracks were a mass of gumbo, making it impossible for vehicles to travel, so United Nations well-digging operations were suspended in the rainy season. During this time, equipment was often taken downriver to Yundum, near the capital city Banjul, for repairs. Many men from the project stayed there with family or friends.

Finally, we arrived at what was known as the UN (United Nations) Compound. The volunteer, Howard, whom Bruce was to replace, happened to be downriver at Yundum overseeing equipment repairs, so we pretty much had the place to ourselves.

Howard's hired help, Tombong, greeted us. An older, friendly Mandinka fellow, he had worked for Howard, doing his cooking, laundry, and "cleaning." Although I immediately liked Tombong, after a quick look around, I wasn't impressed with his housekeeping.

We would live in two structures. One, an oblong mud-brick building, about 10 feet wide and 30 feet long, with a corrugated tin roof, had been built by Howard's predecessor and had three small rooms, one used for cooking, the middle as a dining-living room and the third as a spare bedroom. One of the drawbacks of this structure was that flying insects could easily enter in the space between the top of the wall and the corrugated roof. Just a few steps away stood the second structure, a traditional round hut.

Because travel at night was difficult, UN people coming and going from Banjul to Mansajang needed to have a place to spend the night, so they slept in the oblong house which was already equipped with a bed covered with a mosquito net.

Howard used the round hut as a bedroom, as would we. The large round hut, about twenty feet across, had double-wall construction with perhaps four feet of space between walls, two fully screened doors, and topped with a cone-shaped grass-thatched roof. We loved the arrangement. Actually, we probably had the best volunteer housing in The Gambia.

Besides our two structures, there were three other huts. In one, a UN project mechanic and his family lived. The other two were empty but often temporarily housed UN drivers who needed a place to stay for the night. None of the structures in the compound were painted or whitewashed, but were all made of mud-brick smoothed over with a thin layer of concrete.

Everyone in the compound shared one latrine. About two hundred feet from our hut, the latrine had been dug as a practice well. A deep concrete-lined hole, it was actually quite nice by local standards. The few latrines I'd used had dirt surrounding the hole. No outhouse, but krinting, the fencing commonly used consisting of coarsely woven reeds, provided privacy. Naturally, upon arrival, my first stop was to the latrine. One simply squats over the hole, and when I did perhaps 200 flies buzzed out of the hole, banging against me. I shuddered and wondered if I'd ever get used to that.

Krinting surrounded the entire compound, as in other compounds we'd seen. The fencing provided privacy but its real purpose was to keep roving stock, cattle, sheep and goats, out. Chickens wandered about and I saw no chicken coops. A few sparse patches of grass poked through the sandy soil.

We walked to Bruce's shop a short distance away, and met a few of the crew who weren't downriver working on equipment. George left Bruce with them and took me to the home of Sister Roberts, my future boss. After greetings and introductions, George left to visit friends.

I immediately liked Sister Roberts, who was not a Gambian, but from Sierra Leone. The "Sister" title, the equivalent of Registered Nurse (RN), was the result of her training in England. She spoke beautiful English. I would learn more about the details of my job later, but she made it very clear she wanted me to take over record keeping. "Other than that, Mariama, you should do what you want to do. There's plenty of work. You'll need to talk to Sister M'Boge at the Health Department in Banjul. She's in charge of Peace Corps health workers."

It felt good to have something solid to work toward.

Bruce didn't come away with that feeling, however. No one he talked to at the shop seemed to have a grasp of the situation. Those who were knowledgeable were no doubt downriver at Yundum.

As planned by George, Billy, a volunteer who had been in country for more than a year, stopped by that early evening and invited us out to dinner. At George's suggestion, we told Tombong that we wouldn't be having dinner at the UN compound, but that we would have breakfast there.

We rode to the restaurant in Billy's project car, a Suzuki. Nathaniel would join us at the restaurant, together with his fellow volunteers Norman and Annie. They had visited many of the small businesses with whom they would work, and were in Basse for the night. Norman and Nathaniel would spend the night at what would be Nathaniel's living quarters in a row house; Annie would spend the night with us. We were to meet George at one of the local restaurants, Jobots All Necessary Foods.

Jobots was an adventure in itself. The roof and walls consisted of scrubby corrugated tin. Tables and chairs, obviously made of scrap wood, were cobbled together and none matched. Hot and muggy, the sweat poured off us, but Billy warned us not to drink the water. It was a Muslim establishment so beer wasn't served, but he slipped a local boy, who looked to be about ten years old, some money and a round of beer appeared. After a short while Billy announced, "Well, I'm going to order."

Bruce and I were starving and it was late, but I assumed we were to wait for George.

"You guys do what you want, but I learned a long time ago that I don't put my life on hold waiting around for George Scharffenberger. I'm ordering."

We agreed and ordered, Bruce an omelette and I "bif stek," thinly sliced beef. Wonderful bread came with all dinners. It was the best food we'd had in The Gambia.

George didn't come for at least another hour. "Oh, you started without me."

Billy nodded. "We didn't know how long you would be. These guys are beat."

Indeed we were. It had been a long dusty drive, a busy day, and we were hot and tired. George seemed to have infinite energy and saw more people he knew and had great, loud conversations with them in Wolof.

After finishing our dinner, Bruce and I thought we'd head back to the UN Compound and invited Annie to walk back with us.

As we passed the restaurant's kitchen we made the mistake of looking over the partition. On the dirt floor, a variety of food simmered on several charcoal cookers. No wonder it was so hot in there. Chickens pecked away at the woven bread baskets strewn on the floor, the very baskets that would be placed on tables. As a man prepared a tray to take out to a customer, he dipped a glass into an open jug of water. Sanitation didn't seem to be a high priority. But, the food was good.

As Annie, Bruce and I made our way the mile and a half home, we were amazed how dark it was. No lights of any kind guided us except for an occasional flash of lightning. We followed the gravel crunch of our steps on the road leading to the compound. We learned from that experience never to go anywhere without a flashlight, "torch," as they were called locally.

The next morning we had time to assess the house and hut. The house was ample in size, but, to my way of thinking, inconveniently arranged. The kitchen was a nightmare with limp greasy curtains on the single window and hung on the doorway between the kitchen and living room. I watched Tombong fix our breakfast of left-over rice and tea and as he perspired, he wiped his face and hands on the doorway curtain. I cringed at the greasy dishes and silverware (at least there was silverware).Cooking pots and dishes, heaped together, bore traces of food and were a haven for flies.

We decided we would not hire household help. We needed privacy and, after keeping house for more than twenty years, I knew an efficient house was important to me. It was going to be tough to tell Tombong, but we were adamant about our privacy.

Mid-morning George dropped Annie off to continue her tour with Nathaniel, Norman and their Gambian counterpart, and took us with him to visit more volunteers and then we returned to the village of Mansajang, a short distance from the UN Compound, to have dinner with Peggy. Peggy, a volunteer around twenty-three, was a health worker who had a hut to herself in a large family compound consisting of six huts. A woman served our dinner in Peggy's hut and we sat on the floor around a large bowl to eat what pretty much amounted to fish heads and rice. Peggy explained that the food in her compound wasn't very good, that the meal was typical. Many volunteers, she said, enjoyed much better food.

This worthwhile upriver trip gave us many insights so that we could prepare in confidence for when it was time to live there.

The three weeks at the seminary had flown by. Although it took awhile to appreciate it, we had been treated like royalty. We would need to draw on that memory in the coming weeks.

View from Seyhou Sanneh's apartment in Banjul

Chapter 5

*I*t was time to move on to our technical training. Since Bruce's work was at Yundum for the rainy season and I could access local health facilities, we would live in Banjul, the capital city, for the next three weeks.

Peace Corps volunteers who arrived six months earlier had consisted almost entirely of about twenty health workers who had the advantage of a detailed course of technical training. I was the only health worker in our group, so it was pretty much up to me to learn what I could. George gave me a book on rural health which contained valuable information.

Annie, as a small business advisor, would also be working in Banjul. As it happened, the three of us were together again, a happy arrangement.

We were to stay in Seyhou Sanneh's Banjul apartment. A good natured, husky Gambian, Seyhou worked for Peace Corps as a coordinator for trainees. The apartment was available to us for the three weeks we would be in Banjul.

Seyhou Sanneh would remain at the seminary as a former Peace Corps group was arriving for advanced training. He explained that a Gambian boy, a student who lived with him, would help us get settled, do our housework and help us find our way around the city.

Peace Corps continued to take care of all expenses, increasing our "walk-around money" to cover the cost of food.

Our language instruction was reduced to two hours a day. Our language teacher, a man we hadn't met before, lived about three blocks from our apartment and we were to meet him there at four in the afternoon six days a week, every day but Sunday.

We took all our belongings with us and moved into Seyhou's apartment. From the outside it looked decent enough. Once inside, however, we weren't so impressed. We climbed an inside flight of narrow stairs. Surprisingly, the apartment had three bedrooms. Later we were to learn that the apartment was really upscale by local standards. The apartment didn't have running water, but it did have a gas stove and electric refrigerator. Water was available at a spigot in the back yard. There was no bathroom, but each apartment had its own outhouse.

The apartment building had two units, one upstairs and one downstairs. The upstairs was very hot with no ceiling fans, certainly no air-conditioning. The screens on the louvered windows were either full of holes or non-existent, so flies and mosquitoes were abundant.

The young man who lived with Seyhou greeted us in Mandinka, though he spoke good English, too. Ma-Insu was helpful in getting us settled. He helped Bruce carry our heavy trunks up the narrow steps and showed us around the apartment.

Bruce's stomach and intestinal trouble had steadily grown worse. The move, the heat, and the repeated trips to the outhouse made him irritable and I didn't blame him. Ma-Insu cooked our first meal, typical Gambian food which I thought was quite good. Bruce's stomach rebelled at almost everything offered. He longed for me to cook something familiar.

That evening Ma-Insu left to visit friends and the three of us sat in the living room reading. Suddenly a bat flew in through a gaping hole in the louvered living room window screen. Bats are known carriers of rabies, and the nurse Ann Saar had warned us to avoid them. The bat flew around the room, banging into walls and the one lamp we shared. Bruce finally captured the bat by throwing a towel over it and then carried it downstairs to free it. Afraid it would return through the window, we turned out the light and went to bed. Annie's room was down the hall from ours, a small room with a single bed. Ma-Insu's room was on the other side of the kitchen. Bruce and I were to use Seyhou's bedroom.

We went to bed, but not to sleep for a long time. The bed frame, wire mesh with no supporting slats, permanently sagged from Seyhou's considerable weight. The straw mattress, besides sagging, was alive with crawling things. I called it our "living mattress." We got up and tried to fluff up the mattress, but to no avail. It was like a hammock and a back-breaker when we tried to sleep on our sides. The hot room buzzed with mosquitoes. Constant noise from the street drifted through the louvered windows: cars honked, brakes screeched, loud voices rose in a heated argument, a woman screamed.

It seemed we had just drifted off to a restless sleep when a loud chant made us sit up in alarm. It was the 5:00 a.m. call to worship from a neighborhood mosque, amplified and played through large outdoor loudspeakers. We were so uncomfortable, going back to sleep wasn't a possibility.

Ma-Insu didn't know what to do for us for breakfast. Gambians don't traditionally eat until mid-morning. I sliced bread and brewed a pot of tea for the three of us. My plan that day was to look over the material George had given me and make a study outline for the three weeks. Annie left to meet with her counterpart. Bruce walked to the Peace Corps office to see Ann Saar about his stomach troubles.

Although the office was to open at 8:00, no one was there. To make matters worse, Bruce badly needed to use the latrine. There was simply no place to go, so he had to do his business in back of the building. He had told his ride to pick him up at the Peace Corps office at 9:00, thinking he was giving himself plenty of time. Peace Corps staff finally arrived and Ann gave him some Imodium and took some stool samples to be sent to Washington, D.C.. His ride picked him up and they proceeded to round up the other workers.

The month of Ramadan, an annual Muslim period of fasting, occurred while we were in Banjul. For Muslims, it is particularly difficult. They don't drink or eat anything during daylight hours, not even to swallow their own saliva. In the evening after sunset they eat and drink water. These rules apply to all but small children, pregnant women and the very elderly. As a result many don't go to sleep until much later than normal, making it tough to get up the next morning.

It's risky standing by open bus windows, or anywhere, really, during Ramadan. People spit constantly to avoid swallowing saliva. During Ramadan people are more tired than usual and often short-tempered.

Bruce was appalled when he and the driver first starting picking up the crew to go to the shop. Most of them were still in bed! Following the driver's example, Bruce actually went into their homes, prodded them out of bed and even handed them their pants to climb into. As he was to learn later, people rarely get fired from their jobs. So, if he was going to have a crew, he needed to get them up and to the shop.

For someone who had always lived by the motto, "No matter how you feel, get up, dress up, show up," the local attitude about work rubbed against the grain.

Of course, once at the shop, they were still tired. That first night Bruce came home hot, tired, and miserable with his health condition, though thankfully they did have a latrine at the shop. He was also discouraged with his work and the total lack of progress.

He'd never seen people sleep in so many ways: across the hood of a truck, under a truck, on the truck's seat, tucked back next to a wall. Bruce prodded them awake, only to see them snoozing a few minutes later. All that day, they made no real progress, unless Bruce did it himself. His job was mechanical advisor. He was not there to do the actual work of repairing vehicles. For one thing, it was more than one man could do; for another, the Gambians wouldn't learn what to do if Bruce did it for them. There were a few men who had the energy and interest to do a good job, but they were the exception.

Annie came home discouraged, too. She couldn't imagine how she could get anything done. Being a woman, especially the small soft-spoken woman she was, worked against her. She felt no one listened to her; in fact, they ignored her.

My day had gone better. After I studied for a few hours, I needed a break so Ma-Insu and I went to the market. I told him I wanted to cook, that I had always cooked and I missed doing so. I really didn't want to hurt his feelings, but Bruce absolutely had to have food he could easily digest. Ma-Insu was anxious to show me how to make market purchases and wanted to take over. No leisurely walking around with him. "Okay, Mariama, what's next?" I bought some beef at the butcher shop. "Okay now what?" Potatoes and squash at the open market. "Is that it?" No, I needed some coffee and we bought a small tin of Nescafe' at a small store, and good French bread at another small store. Ma-Insu carried my groceries home and then left. I appreciated the effort he was making to be helpful, but I was dying to be on my own.

Mid-afternoon a neighboring woman walked into the apartment and, at the bottom of the stairs called up to me, "Konk konk." I was startled to see her already inside but invited her to come upstairs. She couldn't speak a word of English, only Wolof, so we couldn't converse. She sat staring at me. I didn't know what to do with myself. It seemed rude to sit and read when I had a guest. I fixed some tea and we sort of mimed a conversation. Thankfully, she left after a very long hour.

Our days settled into predicable patterns. Of the three of us, I had an easier time of it, but I had my frustrations, too. The lady who came that first day, came the next and the day after, but with friends. It was always the same thing, just staring at each other, drinking tea and talking among themselves. It's entirely possible that my guest wasn't all that thrilled with coming over, but she thought it the neighborly thing to do. She no doubt thought I was a crashing bore.

For years, I've been a walker. When we were at the seminary, Bruce and I found places we could walk. Now when he came home, he was so tired he simply wasn't in the mood, plus he needed to stay close to the outhouse. In any event, Banjul wasn't conducive to walking, it was a challenge of dodging cars and avoiding open sewers.

I occasionally walked to the Peace Corps building, just a few blocks away. I always seemed to see the same bunch of young volunteer women talking and laughing. I vowed I would never succumb to that. There must be better things to do with my time than to sit around with tubobs all day. I couldn't imagine why they weren't doing something productive. Didn't they have jobs?

While at the Peace Corps office, I tried to make an appointment by phone with Sister M'Boge, the Health Department person to whom I would report, but couldn't get through to her. She was apparently a very busy woman. Like Sister Roberts in Basse, Sister M'Boge had also earned her nursing degree in England.

After the second visit to the Peace Corps office, I was about to return to the apartment when a Peace Corps volunteer I hadn't met introduced herself to me. Shirley, probably in her thirties, worked half way up the country but had come to Banjul on business. She invited me to join her for lunch. That lunch was so well-timed for me. Here was a person dedicated to her job, had a firm grasp of it and actually seemed to have a purpose. I mentioned to her that I'd wondered about those five or six young women I always saw in the office.

"They are in my group, six months ahead of you. Those girls just don't know what to do with themselves and spend much of their time in the Peace Corps office."

"But don't they have villages they're assigned to?"

"Oh, sure. But they just can't find anything to do, or want to do. They live in villages close enough that it's easy for them to come into Banjul."

"How about you? You apparently found something to do. And on our trip with George we saw many volunteers at their villages."

Shirley nodded. "I have the advantage, as you do, of having worked before. You have to find your own niche here. And be prepared for resistance if you're trying to change anything. Many volunteers have come here directly from college. They haven't developed the initiative to carve out their own work; they keep waiting for George or someone to show them what to do."

"How can George put up with that?"

"Oh, every once in awhile he chases them back to their villages, but it doesn't last."

"But they've had training, better than I'm getting."

Shirley shook her head and shrugged. "I guess they just don't know how to apply it." She worked at a clinic and seemed to be satisfied, though she said at times it was frustrating. "People here are pretty set in their ways."

I enjoyed having a conversation with someone I could relate to, someone who actually worked in the field.

Now that I did the cooking, Ma-Insu was rarely there. Amazingly, he insisted on doing our laundry. I tried to pay him, but he refused, saying that Peace Corps paid him to take care of us. He washed our clothes by hand and hung them outside on the fence to dry. He was gone most days and returned late at night, though he never shirked his duty. I suspected he had a girlfriend. He was a college student, but was on summer break

One evening Annie sat in the living room reading, Bruce, suffering with cramps, had gone to bed early, and I sat at the table typing a letter home. Among our precious belongings, and despite the 40-pound luggage limitation, I had insisted on bringing my portable typewriter. Suddenly, I felt my throat constricting. Something smelled so awful, it actually affected my breathing.

"Annie, do you smell something?"

"Yes, I just noticed it."

"Me, too," Bruce's muffled voice came from the bedroom.

I ran into the kitchen. The stove was fueled with butane—could it be that? No, the smell wasn't as strong in the kitchen and the valve was screwed shut. The smell was apparently from outside. I feared a gas leak in the neighborhood.

I ran down the stairs and outside to the porch. Seeing light underneath. I walked around to an opening under the enclosed porch and there a tiny old woman stirred a pot of the most terrible smelling concoction imaginable. She had a fire with what appeared to be charcoal with a large pot balanced on three rocks. She didn't look up, but kept stirring, like a witch. Spooky, very spooky.

I returned to the apartment. "I think it's okay, someone's cooking under the porch."

"Oh, my God," I heard Bruce mutter.

On my next visit to the Peace Corps office, I told Ann Saar about the incident and she told me what had probably been brewing. "I know exactly what you mean. It's called 'm'baha' and looks like goat turds. Actually it doesn't taste as bad as it smells."

Hopefully I'd never know.

I also talked to Ann Saar about Bruce's condition. "It just doesn't clear up. The poor guy's miserable."

Ann suspected Bruce had picked up something from the water. Although they were to boil all the water we drank at the seminary, she suspected they didn't always bring the water to a full boil. Apparently Bruce had picked up a bug, but I didn't, nor did anyone else in our group.

Once I noticed Ma-Insu boiling water for us. As soon as little bubbles formed on the bottom of the pan, he took the pot off the stove. I pointed out to him it hadn't boiled long enough. He shrugged. I put the pot back on and boiled the water for the recommended ten minutes. Now that Ann mentioned it, I could imagine that's what happened at the seminary.

At home in Washington, camping was one of our favorite pastimes and in the course of visiting campgrounds, we had encountered many outhouses. Campground outhouses were usually pit toilets, or self-contained toilets that flush into something. Not here. The outhouse at Seyhou's had a bucket. During the night, it was emptied from the street via a small door in the back of the building. The problem was that the collectors weren't used to so many using the outhouse at that address, they were used to dealing with waste for one or two people. Especially with Bruce's condition, we were filling that bucket at an alarming rate.

I suggested to Ma-Insu that he tell those responsible to empty it more frequently, but nothing seemed to be happening. The pail was actually full to the brim. "Ma-Insu," I said, "who should I see about that bucket?"

He was horrified. "Oh, no, Mariama, I'll see to it."

"Okay, but we can't last another day."

We didn't have to. Somehow Ma-Insu contacted the right people and from then on they emptied it twice a week sometime during the night. It helped, but that outhouse was still a dreadful place to "go."

With no running water to the apartment, or in most places in The Gambia, a bucket bath is the only way to take any kind of a bath, short of going into The Gambia River, which is ill advised. To take a bucket bath, we filled one or two buckets with water, refreshingly cool water straight from the tap. We wet down with a scoop of water, soaped up, then rinsed. I preferred to use two buckets for my bath to feel really clean, but often managed with one. Our bucket baths weren't at all pleasant. An outhouse environment isn't a place where you want to linger.

At the end of the first full week in Banjul, Annie announced after dinner that she was leaving. She felt she could not make a worthwhile contribution and felt her time would be better spent at home in Texas. "I hate giving up, but I just don't fit in here." She graciously told us that any good moments she'd experienced had been with us, and thanked us for so often including her.

I could see in Bruce's eyes that he would like to leave, too. It's miserable to be sick, especially when you're away from home. He had so little control over things at work and felt he wasn't making any headway with the projects that needed to be done.

I really wasn't experiencing any of those problems. Although I hated Banjul. I couldn't wait to get started on my projects, on our own, in Basse. I couldn't dream of giving up. My life here hadn't begun.

So we said our goodbyes to Annie. I was sad to see her go, but I did understand.

Once, when Bruce stopped by the Peace Corps office to see if we had mail, George spotted him and asked how the work was going. Bruce unloaded some of his frustrations. George showed sympathy for the workers and mentioned how hard it was for them during Ramadan. "It's not easy being a Muslim."

"It's not easy trying to get anything done, either," Bruce replied. "We're supposed to be getting this equipment ready to take upriver, and it's not getting done."

"Well, just try to understand."

Bruce came away disgusted and even more discouraged with the lack of support.

I had looked forward to Sunday, our day off, and maybe a walk to the ocean. We had been warned not to swim in the ocean near Banjul, but we could go for a walk, I countered, and not have to dodge open sewers. But Bruce was so miserable we didn't do anything. He'd mingled with people all week and craved the peace and quiet at the apartment, bugs and all.

At this period Bruce and I were at opposite ends of the spectrum. He had more action than he felt up to with constantly prodding guys to do their job, being given dirty looks, only to do it all over again, time after time. The guys who did a conscientious job didn't take the role of leadership, they simply did what they could to get the job done.

I, on the other hand, did nothing all day but read and study my language. The inactivity got to me and when I couldn't stand it any longer, I'd walk to the Peace Corps office to see if we had any mail and to try again to call Sister M'Boge. I never lingered, but almost always saw the same five or six women chatting and laughing.

One time, after again trying to reach Sister M'Boge, I stopped in to say hello to the nurse and found a doctor there, too. Steve was the Peace Corps doctor responsible for volunteers in five African countries. My arms and legs had been itching and while they were both there, I showed them my arms, full of bites from our living mattress. "Is there anything I can put on these bites?"

Horrified, Steve said, "Flea bites!" He turned to the nurse, "Where is she staying?"

Ann nodded as though this was something they'd talked about before. "Seyhou Sanneh's."

"Never again," the doctor said. "No one else is to stay there. That place is unsafe. Look at her arms! They're just waiting for an infection to happen." He quickly examined the rest of me. I had a few bites on my legs, too, but for some reason my torso was relatively free of them.

They gave me some ointment. We were about half way through this phase of our training and I didn't want to go through moving to another place in Banjul. I shrugged it off and said I'd use the medication, that I was sure it would be all right.

As I made my way down the hall to check our mail, I heard him say. "I mean it Ann, no one is to stay there again."

We never got used to that horrible bed. For some reason, I was affected by bites more than Bruce. That was good, Bruce had all he could manage with his intestinal troubles.

I finally managed to reach Sister M'Boge and we made an appointment for the following Friday. I could hardly wait. At his suggestion, I also made an appointment with George for that same day so that I could go over with him beforehand the things I might discuss with Sister.

The day of my appointments, I arrived at the Peace Corps office to talk with George. At our appointed time he was on a long telephone conversation. It cut into our time, but as soon as he was off the phone, we got right down to the business of my outlined agenda. We were barely into it when Darlene, also from the group of six months earlier, stopped at George's office door.

"Oh, good, George," she said, "you're here." With that she plopped into the chair next to me and proceeded to spread her papers on his desk, some of them over mine

George, ever polite, introduced us. She said a vague "Hi," and launched into a plan she had. Their conversation went on for some time. I glanced at my watch and realized I needed to leave. I gently raised Darlene's papers so I could get mine out from under them, and began gathering my things to leave.

"Oh, wait, Mary," George said, "we haven't finished."

"I need to leave now, my appointment with Sister M'Boge is at eleven."

Darlene gasped. "Oh, I'm sorry. Did I interrupt something?"

"Mary," George said, "you'll have to get used to time here." He shook his head in mirth and Darlene chuckled.

I bristled. "My appointment is at eleven. If Sister M'Boge is late, that's fine and I'll wait patiently, but I'm going to be on time."

I could see their startled looks, but I left George's office on time with my papers intact, and walked the several blocks to the Health Department. Following her phone instructions, I found Sister M'Boge's small office in the basement.

"Hello, Sister, I'm Mary Trimble."

A stout woman wearing a white nurse's uniform stood and shook my hand. "I appreciate your promptness."

Mary studying her Mandinka lesson

Chapter 6

Some days Bruce felt better; other days miserable. He'd stopped by the Peace Corps office again, but Ann Saar hadn't yet received the lab results from Washington, D.C. She gave him stronger medication. I could see he had lost weight, though his appetite was better now that I was cooking.

My days continued with health care reading. My visit with Sister M'Boge had been rewarding and she offered suggestions about what I might do with my time in Banjul. Sister suggested I visit a few clinics, just to get a feel for the type of work I might be doing. She knew I didn't have a medical background but thought it would be worthwhile to get a grasp of their services so that I could understand record-keeping needs.

I became a little more familiar with Banjul and the surrounding communities. I often heard the name "Half Die," south of Banjul. What an odd name. I wondered what it meant. I asked one of the Gambians who worked at the Peace Corps office.

"Half Die. That's English, Mariama. Years ago, half the people in that village died from yellow fever, so they renamed that village Half Die."

At one of the clinics run by Catholics, I had a delightful visit with the nuns who managed it. They were enthusiastic about showing me what they did and the kind of record keeping they maintained. Another visit, to the Bakau clinic, proved worthwhile, too. Also, the British Medical Research Center just outside Banjul offered a glimpse of cases focused on tropical conditions, such as malaria. One of the pleasures of visiting clinics was getting out of Banjul. Even a few hours away offered much relief.

Barbara, one of the earlier group's health workers, happened to be in the Peace Corps office when I stopped by. I imagine Barbara was about my age, in her early forties, an experienced worker. She clearly had a job that kept her busy. She invited me to visit her work place on Friday when they held their well-baby clinic. I took a ferry across the river and walked the short distance to her village, Essau. What a wonderfully encouraging experience! I could see how she fit into the scheme of things and how well she was accepted.

Sister M'Boge also gave me some practical reading material to study. She complained to me that many of the health workers, the group ahead of us, didn't check in with her, but she hoped she and I could meet on a regular basis. Of course, she realized I would be a distance away. I assured her I would be in regular contact with her. Sister, a Gambian and educated in England, had a keen understanding of the difficulties we tubobs encountered adjusting to the Gambian culture.

In Banjul, I missed exercise. I craved getting out and walking in my normal stride, not mincing my way around open sewers and crowds of people. I decided to go to the ocean. Of course it wasn't recommended that a woman go anywhere alone, but Bruce never felt up to it on his days off. I hesitated to go to the Peace Corps office to look for a walking companion; they seemed content to sit and chat for hours at a time. So I set out, wearing my modest Gambian-made dress.

Banjul's bleak ocean beach didn't smell like oceans are supposed to. The sand was a brownish gray. I didn't know just where sewage dumped into the ocean, but I imagined it would be a distance out. I had brought a book and thought after a nice long walk, I would sit on a log and read.

I had just begun my walk when a group of boys, maybe twelve years old or so, spotted me. "Tubob! Tubob!" Over and over they chanted it as they ran toward me. The group, at least a dozen, surrounded me, all talking at the same time and reaching out to touch me. We went through the typical greetings, but this crowd seemed unfriendly to me. One young fellow felt my breast, another started to.

"No!" I said sharply, roughly brushing their hands away, and giving them my sternest look. The boy who had touched my breast smiled slyly, like a challenge. I was actually becoming quite frightened, my knees felt like jelly. I saw an older man walking our way. I didn't know if that was good news or bad. He shouted something to the boys in Wolof and they scattered.

His English was broken, but I clearly understood him to say to me, "You go." I thanked him and left very quickly. A patch of bushes lined the walkway and I feared the boys might pop out from behind one. I made it to the end of that passage and to the street, then looked back. The old man stood watching me. I waved to him and he waved back. I was so grateful for his intervention. My dress was drenched with sweat, more from nerves this time than heat. Not a terrifically satisfying walk.

I didn't share this experienced with anyone at the Peace Corps office. For one thing, I shouldn't have been there. For another, what good would it do?

About one week later, I had another bad experience. I had met with Sister M'Boge at the Health Department, reporting back on my visits with the clinics. Afterward, I planned to stop in at the Peace Corps office to discuss my visit with George. The streets were crowded and very noisy. Suddenly two men stepped right in front of me. One reached out and grabbed my crotch. I instinctively reached down and pressed against his arm, trying to push him away. He was very muscular and I'm sure if he'd wanted to, the whole ordeal could have lasted much longer. He had an evil look in his eye and a terrifying sneer. I later realized his companion shielded the deed with his body so passers-by couldn't see. I didn't utter a sound, truly shocked to the core.

It was over in seconds but I reeled from shock. I continued on to the Peace Corps office, walking at a fast clip. Luckily, George didn't have anyone in his office and I burst in, closed the door, and sat down. He knew immediately something was wrong.

"George, a man just grabbed my crotch." I explained to him what had happened, fighting tears.

"You know, Mary, people in Banjul aren't in their regular environment. They..."

I leaned forward and looked George in the eye. "George, grabbing a woman's crotch is an international no-no. There is no excuse."

He sighed and nodded. "You're right. I'm sorry it happened. I really doubt though that they were Gambians. Gambians just don't do things like that."

I relived that scene many times, wishing I had called out, screamed, had done something to attract attention to those creeps. This was the second time I had been fondled and, by God, it had better be the last.

It was a long three weeks. We'd had a glimpse of a life upriver in Mansajang and that kept us going. Although I had it much easier in Banjul than Bruce, it was still very trying. I'd never felt so stir-crazy. Even with small children in my home state of Washington, I found ways to exercise. Sunshine, rain or snow, I'd bundle the kids up, put them in a wagon or sled, and walk, for miles sometimes. This sitting around was killing me. To top it off, I felt unsafe in Banjul.

Ann Saar finally received the results of Bruce's tests. He had giardia lamblia, an intestinal parasite undoubtedly caused by ingesting impure water. Now she could treat the condition with specific medication. Her scales showed he had lost thirty pounds in thirty days.

I managed to have a dress made in the typical manner of The Gambia. I'd met a school teacher, Ginny, at the Peace Corps office and admired her dress. She suggested we meet the next day after school and she'd bring her dress so I could borrow it to show the tailor. She also suggested which tailor I might use and where to buy fabric. I followed her instructions with marvelous results.

I admired Ginny's tailor. I showed him the style of dress I wanted and he took my measurements. For comfort, clothing is worn loose so he merely measured my height and across my shoulders. His treadle sewing machine was set up in front of the fabric store where I bought the material, a floral print. Some coarse fabrics, called strip cloth, are woven in The Gambia, but finer textured material is imported.

The next late afternoon I again met Ginny to return her dress. I found her agitated and she invited me to go with her to get something to drink. We walked a block away to a German restaurant popular with tubobs. We both ordered soft drinks and she launched into her disappointing day.

Ginny had invited Yvonne Jackson, the country's Peace Corps Director, to visit her third-grade classroom. She had worked on a cute program with the children and they had decorated the walls especially for the visit. It had been fun and the children were excited to have a guest. The time came and went, but Yvonne failed to appear. Ginny was embarrassed with her fellow Gambian teachers who knew about the impending visit, and sad about the children's disappointment.

After school, just before she and I met, Ginny approached the director. "Yvonne, we were disappointed that you didn't come to our school today. We'd planned a special program for you."

"What?" Yvonne responded. "Oh, that's right. I forgot. Where do you teach?"

Ginny looked at me and shook her head. "I won't invite her again. What a letdown, to say nothing of the lack of support."

I felt sorry about the incident. Ginny seemed to be a dedicated, hard-working volunteer. This had been a bad day, but from what I'd seen, she was normally cheerful and positive. I asked her how she liked Banjul.

She shrugged. "I've gotten used to it. I have nice living arrangements and I love my Gambian family. It's mostly been a good experience."

That was good to hear, but I personally couldn't wait to get out of Banjul.

At last, this three-week portion of our training slogged to its conclusion. We were both eager to leave. Saturday morning Ma-Insu helped us pack, making sure all our clothes were accounted for. It had been a pleasure knowing him, and looking back, I would expect great things from Ma-Insu. I didn't realize at the time how advanced he really was and how perceptive. His family's village was half-way up country, so his background was as a village dweller, but since he'd been at the capital city, he'd acquired a sophistication rarely seen. I insisted he take some money as a gift from us.

"Please," I said.

He sighed, "Mariama," but let me put the money in his hands.

I had been aware that the previous group had been at the seminary for two weeks of advanced language training. The Peace Corps office had been very quiet lately without "the group." Their training at the seminary had ended Friday afternoon and now the staff at the seminary expected our group back for one week, then we'd go to another destination.

We arranged for the Peace Corps driver to pick us up at Seyhou's and take us with all our belongings to the seminary. He dropped us off and we passed Seyhou in the yard. We thanked him for the use of his apartment, never mentioning his permanently indented, living mattress, or the flea bites, or even the Peace Corps doctor's opinion of his place. We did tell him, however, of the very helpful, courteous way Ma-Insu had treated us. Now that we were back at the seminary, we asked if we were to have the same room as we had before.

"Yes, of course. The same room."

So we lugged our things upstairs and opened the door to the room to find stuff strewn about. The room was obviously occupied. A volunteer walked by, her hands full of her belongings as she moved out.

"Do you know who's staying here? Seyhou Sanneh said we were to use this room."

She mentioned them by name. I knew they were two whom I saw nearly every time I went into the Peace Corps office. She nodded her head in the direction of the room. "I think they plan to stay and take a few days vacation. They're at the beach now."

Vacation? Vacation from what?

"I'll go ask Seyhou," I volunteered to Bruce. He was beyond weary of this whole thing.

"Seyhou," I said when I found him again, "our room is occupied."

"No, it is not occupied."

"Apparently the two in there plan to stay, take a vacation."

"No, they are not staying. Why would they stay? We are not running a resort here. They are to go to their villages." He turned to leave. "Come back in a few minutes and move in."

We took the opportunity to go to the neighborhood small store and buy snacks of crackers, canned cheese and jam.

When we returned, the former occupants' stuff was in a pile in the hall. I heard their dismay when they returned. I opened the bedroom door. They looked at me with accusation, but I said with all honesty, "The staff must have moved your things out. Seyhou Sanneh told us to move into this room."

We again pushed the two beds of different heights together. We marveled at the luxury of the seminary. Why hadn't we noticed this before? It was wonderful! The open windows were tightly screened, keeping out flying insects, the ceiling fan kept us cool, well, cooler, and the mattresses were smooth and flat. Actually, the mattresses were made of foam rubber, typical in The Gambia. At least they didn't harbor living creatures.

Our former language instructors were back and determined where we were in our training. As it happened, Bruce and I had kept up better than some of the others. We resumed our language lessons in earnest, several hours a day.

At this point, three fisheries volunteers joined us. They had received their technical training elsewhere, but now were to join our group. One of them, Perry, had already served two years as a volunteer in Zaire. Our group of eight grew to eleven.

In the late afternoons, we were delighted to again walk the few blocks to the Chargé d'Affair's and to the ocean. It was a glorious week. Bruce tried to put his bad experience behind him. He wouldn't have to think about his job for almost a month. His health improved steadily. People commented on his weight loss. I worried a bit about going back to Gambian cooking, but taking the new medication helped Bruce's general outlook. He rarely had emergency trips to the bathroom. Even when he did, it was so much better than Seyhou Sanneh's cringy outhouse.

We celebrated my August 31 birthday by joining some of the others who often went to LaPizza. I could see the big attraction with indoor and outdoor eating. We chose to sit outside at one of the long tables under an umbrella. No wonder it was a favorite with its cold beer and delicious pizza prepared in brick, wood-burning ovens. Monkeys swung from tree to tree, screeching. A brilliant yellow and red parrot walked right up to our table and said something, but I couldn't understand it. A couple near us, the Tatums, said it spoke Danish, the nationality of the restaurant owners.

We became acquainted with the Tatums, also Peace Corps volunteers who by this time had only a few months to go before they finished their two-year term. They had helped set up GamCo, a co-op outlet selling Gambian-made crafts. We later visited GamCo and over time bought many articles from them to take home as gifts, including leather goods, batik wall hangings, and wood carvings. The Tatums were a valuable asset to Gambian artisans, helping them set up and maintain a successful cooperative business.

During this week at the seminary a Peace Corps volunteer died at home in her village mid-country. I had met her briefly at the Peace Corps office. Although a member of the group ahead of us, she wasn't one of the young women who continually hung out at the office. The cause of death seemed mysterious, but it appeared she died from an overdose of Aralen, the drug we took to prevent malaria.

A memorial was held at the Chargé d'Affair's home with most of the in-country volunteers in attendance. Yvonne Jackson, the Director and George Scharffenberger, Assistant Director, both spoke, as well as some of her closest friends. We also attended a Mass at the church in Bakau. Ann Sarr, the Peace Corps nurse, accompanied the body home to the United States.

The volunteer's death was a sobering and sad situation. We'd never know the circumstances of her death, but were sorry her time in The Gambia had come to such a tragic end.

Bruce and I both looked forward to the next phase of our training to be held at Jenoi, about half way up-country.

Musicians at a celebration

Chapter 7

We were scheduled to leave the seminary at 9:30, but it was closer to noon when our caravan pulled out. It takes a lot of work to move 20 people, the eleven of us and all our belongings plus workers with their equipment and luggage. A big flatbed truck sagged with kitchen equipment including two refrigerators and a freezer, plates and cooking pots. Much of this equipment was necessary because they still tried to satisfy tubob tastes. Strictly Gambian food would not have required as much equipment. Although the training camp had beds, the staff supplied sheets, pillows and pillow cases. Blankets were not needed in that heat. A Peugeot truck carried our personal belongings. Some of us piled into a van, others in an ancient station wagon and a jeep. Quite a caravan.

Jenoi Agriculture Training Centre, near the village of Jenoi, was used as an instructional center for several groups: agriculture extension workers, farmers, and Peace Corps, to name a few. Two long concrete buildings faced one another with grassy space between them. The two buildings each had six rooms with a bathroom and shower at the end of each building. A dining room/classroom stood at one end, forming a sort of U.

We moved in, two to a room, and found the rooms nice with large windows to let in light and breezes, screens on the windows, and woven shades to keep out the sun, two open closets with built-in shelves. The concrete walls and floors were clean and the walls painted white. Again, we pushed the two single beds together, both the same height this time, and settled in.

Many of the kitchen staff from the seminary joined us in Jenoi. However, the local village women washed our clothes. Whenever possible, Peace Corps hires local people to help boost the local economy. Here the women spread our clean laundry on the dining room tables and we gathered our clothes from the different piles of folded shirts, pants, dresses, and underwear.

Thankfully, Bruce's health continued to improve. The medication seemed to be doing the job, though he was warned that giardia symptoms might come back from time to time.

In Jenoi, the main focus was language training, up to five hours a day. I loved our language sessions. Yaya and Sainey had a way of making them fun but instructive. We again found a place to sit outside in the shade when the weather allowed. It occasionally rained, a hard, driving downpour. But when it stopped, the sun beat down and the sandy ground dried quickly.

During this phase of training, three Canadian (CUSO) and two English (VSO) volunteers joined our group. CUSO and VSO are similar to Peace Corps, but usually have much better working and living conditions and a larger "allowance." Over the next two years, I often encountered these volunteers and they seemed to be doing a good job and were generally more physically comfortable than most Peace Corps volunteers. Typically, there weren't as many of them, as in this case, and they held more technical jobs. Our training group now numbered sixteen.

On the first evening people from the village of Jenoi visited our camp, led by their village chief, Alkala Jobe. The Chief walked with a decided limp and I noticed one leg was deformed, possibly a birth defect or perhaps a broken bone not set properly. They welcomed us with lively drumming and dancing. It was a wonderful ceremony. Alkala Jobe, a lovely old fellow, assigned each of us Jenoi families and encouraged us to visit them from time to time.

The next day after language training, Bruce and I visited our Jenoi families. By now, our Mandinka had progressed to where we handled ourselves adequately in greetings and could follow a bit of what people said. The people of Jenoi were used to trainees and had learned to speak slowly for our benefit. We first went to Bruce's family.

In Bruce's family, the head of the compound had three wives, common in Muslim families. The husband didn't have a hut of his own, and rotated between the wives. The family treated us well and took time to talk to us. The children in this compound were perhaps ten years and older.

The man in my family's compound had two wives and each wife had her own hut where she and her children lived. The man had his own hut. In this case, the wives rotated visiting him. A dozen or so little children ran around. On that visit, one of the wives invited me to sit and, taking a baby off her back, handed me the infant to hold. The baby, wide-eyed, stared at me and reached up to touch my face and hair. Babies were normally naked, sometimes with a cloth loosely placed around their bottoms. When a mother handed me her baby, she often put on my lap the cloth she used to hold the baby on her back. Amazingly, the babies never wet on me.

The wives seemed friendly to one another, more like sisters. With both our families, there appeared to be one older wife, close to the age of her husband, and then younger ones. The women loved to hold their arms up to mine for a color comparison. We always laughed with the contrast of ebony-black and stark white. Although by this time I'd acquired a bit of a tan, next to them I appeared pasty white.

I found the huts sparse, normally with one bed and possibly a single wood chair with a perfectly flat seat with no effort to shape it for comfort. Colorful floral sheets adorned the beds. Apparently the children slept on floor mats. Gambians didn't sleep outside; it's considered unsafe because of snakes and wild animals.

Bruce often preferred to stay in our room to read, but many afternoons I visited my family and found the women delightful, fun and always glad to see me. Compounds usually had five or six huts for extended family, sometimes with an outsider or two, usually single men, living there. The village of Jenoi was quite large with many family compounds.

I admired these women. They worked very hard and I watched as they did their family's laundry, pounded grain with large pestle and mortars, swept the sandy compound, and nursed their babies, who spent most of their time on their mothers' backs. I marveled that the strips of cloth held babies so securely. On each visit, some of the women were away from the compound, working on the farm which consisted of cooperative fields where produce or rice grew in season.

Yaya encouraged us to buy kola nuts to present to the village elders, or the head of a compound. About the size of a chestnut, the kola nut is a stimulant with more caffeine than coffee and is believed to "clear the mind, fight fatigue and increase energy." To our taste, the kola nut was bitter and unpleasant, but Gambians love them and always graciously accepted this gift of respect. At the market, we found them expensive, but we always kept a small supply of kola nuts to give as special treats.

As at the seminary, Landing served dinner around 7:30. Bruce and I followed our usual routine of late afternoon snacks, which we called our "party," to tide us over. Many of the others took a taxi into Soma, a village with a nice market and a few tiny restaurants.

Our mail situation improved with regular letters coming from my family and sister, Bruce's parents and brother, plus an occasional letter from friends. Gaps in mail service occurred, of course, with no one getting mail, but, although we had moved from place to place, our Peace Corps address remained the same. Sometimes our letters were waylaid and caught up with us, sometimes with a tire track across the envelope. We usually hadn't a clue where the letter had been, but were just glad to receive it. We continually wrote letters home, adding to them until we heard of someone going back to Banjul who would mail them.

On Sunday, three of the instructors offered to take us on a picnic to the North Bank, a district on the other side of The Gambia River. Normally, cars can go on the ferry, but that day because of low tide the ferry couldn't land close enough to allow cars to board, so we parked the Peugeot near the landing. Ocean tides affected the river, one hundred miles upriver.

Much to my surprise, we had to wade out to the ferry. The men carried the lunches Landing had packed into two cardboard boxes, so I had to worry only about myself and my small purse, plus holding my dress out of the water, which rose nearly to my knees. Then we had to climb a slippery ladder to board. It seemed quite bizarre.

Back home, my brother-in-law was at that time the manager of Washington State Ferries and he would have had been shocked to see the condition of these two ferries that crossed at Jeno. Huge gouges gaped from the sides, either from banging into things or just from rot. On the aft deck, a noisy gas pump, with a hose held together by string, strung over the deck and off the side, constantly pumped an amazing amount of bilge water. The filthy boat offered no clean place to sit.

I stood, bracing myself by a cable, and watched the activity. A deck hand, bringing in lines, worked near me and occasionally glanced my way. Finally he said in English, "I like the way you look."

A little startled, I just smiled and said, "Thank you."

Soon reaching the other side, we waded to shore and then walked a short distance to a village where we met friends of Mr. DeCosta. On the outskirts of the village we visited the site of an old fort, a lovely place with shade to eat our lunch. Landing had packed a picnic of canned beans, various lunch meats and bread. He had filled several bottles with water, which by this time was warm, but still welcomed. For this occasion, we used paper plates and plastic silverware. Napkins were rarely furnished. I used a bit of bottled water to rinse my fingers after eating.

As we finished our lunch, we placed the trash in one of the boxes. Then, much to our dismay, one of the instructors took the box over to a log and dumped the contents. We gasped, horrified at this act of littering.

I couldn't resist saying something, at least. "Why don't we take that back with us and throw it in a trash can?"

"Carry garbage back with us? Why would we do that?" The conversation ended there.

We made our way back to the ferry, climbed the ladder to board, crossed the river, again waded to shore though by this time it wasn't as deep, then piled into the truck at the other side, satisfied with the day's excursion...except for the littering.

The next morning as we walked to the dining room for breakfast, we noticed one of the instructors reach for a cigarette and then throw the empty package on the ground. Interestingly, the staff's side of rooms was often cluttered with trash while our side was clean. We obviously had different views on littering.

When Mr. DeCosta began a discussion on cross-cultural training, one of the trainees asked a question, as we were encouraged to do. The trainee mentioned that he was surprised to see our picnic trash thrown on the ground. He went on to explain that in America people used to do that, but now we had anti-litter campaigns. I added that even here at Jenoi people threw cigarette wrappers on the ground, rather than toss them in a garbage can, which happened to be right by the dining hall.

Mr. DeCosta and the other instructor with us, Musa, seemed surprised. Musa just shrugged and waved his hand vaguely."That woman will clean it up."

My hackles rose, but it did seem to be the women who kept things in order. When we visited villages, compounds were normally tidy, with the sandy grounds swept clean by the women.

I mentioned that in the United States our family camped and we'd noticed through the years how much nicer the campgrounds were nowadays than even a few years ago. People seemed to be aware of the importance of keeping places litter free. We didn't seem to make an impression on the Gambians and the discussion went on to another topic.

I gathered my courage and asked why Gambians talked so loud. Mr. DeCosta threw back his head and laughed. Loudly. "It's an old Mandinka custom, Mariama. When the men are talking they want their women to know how intelligent they are, so they talk loud enough so the women in their compounds can hear."

One evening after dinner, Alkala Jobe, village chief, walked the short distance to the camp and escorted us back to the village. The village people had gathered and formed a circle, with a special chair for the Alkala. They made room for us to join the circle and the drumming began. I loved the African drumming. A woman jumped into the circle and briefly danced, then darted back to be replaced by another woman, then another. They moved very quickly. Each modest dance only lasted seconds.

With a flourish a male dancer took his place in the center, a magnificent figure in a heavily decorated robe and hairy blue hat. Leather pouches of different sizes swung from his waist. He both sang and danced. Sometimes he sang a phrase and the people chanted back in their broad full-bodied voices. The dancer's steps always kept time to the drumming, sometimes in small steps, sometimes in great leaps.

Some people handed the dancer coins, but the gesture was more symbolic. I learned later that this is how the man makes his living and he is paid generously by the group hosting the party. When he received coins, he formed claws with his hands, looked very sinister, and his dance became more frenzied.

The event lasted about two hours. Afterward, as we made our way back to the camp in the dark, it all seemed like a dream. Drumbeats still resounded in my head. Bruce described it well when he said, "It was like a really good National Geographic special on T.V." But so much more. We were there, stood in a circle with Africans, and actually participated. I thrilled to the core.

One early afternoon, a boy, around ten years old, wandered into camp. We exchanged greetings in Mandinka and then he said something I couldn't understand. Finally, I said in English, "I'm sorry, I don't understand."

He said, *in English*, "We are to talk to you only in Mandinka so you will learn!"

Bruce came along, and I introduced him in Mandinka. *"Nying mke le, Dawda Kenteh."* This is my husband, Dawda Kenteh.

The boy's face lit up in a big smile and he said, *"Ke ning musa."* Husband and wife.

We often came upon the village people and made a point to carry on conversations, greeting them, telling them where we were going, etc. The people were lovely, patient and friendly. Unlike Banjul. I felt safe here. I wondered how our assigned village, Mansajang, would be.

In the late afternoons, after our "party" and before dinner, we often walked. The only place to walk was to the village or just down the dirt road. Walking along the road could be uncomfortable with the constant flow of honking cars. Sometimes a period of time went by with no traffic, then invariably two cars would pass us, one going each way, both honking. We called it "The Gambian Effect."

Sometimes we saw hitchhikers along the road, arm extended straight out with hands slowly moving up and down. Often, a car coming from the opposite direction stopped and the man climbed in. We were often puzzled by this. Did it not matter where he was going, he just wanted to go someplace? Or, did he figure that the vehicle would eventually go in the direction he wanted to go? Maybe he knew the driver and just wanted to chat. Lots of mysteries in The Gambia.

On one of our infrequent trips to Soma, we hired a tailor to make a special dress for me for the "swearing in" ceremony and a fancy shirt for Bruce. My dress was long with green and pink swirl designs and flowing long sleeves. Bruce's blue tye-die, short-sleeved shirt had an open neck with machine embroidery adornment.

An attractive strip cloth is woven in The Gambia and Bruce had another shirt made from it, white with a stripe of red. About twelve inches wide, they simply sew the strips together, two on the front, two on the back. The shirt was basically sleeveless and wonderfully cool.

The market in Soma was fun to visit, much calmer than in Banjul but with not quite the assortment of goods.

Yaya approached Bruce late one afternoon to say that Sainey, the other Mandinka instructor, was very sick. "Would you look at him?" We had no medical person in camp.

Bruce called on Sainey and found him in bed, his drenched bedsheets twisted around his body. Bruce talked with him awhile, then returned to our room to get our thermometer–apparently the only one at camp–and a few of our Aralen pills. We always had an ample supply, so we weren't risking our own health.

Most Africans don't take a preventive medication for malaria because they have some natural immunity. But they do take it on occasion for treatment. The most fatal type of malaria, cerebral malaria, is common in The Gambia, and that's what Sainey had. He'd had it before, he told Bruce, but this time it was much worse. Besides his high temperature, and shaking chills, he suffered from a nauseating headache.

Bruce found Sainey's temperature to be dangerously high. He gave him the medication, plus aspirin, and constantly bathed him until his body cooled. He spent the night with his patient, bathing him and encouraging him to drink plenty of water.

The next day the young instructor felt much better, but was very weak. He thanked Bruce for taking care of him. "You saved my life." It's likely Bruce did. I thought it interesting that Yaya had come to Bruce for help, but that's the kind of fellow Bruce is, he radiates confidence and efficiency. Other than advanced first aid, he'd had no medical experience.

One night the instructors built a big fire outside and we sat around it enjoying each other and the evening. Bruce had brought his guitar to The Gambia, but because of the close living quarters had rarely played it. Mr. DeCosta had seen the guitar and asked Bruce to play. He did, and sang in his rich voice. Others joined in. It was a lovely evening. The gathering reminded me of our annual family campouts back home.

Toward the end of our stay at Jenoi, our meals were getting bleak. Those in our group who often went into Soma for dinner were out of their "walk around money" so were forced to eat at camp. Yvonne, the Peace Corps Country Director, dined with us one evening. She sat on one side of me at a long table, Bruce on the other. Shirley, the Training Coordinator for this segment of our training, sat across from us.

Observing her plate of food, Yvonne said, "This isn't much of a dinner."

Indeed it wasn't. Macaroni with a trace of cheese and flecks of tinned meat, probably Spam, and mashed potatoes, plus a smattering of British canned green beans.

Shirley responded in a defensive tone. "Yvonne, I've been telling you, Landing needs money to run this camp. We can't last the rest of the week without money."

With a bit of an edge to her voice, Yvonne responded, "Shirley, I've told you, the power is off in Banjul and Tobi can't run his calculator." Tobi, a Gambian, was the office accountant and the person responsible for cutting checks.

It was not unusual for the power to be off, and its cause varied, but mostly because generators simply ran out of fuel. Apparently Tobi didn't have a battery-run calculator. Or a piece of paper and a pencil, I thought to myself.

"Can't he cut a check without using his calculator?" Shirley asked, clearly worried about this group and her responsibility.

"Oh, no, he can't do that."

Bruce leaned over to me with a look of incredulity. "Do you want to loan them some money?"

I agreed. This was ridiculous.

Bruce leaned past me to talk to Yvonne. "We can loan you some money."

Delighted, Yvonne said, "Oh, can you? That would be wonderful."

They decided that one hundred dalasi would be sufficient for the remaining days at the camp.

Lynn the musicologist remarked, "Well, it's certainly true that two can live cheaper than one."

I laughed. "I think that's true when you're doing your own cooking and can live in one place, but we're all being taken care of here. Bruce and I just don't go out for dinner."

Our training was nearly complete, though from time to time there would be occasions for additional training, especially for me as a health worker.

We had bought a pretty enamel bowl for my favorite wife of my Gambian family. Enamel bowls are widely used and more common than glass. Selleh seemed thrilled with her gift. She gave me a length of cloth. Later I'd use it to decorate our hut.

On the last day, we were given an oral language test. One trainee at a time, two instructors carried on a conversation with us to test our comprehension and vocabulary. I had studied on my own at least twice as much as Bruce, but we tested at about the same level. Everyone in our group passed training.

Our ten weeks of training was coming to an end. Next step: our swearing-in ceremony.

Bakau apartment kitchen

Chapter 8

*I*n Bakau, the Fajara Hotel was the nicest hotel in The Gambia. It was our great privilege to stay there for the days surrounding our swearing in and only possible because this was the tourist off-season and the hotel had given Peace Corps special rates. Lovely houses graced the neighborhood, homes owned or rented by expatriates or by Gambians of means.

Our room seemed like a dream in its luxury. The hotel perched on a high bank with magnificent views of the ocean. An inviting swimming pool sparkled in the center of a huge patio. Again, we were given "walk-around money" until our regular allowance started. Also, we were given "settling-in money" so that we could buy necessities to live on our own. Nurse Ann Saar encouraged us to purchase small gas stoves so that we could boil our water, if necessary. Thankfully, we wouldn't have to boil water in Mansajang since we knew our United Nations well water would be pure.

After talking with Howard, the former volunteer occupant of the UN Compound, we agreed to buy many of his furnishings he had bought from his predecessor; a three-burner butane gas stove, a table and four chairs, his radio/cassette player, folding chairs, beds, and a few other smaller items. The house we would occupy had basic cooking implements, dishes and silverware. All the items would remain in the house, saving us the trouble of having to move them.

We relaxed that weekend, blissfully free from worries and concerns. On Monday we needed to get a few things done, but for now we relaxed in the pool, soaked up air-conditioning in the rooms, read, took naps and enjoyed good food.

We were encouraged to get two things accomplished in Banjul during these three days: open bank accounts and get Gambian drivers licenses. Each month our Peace Corps allowances would be deposited directly into our bank account.

The first stop, the bank, was unfortunately typical. Throughout our two years in The Gambia, going to the bank would be a frustration. A large group of people elbowed their way toward the counter with no pretense of forming a line. The people behind the counters seemed to move in slow motion. Finally, Bruce and I stood before the clerk.

"Yeeesss?" the clerk asked with a bored expression.

"We would like to open joint checking and savings accounts."

She frowned. "What?"

"We're married, so we want joint accounts."

"Together?"

"Yes, please."

Without a word, she pushed small cards our way. Luckily I had a pen with me, since none was furnished. We completed the cards and then waited many minutes for the account to be processed. I couldn't believe how long this process took.

Bruce needed to catch a bus to the Yundum shop to take care of business, so he walked me to the police department building where I would get my driver's license. Early on, when we stayed in Banjul, Bruce was issued his license so he could drive project vehicles. At the police department, he walked me down dark dingy stairs and along dirt-streaked hallways.

He squeezed my arm affectionately. "Brace yourself. This is going to take awhile." He left to catch his bus.

As it happened, no one was in front of me in line, but still I waited for a long time for someone to help me. Many people milled around behind the counter, but it was hard to tell if anything was actually getting done. One woman slept, draped over her typewriter. Finally, I was given a form to complete and I showed the man my Washington State driver's license. He left for several minutes, then handed me my paperwork and told me to go to another room where they would attach the picture I'd brought to the license. I did as instructed and waited again.

Back and forth I went to four different counters. At the last one, which was also the first, I stood at the window and watched the fellow "process" my paperwork. He shuffled the papers around, then looked at something else on his desk. He went over to another desk and talked with that fellow, glanced at me watching him, returned to his desk, pushed papers around some more. His desk was piled with papers and I could imagine mine getting lost. Like the shell game, I kept watching to keep track of the pea, my application. Seething at this senseless delay, I said nothing but never took my eyes off my paperwork. Finally, he stood, shuffled over to the counter and, without a word, he slid my license toward me.

Three of the five items on the license were incorrect: my date of birth, my middle initial, and the spelling of my last name. I let it go, not willing to make this an even longer exercise.

By this time we had met many volunteers who lived dowriver in the Banjul area. Some were teachers, some worked at government agencies. One married couple, the people who worked in Archives who had visited the seminary, were actually former Peace Corps volunteers and were now employed by The Gambian government. The downriver people often remarked to me that upriver people stayed with them when they came to Banjul for a break or on business. I asked if that was difficult and got a variety of responses.

One said he didn't mind, they just had to buy their own food. He had a typical bachelor pad and it didn't bother him one way or the other who stayed.

The married former volunteers were less enthusiastic. "We're rarely alone." They had a Gambian cook, so meals weren't that much of a worry. "But we're leaving in six months so they'll have to find someplace else to stay." They specifically mentioned the women who were often in the Peace Corps office.

Bruce and I had discussed how awkward it would be to arrive on someone's doorstep and ask for a place to stay, especially since there were two of us. Money-wise, staying at a hotel would not be feasible. The two small business advisors in our group, Nathaniel and Norman, would need to come to Banjul for meetings on a regular basis, at least once a month. Nathaniel would live near us, in Basse; Norman would live downriver, but across the river in Farrafenni.

We approached Nathaniel and Norman about getting an apartment together for us all to use when we came downriver. They were delighted with the idea and set about looking for one. The community of Bakau was definitely more attractive than Banjul, close enough to the capital city to get things done but without the horror of actually staying in the capital city.

Nathaniel and Norman found a great place, a nice, clean two-room apartment in a Bakau row-house. They'd had a lead from a volunteer who was finishing his two years and leaving. We bought several items from the former occupant, a table, two chairs, three-burner butane stove, small refrigerator, cooking pot and pan, a few dishes, sheets and three mattresses. The two-room apartment had no running water, but water was available in the compound. The bedroom had two windows offering cross-ventilation. The double bed consisted of a foam mattress on the floor. Two single mattresses stood in the corner with space for them in the same room, or possibly in the kitchen.

A nice thing about the Bakau apartment was the availability of a flush-toilet bathroom and a separate room with a shower. The whole four-apartment complex shared the bathroom and shower, but that never proved to be a problem.

As it happened, the landlord, who lived in the house in the same compound, was the former police chief, so we didn't have break-in worries, always an issue. Nearby, CFAO, a grocery store, carried tubob food and beyond that the open market carried fresh produce and fresh fish and meat.

The fellows thought a three-way split would be fair because we were a married couple, but we insisted on paying a full half. We all agreed that we wouldn't lend the apartment out to anyone. We wanted it available for any of us when we went downriver. We would try to never be downriver when their meetings were scheduled. Since Nathaniel would live the closest to us and be constantly in touch with Norman on project business, Nathaniel would be the contact when anyone wanted to use the apartment. In the two years we shared that apartment, it worked out beautifully. It proved to be one of our best investments.

The swearing-in ceremony, held at the Chargé d'Affair's residence, was a lovely occasion. The house, though not large, was regally furnished and the dining room table splendid with refreshments. The Chargé d'Affair spoke, as did two Gambian community leaders. We were sworn in as a group, with our names mentioned individually.

After the formal swearing-in ceremony, we were all invited to Assistant Director George Scharffenberger's home for a great party where he served lots of snacks and cold beer. The party was open to all volunteers; thirty or so attended. At that time about 50 volunteers were in-country. We mingled outside in the warm evening. We had worn our new swearing-in clothes and I loved my dress. As usual, not being the party types, we left the party earlier than most of the others.

Back at the hotel, Bruce struggled to get out of his new indigo blue tie-dye shirt. He was so hot, the shirt just seemed to have become a part of him. In desperation, he asked me to just cut it off! I hesitated to do that, it was such a beautiful shirt. If nothing else, I could wear it. I tugged and tugged and, slowly, slowly peeled it off. He never wore that shirt again, but I did.

Following swearing-in, the country's health workers were scheduled to have a 3-day medical language training session followed by a 5-day medical training class at the Fajara Hotel. Although we'd looked forward to getting upriver to our new home, this was a wonderful opportunity for me and I accepted the invitation.

Bruce left for Basse in a project vehicle, taking most of our stuff, leaving only the clothes I'd need for the week. He intended to stop along the way to buy a refrigerator.

Ellen, my roommate at the Fajara, a retired nurse, was so much fun. She talked about her generally positive experiences in The Gambia. With her background she had no trouble finding her niche and keeping herself busy. I learned so much from Ellen.

I was so glad we'd already agreed with Nathaniel and Norman to not open our apartment up to others. Word gets around quickly among volunteers and many asked if they could use our apartment when they came downriver. Each time I explained that there were four of us and Nathaniel and Norman needed it frequently for their work, and we would use it occasionally too, so no, it wasn't available to anyone else.

Gearing language training specifically toward medical terms helped to solidify my vocabulary. To know Mandinka medical words such as, pain, ache, doctor, hospital, diarrhea, fever, was vital to my work. The country kept standard health records, a folder issued to each new baby at its first visit to a clinic, and we were shown how to maintain these records. All entries were made in English.

The 5-day advanced medical training also proved worthwhile. Sister M'Boge spoke several times as did a doctor from Banjul's Queen Victoria Hospital. Our group had been to that hospital on one occasion to receive our hepatitis shots. It was a very large hospital by local standards, but memorable to me was the open drainage ditch that ran from the hospital along the sidewalk to join a larger open sewer running down the street, and eventually into the ocean.

We learned what to watch for, basic symptoms for some of the common diseases in the country, and what to do upon discovering them, such as referring the patient to the closest medical clinic and helping to arrange transportation. Also important was instruction on how to care for ourselves. Everyone except me had been at their jobs for six months, so I had the advantage of hearing their questions and observations.

A discussion about girls' circumcision was a shocking eye-opener to me. I'd never heard of it. Sister M'Boge explained that although it was against the law, it was a tribal custom and commonly practiced. We were not to comment on it or act judgmental in any way. Someone asked why they did it. Sister's answer, "To prevent promiscuity and that's all we need to say," ended the conversation.

The sessions wrapped up mid-afternoon in the heat of the day and taking a dive into the pool was such a treat. The little cliques in that group remained intact, mostly those who spent so much time at the Peace Corps office, but I did get to know more of the "active" workers and felt so thankful to have this opportunity.

Bruce combined a business trip to Yundum with picking me up after the medical training session. We were anxious to be together, on our own. At last.

Baskets of sea salt at market

Chapter 9

*T*he United Nations owned all the well digging project vehicles and they were driven by the project's designated drivers. On the day Bruce picked me up, he and a driver brought a Land Rover down to Yundum for minor repairs, but they needed to get a second vehicle back to Basse. It worked out that Bruce would drive the second vehicle back to Mansajang, a lucky break for us. In the two years we would be in The Gambia, Bruce sat behind the wheel only a very few times.

Bruce picked me up at the Fajara Hotel. Crammed in the back were a small wooden table and two chairs for the hut that we'd bought from an outgoing volunteer and a case of toilet paper Bruce bought at CFAO, the "tubob" store. Anxious to get "home," we drove straight through to Mansajang. Bruce apologized for not doing much to the house, but he knew I'd want to arrange the kitchen myself. While alone, he'd slept in the house bedroom. He'd ordered a large mattress and bed frame for the hut, but they hadn't arrived yet. He found sleeping in the house hot because it was necessary to sleep under mosquito netting, which keeps mosquitoes away, but also blocks breezes.

Bruce had bought a few groceries for that first night, but he hadn't found a refrigerator to purchase, so keeping fresh food was a problem. Our first night's dinner was canned British stew and good local bread from a little store Bruce found nearby.

The first thing after breakfast the next morning, I removed the grimy curtains, slick with grease and sweat. I stooped over a three-foot broom made from straw bunched together and tied with twine and swept every inch of the kitchen. Thick dirt had collected in the corners. Chicken crap and who knew what else formed clumps on the floor. Bruce showed me how to operate the foot pump at the UN well in front of our compound and we filled two buckets. I poured water on the floor and, on my hands and knees, scrubbed it with an old brush I'd found. Next, I cleared the large table of pots and dishes, stacking them in the living room, and scrubbed down the table. Then I heated water and washed the dishes.

We still had use of the Land Rover so we took it to the market. Rules forbade private use of "official" vehicles, but Bruce felt it allowable for our initial settling in. Also, he took one day off from work to help get our home habitable.

The Basse market was smaller by far than Banjul, but quite complete. The building was a corrugated tin roof held up by concrete posts. No walls. Slabs of concrete served as counters. On the outskirts of the market proper, merchants, mostly women, displayed their wares on cloths spread on the ground. The women also sat on their cloths with no back support, legs spread straight out in front of them. Tiny stores lined the streets around the market, many owned and operated by light-skinned Mauritanians. Down the street a larger store, which everyone called "The Blue Store" because it was painted a bright blue, sold a few tubob items, such as beer, oatmeal and powered milk.

At a fabric store, we found a length of oilcloth to cover the kitchen table and the small table the stove sat on, a few towels and dish cloths. I loved The Gambia's colorful sheets with large splashy flowers. These were imported items, but reasonably priced. We bought four sheets to have enough for the guest bed, too.

At another store we purchased a pretty enamel bowl, and two dishpans we'd use for washing and rinsing dishes. We bought two more buckets so we could have a water supply in the kitchen and another in the bathing area.

One of the stores sold used clothing, obviously donated by various charities from Europe and the United States. Many of the heavy knitted synthetic materials weren't appropriate for The Gambia's hot climate, yet we saw many people wearing these clothes, sometimes with humorous results. Local women didn't wear bras, yet we occasionally saw donated bras worn outside their tops. Another interesting and frequent sight was some big, burly guy wearing a knitted, pink baby's hat, complete with tassels on the ear flaps.

We ran into Nathaniel, also setting up housekeeping, though on a much smaller scale. He asked if we had been to Pa Peacock's and learning we had not, insisted we go with him that very minute. He had checked it out with Billy that night during training after we had dinner in Basse.

Pa Peacock's White House Fuladu East Bar was a great little place, not more than ten by twenty feet large, and one of the few establishments that served alcoholic drinks. A cold beer hit the spot that hot day. Pa Peacock asked our names and thereafter always remembered them. The bar, resplendent with liquor bottles of every sort and shape on narrow shelves behind the bar, had a decidedly different atmosphere than other Basse places of business. Obviously not operated by Muslims since Muslims do not partake of alcohol, it seemed different in other subtle ways, too.

Returning to the house, I stacked our cooking utensils and dishes onto the bright new oilcloth. Two stools that came with the house served as stands for washing and rinsing dishpans.

Bruce had mixed powdered milk to have over our breakfast oatmeal, both items packaged in Denmark. We didn't use it all and by mid-afternoon it had soured and was the consistency of yogurt. We needed a refrigerator.

I had just put the kitchen in order when Tombong called on us. I'm sure he expected a job. He saw the kitchen and his eyes lit up. "Oh, fine. Oh, fine!"

"Tombong," I started, "I have cooked for my family for a very long time, for twenty years." I didn't go into the fact that Bruce and I had only been married a year, and that I had been married before. "I like to cook and keep house, so I won't need your help."

I could tell he was shocked and hurt, but he seemed to understand. He nodded. "You will cook in this nice kitchen."

"Yes, but I hope you will visit us often. There is so much we need to learn that you can teach us."

He perked up. "I will come. I will teach you what you need to know."

After the traditional Mandinka greetings, we spoke in English. His English comprehension was exceptionally good and he had a grasp of the tubob way of looking at things. Tombong had been in the army, in central Africa, and had worked with tubobs there, he said. I don't know how old he was at the time. Gambians, especially older people, don't keep track of birthdays, but I imagine Tombong was around 55, perhaps older.

Luckily, he was able to get work at the UN shop and throughout the two years we enjoyed a good, solid friendship.

Bruce's ingenuity made our lives much nicer in several ways. For one, he created a place for bathing in the space between the outside hut walls, a lovely private enclosure. He built a little stand for our soap and towels, and built a slatted board platform to stand on, keeping our feet off the dirt floor. He made a trench so that when we bathed, the water ran off. Later, he would build a little garden patch on the other side of the wall that would receive our cast-off water. Now our bucket baths seemed luxurious.

Another marvelous improvement was a latrine treatment of used motor oil which Bruce poured into the hole to kill the fly larvae. Then he built a cover, one that could be removed and slid back into place with a foot. He explained its use to our neighbors and they followed his instructions. This kept flies out of the latrine with very little further effort.

Another great improvement Bruce accomplished was bringing electricity into the hut. A wire had been strung from the shop to the house, but not into the hut. Now we could read with an electric light, rather than suffer from the heat of a lantern or the danger of an open-flamed candle. One day, hopefully, we'd buy a fan. It might not be the way Gambians lived, but it was a way we could be more comfortable and get things done.

Bruce also discovered that the commonly used bed frames have another purpose. The bed frames, made of a woven bamboo mat on top, had cross-bracing underneath. By placing the woven top to the wall, the cross bracing made ideal shelving. A single bed frame served as our kitchen pantry. There were no other shelves in the kitchen. We also placed a bed frame shelf in the hut to hold our clothes.

Right after being sworn in and on his way to Mansajang, Bruce had stopped at a little village where he'd heard bed frames were built. He custom ordered what we would call queen size, together with a foam rubber mattress to fit. The second day after I arrived, one of the fellows from the shop picked up our new bed frame and mattress on his way back from a well-digging job. Besides the bed, the little wooden table and chairs and the shelves nicely furnished our hut.

We heard of a small refrigerator for sale, very small, about three feet high and twenty-two inches deep. Its top served as a little counter, which was nice since we had few surface spaces. Now we were able to keep things cold, saving numerous walking trips to the market, more than a mile away.

As soon as we settled in, we lived entirely on one monthly allowance which amounted to about $120, and saved the second allowance in our bank account. We wanted to live more on the level of our fellow Gambians, though we obviously couldn't do that entirely. Many Peace Corps people tried to live exactly as their families, but most found their bodies couldn't be sustained in good health on the local diet.

Peggy, the fellow health worker who lived a short distance away, called on us soon after we were settled in. She couldn't believe the transformation. She knew that we wanted to do most things for ourselves, but suggested we might want to hire someone to do our laundry. I thought it a great suggestion. She mentioned that as a member of her compound, she paid a small rental fee and her food was furnished, but she did pay one of the women to do her laundry. I asked what we should pay for laundry service and she suggested a fee.

We had met our neighbors within the UN compound. Africans here were very friendly and, as part of their culture, our neighbors checked in with us daily to see how we were doing. Although Fula and originally from Guinea Bissau, Mosalif Jallow, a mechanic at Bruce's shop, spoke good Mandinka. Binta, his wife, spoke Fula and only a little Mandinka. Their two daughters Jariettu, five when we arrived, spoke only Fula, and Kujah was just months old. Although Muslim, Mosalif appeared to have just the one wife. On occasion, a Gambian might have one wife upriver and one in another village or downriver, but that wasn't the case with Mosalif.

The Fula are generally smaller than the Mandinka or Wolof, lighter skinned, and have finer facial features. I found the Fula to be the most handsome in The Gambia.

After Peggy left, I walked the short distance to our fellow compound dwellers, Binta and Mosalif's hut. When going to a stranger's door, one might say, "konk konk," but when you know a person it is more common to sort of sing out their name. "Biinnttaaa!"

Binta came out smiling, holding Kujah at her breast. Jariettu peeked at me from behind Binta's wrap-around skirt. Binta was a beautiful woman, her body strong and shapely from physical labor. Throughout our two years in The Gambia, I marveled at the African physique. We rarely saw overweight Gambians. Bruce said he'd witnessed men, powerfully built, lifting huge weights in the course of their work. Women's shapely arms and developed backs were the norm here, even among older women.

It took me awhile to get used to what I called "blue smiles." Many women, Binta included, followed the fad of painfully pricking their gums and rubbing in blue henna dye.

As did many Gambian women, Binta wore gold hoop earrings. Some women, though their surroundings were humble, wore such large gold hoop earrings; they wore a string around the earrings, looping over their head to hold the weight. I'd seen a few torn earlobes. Ouch! Large earrings often represented the family's wealth. Binta's were small, perhaps an inch across, which may have been Fula custom.

After the proper greetings, I launched into the reason for my visit. Piecing together a conversation of Mandinda and mime, I asked if I could hire her to do our laundry. She agreed, though looked puzzled.

Later that evening, Binta came with Badou, Bruce's technical counterpart and the lead mechanic from Yundum. He was only in Mansajang temporarily, having brought equipment upriver. Binta had sought him out, apparently because he could speak both English and Fula. Although her husband spoke Mandinka, I think she wanted someone she felt "official" to handle this business transaction.

After greetings, Badou stated his business. "This woman say you want her to wash your clothes."

"Yes, that's right."

"She say you want her to do this two times each week."

"Yes."

"She say you will pay her ten dalasi each week."

"Yes, is that all right?"

"Yes. That is fine. She want to make sure she hear you." The Mandinka word for "understand" and "hear" are the same and often confusing to tubobs.

* * *

Soon after we settled in, I called on Sister Roberts at her home, a short distance from the Basse Health Centre where I would work. She suggested that since she was leaving the next day for Banjul, I not start work until she returned the following week. Having the time off allowed me to explore and leisurely become acquainted with my surroundings.

I found great joy going to the market on my own. I started out early, but it quickly became hot. Waves of 100-degree heat shimmered off the rice fields and dusty road as I walked the distance to market. Carrying my cloth satchel which held a few recycled plastic bags, an enamel bowl, and an empty jam jar, I passed a tired donkey plodding along, his head hung low. He pulled a heavy cart loaded with sacks of millet. The driver whacked the donkey on his bony spine with a heavy stick.

The Gambians' inhumane treatment of animals bothered me. I could understand their not wanting to bear the cost of pets, but we'd noticed they consistently overburdened donkey carts. On our trip upriver with George we had seen boys throw a net over bushes to catch birds. After snaring them, the boys tied a string to one of the captured bird's legs and flew it around like a toy. There were apparently no animal protection laws here.

With each step I took, puffs of red dust settled on my legs and sandaled feet.

What a difference between the life I now led and making a quick dash to Safeway in Seattle.

Many people were on their way to market, both men and women. I heard my name called as I trudged along. "Mariama! *Salaam Malekum!.*" May peace be with you.

"*Malekum Salaam,*" I answered with a smile.

The young woman reminded me that her name was Haddi, one of the wives from Peggy's compound. Haddi fell in step with me and we conversed entirely in Mandinka. She carried a cloth bag on her head, and she had her youngest child, a baby boy on her back. I patted his little behind, encased in a cloth tied securely to his mother. Arriving at the market, Haddi and I parted, each to our own errands.

I stepped around a blind woman being led by a young boy. I had seen this many times at the Banjul market. The blind woman occasionally sang and the little boy rattled a can containing coins. Blind people in The Gambia are often beggers. I was appalled at the number of instances of blindness I saw in The Gambia. Eye care simply wasn't available, at least in rural villages.

I decided to go to the meat market first, get it over with. The butcher's shop, a small mud-brick building with a corrugated tin roof, was somewhat removed from the regular market. A large concrete counter separated the butcher from his customers. Clouds of flies gorged themselves on bits of meat, bone and blood splattered on the counter. Gutted and skinned goat, sheep, and cow carcasses hung from rafters. A worn and bloody log on the counter served as a "cutting board" as the butcher whacked portions of meat for the customers.

The meat market crowd pushed their way to the counter. I, too, elbowed my way through the crowd as I had learned to do with Ma-Insu in Banjul.. Whack! A hunk of beef fell off the carcass, severed with a mighty machete blow. Splat! Blood and bits of bone splattered on my dress and neck. Cringing, I held fast to my hard-fought place. Several flies left the main event, the beef carcass, and landed on me.

The butcher spoke a little English. "What you want?"

"Bif stek, please," I answered. One doesn't order steak, or ribs, or roast. You simply get what the butcher gives you and it's all called "bif stek". One of these days I'd have to try cooking goat or sheep, but I'd stick to beef for now. Whacking off a piece of meat for me, he placed it in the enamel bowl I held out to him. Then, as a treat, he dropped in a little pile of wrinkled grayish-green tripe. Stomach lining. Trying to show gratitude, I smiled, but knew I wouldn't eat it; I'd give it to Binta. As I left the meat market, my personal flies came with me. I considered the benefits of becoming a vegetarian.

Fragrances, both lovely and not so good, bombarded me as I entered the main market, a large open-sided structure. Spices, sold by the bulk, were lined up in little bins.

Large flat baskets displayed freshly roasted peanuts. The peanut vendor tore a scrap of paper--any type of paper--and folded a little package to hold the peanuts, still warm from an earthen oven.

The distinctive aroma of yeast permeated the air. Pankettas, flat yeast dough deep-fried in palm oil, and sprinkled with sugar, quickly disappeared, breakfast for many shoppers.

I skirted around piles of unpleasant smelling, fly-covered dried fish. After visiting the fishing village in Bakau, I never bought it, though I'm sure that's what we had at Peggy's. The fresh fish was lovely though and the catfish appeared to still be breathing. Anything that's still breathing must be fresh. I bought a catfish, slipping it into one of my plastic bags.

Chickens roamed freely, pecking at the ground. Some weren't so lucky and hung upside down, feet tied to a rod. They never seemed to struggle, awaiting their fate. As I shopped, I saw many women carrying live chickens in the crook of their arms as they conducted their shopping business.

The astonishing noise level rose when a bush taxi beeped his horn as he dropped riders off. Donkeys brayed as they arrived with their heavy loads. People shouted to be heard. Children darted about, squealing with their games. I'd never thought Africa would be so noisy.

Sewing machine treadles click-clacked in the background. There were no ready-made clothing shops in Basse. I needed to find a tailor and have two or three dresses made. I decided to wait until I started work so I'd have an idea of what I needed.

We couldn't seem to get enough fresh vegetables or fruit. The country in general had no cold storage so the availability of produce depended upon the season. Tomatoes were still available, since it was so soon after the rainy season. And okra, but I didn't yet know how to cook it. Peggy had told me that all year long we could buy squash grown in The Gambia, and imported onions and potatoes.

A woman signaled me to come to her table. I admired her display, piles of tomatoes. Each pile displayed a similar assortment, perhaps one large, two medium, and two small tomatoes, in various stages of ripeness. I reached out to take one out of a pile and she made a clicking sound in her throat and wagged her finger. I drew my hand back, not understanding. She cupped her hand around the pile, indicating I should take the whole pile. One chooses which pile, but does not take some from one, some from another. I purchased two piles and a piece of squash.

A large rat streaked by my sandaled feet with a cat hot on its trail. A few eyes flickered toward the motion, but no one seemed alarmed.

I spotted oranges, arranged in piles of four. I'd learned from the Banjul market that, although ripe, the orange rinds here were green. Their tough skins required a sharp knife to peel. Once, in Banjul, I'd counted 52 seeds in one orange. Bruce didn't feel they were worth the bother, but I craved fresh fruit.

I remembered I needed rice and crossed to the other side of the market where a vendor sat next to a burlap bag. The man measured rice into my plastic bag, using a porto, a tomato paste can, as his measuring device. Rice grew locally, thanks to the Chinese who taught Gambians to cultivate this essential product. It was good rice but it didn't keep well, turning buggy in just a few days. I bought only enough to last a week.

We'd talked about making pancakes, so I needed flour. A warning stenciled on the side of the 50-pound flour sack read, "This is a gift from the United States of America. Not to be sold." I purchased two scoops and moved on.

We'd made the delightful discovery of Gambian peanut butter, which they called groundnut paste. During training, Landing once served domoda, made from groundnut paste, tomato sauce and a little meat, spiced with hot peppers, and served on rice. Tomorrow I'd fix domada for dinner. I had all the ingredients except for the hot peppers which neither of us liked.

Gambians couldn't believe we tubobs spread groundnut paste on bread, but it had become our favorite lunch. I held out my jar into which the woman plopped four two-inch balls. She held up one more ball to make sure I saw that she'd given me one more as a gift. She had to push it down to make room. The fragrance was heavenly. I would definitely be a return customer to this woman. She told me her family grew peanuts and stored them for use during the year. Before going to market each morning, she pressed shelled fresh-roasted peanuts into a paste using a smooth board and an old wine bottle as a rolling pin.

I loved the coarse-grained sugar from Russia, the only sugar I'd seen in The Gambia. It would have made wonderful sugar cookies, but alas, I had no oven.

Sea salt, displayed in hand-woven baskets piled against a wall, made a pretty picture. I couldn't imagine using that much salt, but I supposed when they cooked for an entire compound they would eventually go through a whole basket. I asked for just a small portion and the vendor scooped a cup full from a basket and wrapped it in a scrap of paper for me.

On my way home from the market, I ran into Peggy and mentioned that I'd arranged for Binta to do our laundry and the subsequent conversation with Badou.

"Ten dalasi!" Peggy gasped. "That's a lot to pay for laundry."

"That's what you told me to say."

"No, I said five dalasi."

"But there are two of us, so I doubled that."

Peggy laughed. "I'd already doubled it for you. Now you're paying twice that. No wonder she got Badou to verify it."

Oh, well. To me it was worth every penny, or batoot, in local currency. Plus, we were happy to boost our neighbor's income.

* * *

While I leisurely learned about African life, Bruce had no
such luxury. Equipment returning from the rainy season at
Yundum needed his attention. It drove him crazy that so
many men aimlessly milled around the shop. Bruce felt that
the tendency of the Gambian government to hire more
people than needed encouraged the attitude of no one
taking responsibility for a job.

Badou, the lead Yundum mechanic, was efficient and
helpful, but he was needed at Yundum to take care of the
downriver well-digging operations and would only be in
Mansajang for a short time.

I found the well-digging operation interesting. A village
applied for a UN well, usually because recent drought years
rendered their traditional hand-dug wells too shallow to bring
in water. Sometimes the walls of older wells collapsed. Or
perhaps the water had been determined to be unsafe. Many
traditional wells were simply holes in the ground and animals
often fell in, fouling the water. Some wells had walls around
the opening, but still were not covered, allowing in impurities.

In some cases, whole villages were forced to move
because they had no safe water. That's a serious situation,
moving a village. Many villages were very old, dating back
generations, and people had strong ties, plus their dead
were buried there.

After a team from the UN determined that the village
would get a new well, an agreement was made that the
village would furnish the sand for the concrete and would
feed and house the workers until the well was complete,
perhaps as long as six weeks. Most of the men stayed there
during the week, but returned home for the weekend.

The concrete-lined UN wells would last virtually forever
and were designed to be operated by a foot-pump.
Unfortunately, the foot pump occasionally failed to work.
When that happened, the village men hitched up a team of
mules or an ox and pulled the lid off. The village would get
word to the shop that the pump was broken and a team

would get out as soon as possible to repair it. Wells in especially remote areas were left uncovered so villagers could get water by dropping in a bucket, often made from an inner tube, and pulling it up with a rope. From the inner-tube bucket, they poured the water into their own pails, thus keeping the well water more sanitary.

Keeping equipment in shape was key to a good well digging operation. Many of these villages were miles away, deep in the bush, and getting equipment in and out was a difficult task. An equipment breakdown in the field resulted in serious consequences.

Bruce felt under constant pressure, but he seemed to be the only one. Men straggled in late, left mid-morning to eat breakfast, which women sold just outside the UN compound. They ambled back and often found a place to sleep. Not everyone followed this pattern. Our neighbor Mosalif was a good worker, and a few others, but they were the exception.

However, once in the field, the men who actually dug wells worked very hard. Bruce often trekked to the bush and came away impressed with their work. They dug the wells by hand, lowering men down in a bucket operated by a winch. Mosalif's main responsibility was to maintain the winches which were brought in at the beginning of a job and remained until the well's completion. The men brought up dirt in the same bucket that transported men. Wells were from 35 to 200 feet deep, depending on at what level they found water.

As they dug, they installed steel mesh fortified with rebar that was placed between the mesh and the well's dirt wall. Steel six-foot wide molds were then placed next to the steel mesh and concrete poured between the molds and the dirt walls. The wells, built from the top down, were a series of connecting concrete rings, which gradually went deeper until water was reached.

Once they reached the bottom and water began seeping in, the men were brought up and they used a mechanical digger, a clam mounted on a big Mercedes flatbed truck. The upriver UN shop had three Mercedes flatbed diesel trucks, commonly used in Europe, that hauled bags of cement, rebar, ring molds, tools and welded steel mesh. Another Mercedes with the clam rotated between the upriver and downriver operations.

The upriver project also had a large dump truck with sides. Besides its dump truck use, this truck hauled workers back and forth to a well site.

If the well diggers encountered hard clay or rock, the project also had a jack hammer powered by a portable compressor mounted on a trailer

Before calling a well "completed," the team tried to dig thirty-three feet deeper than the first sign of water to ensure the well would continue producing water during droughts.

Of the upriver project's five Land Rovers, usually only three worked at one time. With all the coming and going to well projects and runs downriver, the project constantly scrambled to find ways to get what they needed. These no-frills gas-powered Land Rovers were the tropical double layered roof version, with no seat belts, no radio, and no air conditioning. They offered a rough and bumpy ride, but were tough enough to withstand the rugged African terrain. Their biggest problems were with brakes and batteries. It was a constant battle to keep the Land Rovers in running condition.

During the dry season, Bruce's team dug three to six wells at any one time. The nature of the jobs necessitated much coming and going, out to villages, downriver to Yundum to pick up equipment and supplies, such as cement and steel. Keeping the various vehicles in good running condition was essential and one of Bruce's most frustrating tasks. Obtaining parts was difficult and they often had to rob one vehicle of a battery or other part to install in another. The unforgiving terrain with its deep ruts took its toll on vehicle springs and they were often repaired with material at hand, only to break again.

To top off Bruce's frustration, an incident happened that, for Bruce, was that day's last straw. A group of men were working on something that needed a sharp knife. Karafa, the head mechanic, asked Bruce if he had a knife. Bruce reached into his pocket for a treasured pocketknife his father had given him. Some time passed and when he saw Karafa go on to another project, Bruce asked him for the knife.

"Ebrima needed it. I gave it to him."

"But it was my knife. You should have returned it to me."

"Ebrima needed it."

Bruce went to Ebrima. He didn't have it, he gave it to someone else. "He needed it." On and on. Bruce never got the knife back. It might seem like a small thing, but this is a country where articles like pocket knives are hard to find. More than that, Bruce's father had given the knife to him when Bruce turned twelve and he took very good care of it. The incident was indicative of many attitudes in The Gambia. People often didn't take care of things, especially other people's things.

* * *

I marveled that people always looked so clean. Although they might get dirty digging wells or working in the rice fields, or from performing any number of physical chores, they bathed and changed clothes frequently. Men often wore spotless, long white kaftans when they went to mosque or on business. Impressive, since all washing was done by hand.

Traditionally, women and girls hauled the water. To pump water at our UN well, one climbed stairs to a platform above the well that stood perhaps three feet from the ground. When I arrived at the pump with my two buckets, they often urged me to go ahead of them. I usually refused, saying I would wait my turn. One day I watched two girls, perhaps sisters, chatting while they filled their containers with water. The older girl, probably about twelve, filled a large laundry tub; the other, maybe eight years old, a large bucket. After the older girl filled her tub, she slid it aside to the edge of the platform while the younger girl filled her bucket.

With both containers full, the girls returned to the ground and lifted the large tub onto the older girl's head which had a circle of cloth on it to cushion the load. Then, with that heavy load on her head, the older one helped the younger girl heft the pail of water onto her head, never spilling a drop. Throughout the whole procedure they carried on a normal conversation, pausing only briefly to heft the containers, then walked back to their compound, still chatting, the heavy containers balanced on their heads, with perhaps one arm extended to steady it.

The UN well in front of our compound was a popular watering hole for all of Mansajang. Although the village proper did have a water spigot, it often didn't work and people complained of the water's taste. All day long, women and girls came to the UN well to fill their tubs and pails of water, carrying the heavy loads on their heads as they returned to their compounds.

Because washing clothes has such a high demand for water, many women washed clothes right there at the well, then carried their clean wet clothes home to hang on their compound fencing. They used the local soap, OMA, made from peanut by-products. Bruce became concerned about soap residue filtering through the soil into the well water.

He made a circle of rocks around the well a safe distance away and asked the women to wash clothes outside the circle and explained that this would keep the well water clean. It made more work for them, having to haul their heavy tubs farther from the water source, but they obliged him when he was there, and promptly went back to their former habits when he wasn't. Bruce patiently reminded them with good natured banter. The problem, of course, was that the women didn't understand they were jeopardizing their own water supply.

One evening a man from Mansajang called on us and asked Bruce to talk to the village about safe water. This particular man was probably sent because he could speak English. Apparently the village elders had gotten wind of a problem with the well and wanted everyone to understand. Delighted, Bruce accepted his invitation.

"What time should we be there?" I asked.

Surprised with the question, the fellow answered, "After evening prayers. You'll hear the drum." Gambians had a different sense of time than we did. Watches or even clocks were rare. Activities centered around Muslim prayer calls five times a day. When it was time, people, mostly men, stopped what they were doing, brought out their prayer mats, faced Mecca to the east, and prayed.

A word about the drums. Three basic types of drums are common in The Gambia: the rhythm drum, used for dancing; the ceremonial drum, used for more serious things such as funerals or other somber events; and the talking drum. The talking drum has a sort of "boink, boink" sound to it with varying pitches. People understand the talking drum, as they understand their language, whether it be Mandinka, Wolof, or any of the tribal languages. The talking drums provide tremendously efficient communication, especially in areas where there is no telephone.

Knowing that we would hear the drum, we agreed to be at the village meeting place.

Sure enough, we heard the drum soon after we'd finished our dinner. We walked to the center of Mansajang, perhaps a half mile away. The meeting place, a large woven platform under a giant baobob tree, was devoid of people. One lone person walked by.

Our conversation was entirely in Mandinka, I greeted the man, then said, "Where are the people?"

"The people aren't here." Such a typical response. I never got used to it. The man resumed his walk.

"But we heard the drum. We are here for the meeting," I called after him.

He turned to look at me, shook his head and tsked. "The drum said there was no meeting."

Apparently one of the village's important people couldn't attend so the meeting had been postponed.

Gambians found it hard to believe that we could understand, or "hear," Mandinka, but we couldn't "hear" the drums. I'm sure in their eyes we were so hopeless.

Basse hospital with Land Rover ambulance

Chapter 10

I had mixed feelings about my first day at the hospital, excitement about doing something worthwhile, yet apprehension of the unknown. The mile-long hot, dusty walk from Mansajang was about a half mile closer to our home than the market. The hospital, a 2,000 square foot concrete one-story building, had been white-washed, but outside, the surrounding dirt, splashed up from heavy rainfall, stained the lower half reddish brown.

Many people milled around outside, family members who took care of their sick relatives, feeding them and tending to their personal needs. At least one family member stayed at the hospital compound to care for their loved one. The hospital served basic food to the patients, cooked on an open fire behind the hospital. Any special dietary needs were the responsibility of patients' families.

Electricity for the Basse area was often spotty with generators either having mechanical problems or running out of fuel. The water system at the hospital ran on electricity so when the power was off, so was the water.

Stepping into the hospital for the first time, I gagged from the putrid smell. Flies were everywhere. Windows didn't have screens and the front door was left open. Ceiling fans helped circulate air, but enclosed areas were stuffy and hot.

One nurse apparently had been there all night. She didn't greet me, only glanced my way. Later I learned that if a problem arose during the night, one of the orderlies fetched the doctor from his home. Although a telephone sat at the front desk, the phone did not work until about the last three months of my two-year term.

The workday at the hospital started at eight but people didn't start trickling in until around eight-thirty or so. Having arrived at eight, I sat at the front table until others filed in. Sister Roberts arrived, greeted me warmly and introduced me to people as they arrived.

Sister Roberts, the head nurse, had been well educated in England; the two nurse mid-wives were educated in-country, but seemed knowledgeable; the eight or so auxiliary nurses received on-the-job training and my first impression was not good. Sister Roberts and the two mid-wives wore white uniforms, the auxiliary nurses wore pink checkered dresses. Three or four orderlies in green scrubs milled around. The hospital, like so many Gambian establishments, clamored with noise.

It was required that the nurses could speak and write in English, however, they spoke to one another in local dialects. After awhile I could keep up when they spoke Mandinka, but I couldn't follow Wolof, the other main language spoken between them.

Doctor Ceesay, educated in Russia as were most Gambian doctors, enthusiastically greeted me and immediately invited me to accompany him on his rounds.

"Doctor," I said, "I'm not a nurse. I am here to help maintain records."

"Yes, yes, I know. Come." Doctor Ceesay was the only doctor for the 130,000 people in the Upper River Division, one of the country's five administrative divisions.

Sister Roberts and all the auxiliary nurses accompanied the doctor on his rounds. The nurse mid-wives' main responsibility was child-birth, and they immediately attended to two women patients. Actually, women rarely came to the hospital for childbirth. The rule of thumb for hospitalized childbirth was for first births (those "women" were often thirteen or fourteen years old), twin births, and women who had given birth to more than twelve children. In reality, only complicated births normally happened at the Basse hospital.

Going on rounds turned out to be one of the grimmest experiences of my life. Doctor wore street clothes and went from bed to bed examining people with health problems, the likes of which I had never seen. Of course, I'd never seen the inner-workings of any hospital, except when it applied to me or a member of my family, and I had never seen some of the conditions I saw that day.

The staff made no attempt to wash hands between patients, no gloves or special gowns were worn. Linens, stained and torn, were washed by hand. Patients wore their own clothes.

Most patients either stayed in the men's ward, the women's ward, the children's ward or the maternity ward. Two rooms were reserved for those patients whose condition required quiet. A man occupied one of the private rooms, now darkened with a cloth draped over the window. Doctor Ceesay motioned for us to be very quiet. The man had cut his finger, not seriously, but had contracted tetanus as the result. Any noise or bright light would send him into painful convulsions. We stood in the doorway while Doctor quietly went to the patient's side.

"I'll come back later when he's awake," he whispered when he returned to the hall.

We rarely heard of anyone getting tetanus in the United States. Tetanus vaccine was available in The Gambia, but they often ran out of vaccine or the people failed to get periodic injections. Tetanus is very serious, and although this man lived, in the course of two years I saw several people die of tetanus.

In the women's four-bed ward, a young woman lay with her leg propped on a pile of cloths, the leg swollen and raw from a skin infection. Basse had no diagnostic equipment. Rarely, specimens were sent to Queen Victoria Hospital in Banjul for diagnosis. After many weeks, at her husband's insistence, the woman was discharged only to be readmitted and die two days later.

A patient in the two-bed men's ward had a condition that made his scrotum swell as large as a football. As modest as these people were, in the hospital they seemed to have no inhibition and the man flung open his covering to show the doctor and the rest of us. I learned this condition was not uncommon and the patient would eventually die.. A member of the patient's family fanned away flies and made efforts to make him comfortable.

The children's four-bed ward made me sad. Although there were many reasons why a child would be admitted to the hospital, the underlying reason was usually the result of malnutrition. I would later learn the reasons for this and perhaps I could make a difference.

As we moved from patient to patient, Doctor Ceesay made comments to Sister and gave instructions to the nurses. Very little was written on their charts. Occasionally Doctor's temper flared at some obvious neglect.

The hospital had about nine patients in all. People didn't willingly come here for treatment. It was thought of as a place to die, and for good reason. In fact, the Peace Corps nurse Ann Saar warned us against coming to this hospital ourselves, even in an emergency. "Make every effort to get to Banjul and see me. Or send for me."

It wasn't my job to learn about the various illnesses I saw and I didn't want to be drawn into the responsibility of providing treatment, but each day doctor asked me to accompany him on his rounds.

An operating room, or theatre as they called it, stood just off the lobby and contained a set of cupboards, a padded surgical table with stirrups, and a floor lamp. Nothing matched in the hospital, as though they had acquired equipment from various sources over a period of time.

The hospital dispensary, off to one side of the lobby, contained a refrigerator, cupboards, an autoclave, and a large wooden table with a two mismatched chairs. Nothing looked clean. I constantly swatted at flies and tried not to think of where they'd landed before me.

Attached to the hospital, a dispensary was open six days a week. The dresser dispenser, a person with pharmaceutical training, treated less serious injuries and dispensed medications. These were government-run facilities and there was no charge for treatment or medication.

Later in the day I needed to use the restroom. I asked one of the auxiliary nurses where it was and she pointed to a room at the end of the building. I stepped into the dingy room and decided I could wait. The one latrine had no degree of privacy, was a mere hole in the concrete floor and had no sink to wash afterwards. The smell was dreadful. I retreated as quickly as I could.

Nathaniel had shown us his small business advisory office, close to the compound where he lived and a short distance from the hospital. His office had, miracle of miracles, a real bathroom with a flush toilet. I called on him that day and received permission to use his bathroom any time. If he was on trek, he would leave a key in a designated hiding place. What a pal.

That night, at dinner, I tried to tell Bruce about my day at the health centre. I gagged and couldn't continue. What I had seen affected me so deeply, I couldn't even talk about it. Rare for me.

I did share with him my worry about not being able to tell the auxiliary nurses apart. "They all look alike!" I wailed. All were African with black, kinky hair, all wore pink striped uniforms. I didn't know how I'd ever learn their names when I couldn't even tell one from another.

We laughed, remembering when in training I had asked Mr. DeCosta a question when we visited a village. Anxious for us to mingle with the villagers, he said, "Ask that boy."

I looked where he pointed, but saw several boys. "Which one?"

"That dark one."

At the time we thought his comment so funny, they all looked dark. But later I did see that there were shades of darkness.

Now I faced the same dilemma and it worried me. I was to work with these women and it was important I learn their names. But, as it turned out, it didn't take long at all for me to recognize them as individuals and I could laugh at my earlier concerns.

Interestingly, at first Gambians confused Peggy and me. Peggy was shorter and about twenty years younger. How could they possibly confuse us? Soon, through association, they could tell the difference, as I could with them.

It took several days before I could tell Bruce about the grimness of the hospital. I usually waited until after dinner to describe my day.

Each week, the Basse Health Centre conducted an antenatal clinic and a well baby clinic for children five years and younger. Sister suggested that I attend these clinics, where record keeping was vital.

The next day, Tuesday, I helped in the antenatal clinic. The clinic, a separate building in the hospital compound, had rows of perhaps fifty chairs on one side and a couple of tables at the other. Outside, the overflow waited in a covered area. Many of these pregnant women had come from miles away, most walking, some arriving in bush taxis. or donkey-pulled carts. Many carried babies on their backs.

Women and their children stood in line, which was a phenomenon to me. My African experience so far had been crowds of pushing people, at banks, the post office, the ferries and bus stops. But here the woman formed a queue, as instructed, and stayed in line.

At one table, the auxiliary nurses reviewed the woman's personal health record, took blood pressure, and pulled down the lower eyelid to look for pale coloration, a sign of anemia. Many Gambian women were anemic due to frequent childbearing. The woman then progressed to the next table to see the nurse mid-wife while I recorded the woman's name and entered information in a ledger. All during this procedure, I noticed women shielding their eyes from me. Some actually cupped their hands around their eyes to avoid looking at me.

I asked the nurse mid-wife why the women wouldn't look at me. "Oh, Mariama, it's a stupid superstition that if they see a white person they'll have an albino baby."

I had seen African albinos and it is an unfortunate condition. Their skin is white and their eyes affected with extreme light sensitivity. Having an albino baby would be something to fear. It bothered me that the women felt threatened by my presence.

After clinic that first day, I told Sister Roberts about my concern. She also scoffed at the superstition.

"But still," I countered, "I don't want to give them that worry."

We agreed that I wouldn't attend the antenatal clinics, but she definitely wanted me to attend the well baby clinic on Fridays.

I'd noticed a definite reserve among the auxiliary nurses toward me. I believed they felt threatened, that perhaps I would change things. I needed to find a way to dispel these fears. If anything, I needed to learn from them.

A team of one mid-wife, four auxiliary nurses, a dresser-dispenser (pharmacist), and an orderly/driver trekked to outlying villages every Wednesday, rotating to eight different locations for well baby and antenatal clinics. It was agreed I would accompany them the following day. I could hardly contain my excitement.

Wednesday morning as I walked to work, I prayed that I could be of help, and a real part of things. I arrived at the hospital, eager to go on trek. We were to leave at 9:00. By now, I realized that plans and actuality were entirely two different things, but still I had hopes of leaving close to the appointed time. The orderly and nurses poked around, talking and laughing, half heartedly loading equipment into the Land Rover.

The Health Centre's two Land Rovers were used as ambulances and for trekking to outlying villages. The staff futzed around until finally, we were ready to leave. But no, the orderly had to get fuel. Outside of the capital city, there were no facilities that we would call gas stations, but in major areas a government supply center dispensed fuel. So the orderly set off in the Land Rover for fuel.

A few minutes later, the orderly casually walked into the hospital where we waited and said, "Acha," an indispensable, all-purpose word meaning, "Let's go," "Hurry up," "Come on," or even "Get out of the way!"

At 10:30 we all piled into the Land Rover. I was embarrassed by our lateness. While we were dawdling, those women we were to see and their children waited for us, many having walked from neighboring villages. I forced myself to relax. At least we were finally on the road. The orderly pulled into the market and everyone except me filed out. Oh, no. Now what? They came back with food. Of course, they hadn't had their breakfast yet. We drove another little bit and stopped again. This time two nurses climbed out and were gone for several minutes When they returned, I noticed one carried a package of cloth, probably for a new dress. I was beside myself with anxiety. After all the delays, it still took about an hour of bouncing around on rough roads to get there, then more time to set up.

Finally, clinic began. Women brought their babies to the weighing station, then the children were given any injections due. At each step, I recorded treatment on the child's health record, a folder each mother brought. I was impressed with the mothers' dedication and careful attention they gave to their children's health records. I had seen enough huts to know the challenge of keeping any kind of record clean and out of harm's way. Most women kept important papers in a cloth-covered bowl stored in a safe place.

Being unfamiliar with African names, I couldn't at first distinguish clothed baby boys from girls. I soon realized that baby boys often had their heads completely shaved, while girls had a patch of hair left in front. Shaving was done for lice control and continued until the children were about three. Not every family did this. The little girls in our compound did not have shaved heads. On the other hand, our compound only had two children; many compounds had numerous kids, increasing the chance of lice.

In many instances, babies were being seen for the first time, since they were born at home. It was amazing to watch as babies were placed on their mothers' backs. For the tiny newborns, the mother leaned forward while another woman placed the baby on its mother's back and the mother wrapped the cloth around to secure her child. As the babies grew older, the mother slung the baby around by a firm grip to the upper arm and shoulder. The baby seemed to instinctively cling to the mother's back while she secured the cloth.

The older children, up to five years old, more often than not had younger siblings. The children were well behaved, but crying, screaming, and loud talking filled the clinic.

As injections were given, it appeared from where I sat that the nurses were reusing the needles. No, it couldn't be. But with all the noise and confusion, plus tending to my own duties, I couldn't be sure.

The auxiliary nurses' rudeness to patients often embarrassed me. My observations so far in Africa were that anyone in a uniform seemed to lord it over others. If a child was underweight, the nurse loudly scolded the mother, berating her in front of the others.

Although this was a clinic for well babies, mothers often brought sick children in for treatment. Some were given medications and others referred to the hospital. In some cases, if the child were very ill, the woman and child returned to the Basse center with the Health Centre team.

The following Friday, we held the well baby clinic at the Basse Health Centre. Glad I'd had the experience of working the smaller one, I was nevertheless overwhelmed with the sheer numbers at the Basse clinic. We saw about three hundred children that day. Still, even with that crowd, it was orderly with the women forming queues.

To keep track of serum supplies, it was important to tally the numbers and kinds of injections given. To me, the most effective way to tally is by fives: making four vertical lines with the fifth running diagonally across the four. Then one can easily count: five, ten, fifteen, twenty, etc. In Basse, one sheet of paper was used for each type of injection. The nurses simply made a mark on the paper so by the end of the day, the paper was filled with little marks with no order at all, making it impossible to count accurately.

I casually showed the nurses how tallying might be done more efficiently, but in the two years, I could never convince them. Finally, I asked them to count their random marks and place the count on top of the page. In two years that never changed, though they witnessed how I did it and how easily I could tally a final figure.

A variety of tribes comprised the region's population, commonly Mandinka, Wolof, Serahule, and Fula. Sitting at the table with Sister and me was Seri, an elegantly dressed woman, about fifty years old. Seri could speak all those languages plus English, and although she wasn't a nurse, managed to convey instructions to the women in their own language. Unlike most of the auxiliary nurses, Seri was polite and friendly to the women, treating them with dignity.

I learned the hard way that Seri could not read. I couldn't make out the spelling of the woman currently being seen. Many of the names were still unfamiliar to me. I showed the card to Seri and she made that interesting clicking in her throat. That's usually a negative and it occurred to me then that she couldn't read. How impressive. She could fluently speak several tribal languages and English, but couldn't read nor write.

Illiteracy rate was high among women. At that time illiteracy rate among adults in the country was around 93 percent. Seri's instructions were often drawn on a scrap of paper indicating a rising sun, high sun and lowering sun, meaning to take the medications three times a day. Or, she'd draw a pill with two halves, which meant cut the pill in half.

Sister dispensed pills, but only what patients needed for the next two or three days. Containers were at a premium, so pills were packaged in cone-shaped paper packages the nurses made. After awhile I grew adept at making them, too, but it took awhile for me to get them as tight as they did. The paper used was anything at all, certainly nothing sterile.

I paid special attention and discovered that, indeed, they used disposable needles over and over again until the needle would no longer puncture the skin. Only then would they switch to a new needle.

One day I asked Doctor Ceesay about it, trying to be diplomatic, but feeling a need to say something. "Doctor Ceesay, do you think it's safe to use disposable needles more than once?"

We spoke in English, thankfully, because I didn't yet have much of a medical vocabulary in Mandinka. "Mariama, I know your concern. We don't have the money to buy a needle for each time."

"But couldn't they be sterilized?"

"Do you know how much work it is to get a fire going, to boil water? We don't have that kind of time."

"How about the autoclave, wouldn't that work?"

He scoffed, though politely. "That autoclave hasn't worked for years. It was some cast-off to begin with."

I opened the autoclave and found a package of cigarettes, probably one of the orderly's.

"There are a lot of things here, Mariama, that aren't right. We just do the best we can."

How can you argue with that? The injections they gave saved lives, but introduced problems, too. It was a balancing game, choosing the lesser of two evils.

* * *

One of the fisheries volunteers from our group called on us soon after we'd settled in. We liked Kevin and were anxious to hear how everything was with him. He lived in a village a few miles from us.

"Now that things are settled, it's fine, but it was tough going at first."

Kevin went on to say that when we all went to our potential job sites during training, he had made his living arrangements to stay in the Alkala's compound. He would pay a small amount of money, have his own room in a row house, and the fee would also cover meals and laundry.

He'd arrived in the late afternoon and was unsure what to do about dinner and no one approached him about mealtime. Kevin was about twenty-three or so, still hungry much of the time.

He'd gone to bed hungry, so was hopeful about breakfast. He didn't know his way around yet, had no transportation and didn't have a clue about how to get to a market, or anywhere that would have food.

Breakfast time came and went. At that time, he didn't realize that most Gambians don't eat breakfast, they have a mid-morning meal. He saw the Alkala's wife and asked her, but she couldn't understand him. Her husband came along and Kevin asked him when a meal would be served, that he hadn't eaten since noon the day before.

The husband started yelling at his wife, then proceeded to beat her, pounding on her back with his open hand.

Kevin, mortified that he had caused this problem, didn't know the proper thing to do. The wife scurried off and brought back a bowl of cold food, leftovers from the previous night.

The poor guy was still shaken up by the ordeal, but at least now that he knew the routine, was getting regular meals. He was so happy to have dinner with us and have "real food." We saw Kevin and the other fisheries people frequently.

* * *

Chickens roamed around every compound, including ours. They were scrawny things, living entirely by foraging for themselves, maybe given a little rice. I'd never had chickens and loved watching Binta's. When one of her hens had chicks, I marveled at the mother's sense of protection.

Grotesque turkey vultures flew around the compound, occasionally landing on our corrugated roof with a loud thud, then taking off with a screeching of claws on the tin roof, like fingernails on a chalkboard. Up close they were ugly birds, though we found them magnificent while soaring on thermal updrafts.

The hen kept a sharp eye for predators and seeing a vulture, gathered her chicks under her protective wings. She'd hunker down, but we could see tiny feet of perhaps a dozen chicks huddled under her.

Gambians raised chickens for meat; eggs weren't a part of their diet. They felt eating eggs made a person stupid. For us, getting enough protein proved to be a challenge. Meat was available most mornings at the market, but it was tough and stringy. I frequently prepared stews and the long cooking time helped tenderize the meat. On days that I worked, I could only fix meals that didn't take so long to cook. We bought a grinder, but that was a messy job, especially without running water.

We needed chickens to solve our protein problem. I had seen live chickens for sale at the market, but when I talked to Binta, learned these chickens were past laying eggs and sold for meat. She apparently told Mosalif we wanted chickens.

The next morning when Mosalif came to our door to greet us, he asked if we wanted him to buy chickens. Work that day would take him into the bush and he could buy young hens for us. I asked how much money he needed and gave him money enough to buy four.

Unfortunately, Bruce needed to meet with the UN project lead in Yundum and would be gone for two days. But knowing that we would be getting chickens, he had fixed up the other outside passageway of our hut as a chicken coop. Africans didn't coop up their chickens, since they didn't gather eggs. Binta's chickens roosted where ever they found a safe place, often in one of the empty compound huts or on a tree branch. Since we didn't care to have an egg hunt every day, we needed to confine our chickens for at least the night and part of the day.

One half of the space between the outside walls of our hut was our bathing area, the other half a chicken coop.

Bruce cobbled together a gate to keep them in. We found straw for them to make their nests. To begin with, we could feed them rice that had already turned buggy. While downriver Bruce planned to buy real chicken food, a by-product from peanuts. We began grinding up egg shells to mix with their food so that the extra calcium would ensure stronger shells.

At the end of the day, Mosalif stopped by with four young chickens, two of which he said would give us eggs, the other two would produce soon. I was thrilled.

Only having had dogs and cats, I worried that the chickens would run off, maybe join Binta's brood. To make sure they knew where they lived, I tied strings to one leg of each of the four chickens, long enough for them to get to a nest, drink water and eat rice. My intention was to only do this for one day, until they were used to their surroundings.

On that first day Mosalif came over in the early evening to see how I was doing with the chickens. When he saw the strings, he knelt down to get a closer look. Mosalif and I conversed only in Mandinka. *"A mong beteata."* This is not good, he said, watching the chickens trying to walk around, lifting the tied leg high, giving them a strange gate.

"I'm afraid they'll run away."

He looked somber, but in thinking about it afterwards, I'm sure it was all he could do to keep a straight face. "You have fed them, Mariama. They won't run away." He carefully removed the strings. "When it is dark, they will come back to this place. Then you close the gate."

Well, I wasn't at all sure about that, but I'd give it a try. Sure enough, at dusk they all filed into the chicken coop as though they'd done it all their lives. I closed the gate behind them.

During our stay in The Gambia, we derived great pleasure, entertainment and nourishment from our chickens. We were the only volunteers in-country with chickens and I marveled at that. Once a week we enjoyed an egg dinner, usually an omelette, and eggs for breakfast once or twice a week, plus I used eggs in puddings and other desserts. I found I could make a double boiler by inserting my covered enamel bowl into my large pot filled with water and prepare a very good cheese souffle or a delicious bread pudding, both dishes using four eggs.

Even though there were plenty of nests, two or three chickens often crammed into one nest, African style, like people on bus seats. Our flock grew, some we bought, many were given to us. At the most we had seventeen chickens.

We named our chickens, names that seemed to fit their little personalities: Ruth Schultz, Blue, Kunta Kinte, Myrtle and Penny, who was the color of a copper penny.

* * *

As weeks became months, we fell into a daily routine. The first thing we heard in the mornings was the sound of women pounding grain in their large wooden mortar and pestles. Often, two women pounded together, alternating strokes. It made a lovely, rhythmic sound. Once, on an early morning walk, we watched as a woman and girl pounded millet. They greeted us and I asked if I could try. It was a lot harder than it looked—that pestle was heavy. No wonder those woman had such strong physiques.

On a workday morning, while Bruce fixed breakfast, normally oatmeal from Denmark or possibly eggs, I swept the hut. With a thatched roof and the subsequent grass particles and termite droppings, bits and pieces landed on our bed and the floor. In the hut, we didn't need mosquito netting but we soon learned to rig a sheet over our bed as a canopy to protect us from droppings. Still, I needed to shake out our bedding every morning. The poor quality concrete floor continually produced a fine powder. The amount of sweepings amazed me.

Frogs permanently resided with us, particularly in the house, though they occasionally made their way into the hut, too. We had one of our trunks in the house bedroom that we used for storage. When I pulled out the trunk to clean behind it, I often saw the frogs stacked up, crowded into a tight corner. After I recovered from my first jolt of surprise, I didn't mind the frogs, knowing they ate bugs. Of course, it was a trade off. The frogs left their droppings around the house. Well, never mind. I'd rather put up with frog turds that bug bites. I swept every day anyway.

Tombong usually stopped by in the mornings on his way to work. After the traditional greeting, we often had questions for him. Where to buy things, how much should we pay, what did it mean when people said a certain thing. It was wonderful being able to talk to someone in our own language, yet someone of a different culture who could explain a word or translate a meaning.

Another frequent morning guest was Alieu, a boy of about ten years old. Other children occasionally came, many begging for money or candy, but Alieu came just to see us, never asking for anything. He was frank. "I want to see how the tubob live." Fair enough.

Alieu, a delightful boy, found his way into our hearts. Once he brought his little sister, probably about two. She sat next to him, on the same chair, never making a sound. He occasionally spoke to her, she merely nodded, eyes big with all those new things.

In addition to brief morning visits, Mosalif, always dignified and respectful, stopped by when we had guests. It gave me great pride to introduce him to our friends. Sometimes he'd come to greet those he'd met before, like Nathaniel or Peggy. He wouldn't stay long, just long enough to pay his respects.

Bruce had a short distance to walk to work, so left the house around eight. I straightened and swept the house, then left around nine, depending on the day's plan. On well-baby days I left earlier, around eight. I didn't work on Saturdays, so while Bruce worked a half day, I caught up on chores.

Mid-afternoon most days found us both at home. Nothing at all went on at the health centre. All of my business was conducted earlier in the day, even treks to outlying villages. Bruce found mornings the productive time at the shop and after teams left for the bush there was little that could be accomplished in the heat of the day. In any event, he was right next door if needed. Bruce often accompanied teams into the bush to oversee repair of a well pump or perhaps broken equipment and he could be gone most of the day, sometimes into the evening, but most days found us both at home at least by three.

Afternoons were generally quiet. Commonly, the only sound we heard was the soft cooing of doves in the large acacia tree at the back of the property at the adjacent UN shop.

We resumed our earlier habit of having dinner around six. I tried to avoid washing dishes in the dark since the light in the kitchen attracted bugs. Once, when we had eaten late and I stood at the stool washing dishes, I felt something on my neck and raised my shoulder to get it off. A painful stinging followed. I'd been stung by a blister beetle and the subsequent trail of blisters were an annoyance that lasted for days.

We often sat on our stoop at dusk and watched our chickens file into their coop, listening to their low mummers as they settled down. We'd wait a few minutes, then close the gate, not to be opened until mid-afternoon when we'd let them out to forage for bugs and what scraps of vegetation they could find.

In the early evening, as heat of the day subsided, we walked a mile or so, many times longer, always taking with us our flashlight, a snake-bite kit, and water. We grew accustomed to shining the light ahead of us a few feet, looking for snakes, then turning the light off to enjoy the peace of night as we walked.

Night skies in Gambian rural areas are spectacular. Because of the pure air with very few pollutants and the lack of city light, the sky and especially the moon look to be within touching distance.

Sometimes our evening walks took us through Mansajang, following paths that wove between the many circular family compounds. Most compounds were enclosed by krinting fences, some only waist high, some taller like ours. It became obvious which families were poor: those compounds where the krinting fence was cut in half, or broken with jagged holes. The huts might have uneven grass-thatched roofs or the hut itself sagged from years of weather. Chipped, worn pestle and mortars often indicated the family's financial status.

Between the compounds, stringy vegetation grew, plus a few trees that managed to survive drought conditions. The baobob and mango trees seemed to thrive in that climate and offered shade and, in season, fruit. Young people gathered in open spaces and we often stopped to watch and listen to drumming, singing and dancing. The drumming continued on into the night.

If our walks took us farther than Mansajang, we walked along common paths or back roads. To walk through a village, protocol would dictate we first call on the Alkala and state our business. We could walk freely in Mansajang where we lived and where people were used to us.

Between villages, open fields had more vegetation. Sheep and goats were often tethered for the night, sometimes tied to a tree, or staked. To us they all looked alike, but apparently their owners could tell one from another. Bony cattle also roamed, but they normally had a Fula herdsman with them, often young boys. Sustenance for sheep, goats and cattle was only what they could forage, thin grass and leaves from shrubbery. Tree branches bore an almost straight line where cattle stretched their necks to crop off leaves. During the rainy season, the foraging animals had better fare, but for much of the year it was slim pickings.

After our evening walk, we usually sat outside and talked. We never tired of that nor ran out of conversation. On some evenings Bruce played his guitar and sang. Around nine o'clock, a breeze cooled us. We usually waited until dark to take our bucket baths so the coolness would last.

Nightly we drifted off to sleep with the sound of drumming in nearby Mansajang. Sometimes we heard singing, but always drumming. We loved the African rhythm. Lynn, our volunteer musicologist, told us that Gambians have an extra beat and once she identified it for me I, too, could hear it. Spectacular!

Sometimes during the night we awakened, drenched in sweat. We found that if we got up and poured a scoop of water over our heads in our bathing area, we could get back to sleep before it dried.

We were comforted to have each other, but during the hot season we could be little more than good friends. Closeness was simply too uncomfortable. It seemed impossible that we would be doing this for two years. Just living was hard work, devoid of many conveniences we'd taken for granted: ready transportation, easily accessible food, running water, clean, comfortable surroundings, flush toilets, availability of sanitary medical facilities. We had committed to this for the long haul, but could we last two long years?

Nurse holding malnourished child

Chapter 11

We often invited nearby volunteers Peggy and Nathaniel for dinner. Nathaniel's living situation was good and he enjoyed his compound family's food. Sometimes he cooked dinner and invited us over. He was a self-sufficient fellow and became one of our best friends. Fun and funny, he was easy to be with and we shared many common interests.

Although often frustrated, Nathaniel went about his job as small business advisor with energy. It was tough gearing down to the level of the local "small business." His clients ran stores that carried perhaps five items at the most: tomato sauce, bread, cigarettes, which were most often sold in ones and twos, perhaps produce in season. Gambians first loyalty is to family, but that generosity is often short-sighted to the western mind. For instance, all of that month's profit might go to satisfying a brother's need to repair a bicycle. The problem with that is that the merchant now has no money to buy products to sell. Planning for the future is almost non-existent. Still, Nathaniel found creative ways to advise his clients and became a respected business resource for them.

Bruce and Nathaniel set up a once a week program for what they called a "knowledge exchange." Nathaniel, a graduate of Duke University specializing in international business, felt woefully inept dealing with radio and electronics. Bruce, on the other hand, wanted to learn trigonometry and other higher math principals. They traded books and set up lesson plans for one another. I got into the act, too, when Nathaniel mentioned to me he had a college level accounting book and asked if it would be of interest to me. Our study evenings often included dinner and it was a time we cherished.

Peggy's living arrangement was also pretty good and she was an accepted member of her compound, but the food wasn't very good. Although we did eat there a few times, more often Peggy joined us for dinner.

Peggy's working situation was a frustration to her. As a health worker, she had been advised to work with the Upper River Health Inspector. Although I wasn't involved, what I observed was that Peggy had pretty firm ideas about how that department should be run. The Health Inspector seemed happy with the situation as it was. With meeting dates not kept and change non-existent, Peggy's frustration with the Health Inspector grew, but rather than turning to other projects, it seemed she just waited for things to improve.

Many volunteers who recently graduated from college were challenged when they tried to find their niche in The Gambia. Unsure of what to do, unsure of their own potential, they often did almost nothing productive. From my perspective, that was the problem for many of the volunteers I had so often seen in the Peace Corps office. Now that I was in the field, I could appreciate their frustrations. What so many volunteers lacked was the self-confidence to forge ahead and create their own job. They could only envision possibilities one way and if that didn't work, nothing worthwhile happened.

That's how I viewed Peggy's situation. Her language skills were excellent. She spent hours sitting and talking to people in her compound. It's true they may have exchanged valuable ideas and perhaps that's enough. For my innate sense of purpose, it was insufficient and I felt that Peace Corps looked for more.

According to Sister M'Boge and Sister Roberts, so much needed to be done and they looked to outsiders to share our knowledge and lead the way. Sometimes I found this intimidating. What if our ways simply didn't work for them? I decided I would attempt basic projects, concepts that people could relate to.

I have so often found that once I make up my mind to do something or feel as though I should do something, a door opens to show the way. During that week's Friday Well Baby Clinic, we saw several seriously malnourished children. Two of them were so seriously endangered that Sister Roberts admitted them to the hospital.

As Sister and I gathered our papers after a long session in which we saw about 350 children, she said, "Mariama, rather than go on trek to the outlying clinics with the team, what would you think about following up on the malnourished children, those we admit to the hospital? Talk to the mothers while they're here at the hospital with their children, then when they're released, follow up at their villages?"

There it was. My chance. "Talk to them about nutrition? You bet! I'd love to do that. I could also follow up on the ones we see but don't admit." My mind whirled with the possibilities.

I had learned from my reading and then later saw for myself the terrible effects of malnutrition. Malnutrition often doesn't come from poverty–food was readily available here–

but from lack of education. Two types of malnutrition commonly seen in The Gambia was kwashiorkor and marasmus. The kwashiorkor child eats enough, but it is the wrong kind of food. For instance, he eats only starchy food. At first glance, he looks fat, but his muscles are thin, his skin dull and hair reddish. I saw a lot of kids who fit that description.

The marasmus child looks very thin, the typical starving-to-death look. This is often seen among those children who have been suddenly weaned. The child balks at regular food, or he gets diarrhea from an abruptly changing diet, weakens and dies.

Breast feeding is the norm in The Gambia. African women have great quantities of milk. Lack of mother's milk is rarely a problem. Unfortunately they often breast fed exclusively for too long. Breast feeding is a wonderful, sanitary way to feed infants, but local practice was to breast feed until the child was two years old, or until the mother became pregnant, and the child then suddenly weaned. When offered regular food, the child often balked and quickly became malnourished. Unfortunately, this was not an uncommon scenario. The death rate between birth and five years at that time was 50 percent. This was a terrible statistic and the cause of death often avoidable. There were several reasons for a child's death, but malnourishment due to sudden weaning was one of the most common.

After talking to Sister Roberts, I went home all fired up. This was Friday. By Monday I would have my materials ready to talk to mothers of children in the hospital.

From information furnished by Peace Corps and supplies I had bought in Banjul, I traced pictures to make posters to teach mothers in their own village surroundings. The first picture showed a mother breast feeding. Bottle feeding was never promoted because of the serious sanitation issues, the lack of formula availability and impure water. Breast feeding was by far the best protection a baby could get with vital nourishment and antibodies against diseases.

The next poster showed the baby at four months old. The age was shown by four moons. The baby was pictured nursing, with another picture of a small bowl containing pap, the local name for hot cereal made from mashed rice or millet, egg and oil. Although Gambians traditionally didn't eat eggs, an attempt was made by health workers to introduce them into the diet. Sister suggested I tell them we fed our children eggs and they were strong and bright.

The next poster showed a six-month old baby nursing, eating pap as shown in the previous poster, plus mashed bananas, sweet potatoes, eggplant, juice of lemons and oranges.

At eight months, the baby was shown eating all of the food previously shown, plus mashed peanuts, beans, and carrots.

The last poster showed a mother cooking her family's meal in a large pot over the fire. At one year old, the baby could eat whatever the family ate. It was now safe to wean him, or even continue breast feeding along with the food.

To add to this, I needed to explain to the mothers how to make this happen. Since Gambians don't have a cooked meal in the morning, it was simply not feasible for mothers to build a fire for one child's meal. The previous night, before feeding her family, the mother must put aside cooked rice or millet. As the baby matures, the mother can also take out of the pot other ingredients suitable for the baby.

This sounds simple, but Gambians often looked at death as though it was Allah's will. They didn't realize that Allah had given them the tools to take responsibility for their own health. Then there were food taboos. Most food taboos weren't against their religion but were tribal related, equally strong and frightening. About eggs, for instance, and their fear it would make children stupid.

By Sunday afternoon I had my little demonstration ready. Each 8 ½ by 11 poster was made of regular typing paper, but I placed each one in a clear plastic page protector. Hopefully, one day we could have something of this nature printed to pass out, but for now this would have to do.

From what I had seen, Binta only breast fed Kujah. Although I was hesitant to interfere with our neighbor's life, I decided to talk to Binta first. My practice run.

All during our greetings, Binta's eyes strayed to the posters in my hand. I told her I wanted to talk to her about feeding Kujah. She was most receptive and invited to me sit down next to her on the bed. Jariettu, about five then, stood at my shoulder and watched, never uttering a peep. I had to remind myself that pictures, books, even paper itself were rarely seen in local households.

I asked Binta how many months old Kujah was. She held up seven fingers. I began my little talk, keeping in mind I actually knew more Mandinka than Binta. I managed to get my message across. She worried that it was already too late, but I assured her that Kujah was a healthy baby and she could start now and it would be fine.

"Doman, doman." Do it little by little. I explained that, besides breast feeding, she should feed Kujah pap for two months, then go on to the next step, and by one year she could continue to nurse, but the baby could eat whatever they ate.

I couldn't believe how thrilled Binta was by our talk. She gave me her widest blue smile. What a delightful woman. This welcomed reception inspired me to spread the word.

Monday morning, as I headed for work, posters in hand, Binta called me to their hut. There she sat, holding Kujah, dipping her finger into pap and putting it into Kujah's open mouth. The baby loved it.

At the hospital, implementing a new diet was a little more difficult. For one thing, these children were already very ill. But I found the mothers receptive, even eager. They could obtain cooked rice to mash from the hospital kitchen, which was a start, anyway.

So that I could follow up with children at risk, I asked where they lived. The only address was the name of a village. Once there, I asked for directions or someone took me to the compound. This worked well. I could see that these mothers wanted to do what was right for their children. I decided to branch out.

With Sister's permission I asked Sainabou, one of the more friendly auxiliary nurses, one who also spoke pretty good English, to go with me to a nearby village to talk to the women. At Sister's suggestion, I'd had the orderly/driver take me to the village a few days earlier to ask permission from the village chief, the Alkala, to speak to the women of the village. The Alkala seemed surprised at the request, but said the women would be there.

When we arrived, women were already gathered, with others heading our way. One woman, a polio victim according to Sainabou, dragged herself toward us. A beautiful woman, she pulled herself along on the ground with her arms. As she arrived, someone offered her a chair. She removed the cloth she'd used to protect her clothes and pulled herself up onto the chair. She was beautifully groomed and casually shook out the protective cloth she'd wear to return home. I was stunned and humbled that she'd made this effort.

How much easier her life would be with crutches, but that was beyond the financial means of most villagers. A wheelchair, impractical to use on the sandy soil, would be financially impossible in any event.

At that point, I didn't feel my Mandinka was good enough for public speaking so I gave my little talk in English and Sainabou translated it into Mandinka. I showed the pictures, walking around so everyone could see. The women were entranced.

A orderly had driven us to the village. On the way home, as we bounced along in the Land Rover, I asked Sainabou how she thought it went.

"Oh, fine."

"Would you like to do that again with me?"

"Of course."

"Why don't you choose the next village?"

"Yes."

"But we'll have to get the Alkala's permission."

"Isn't it."

We heard "Isn't it" often, even when Gambians spoke among themselves. We surmised it meant "Isn't that true," or "Isn't that so."

Our programs came together quite well. One week we would get permission and the following week give our talk. I was amazed and encouraged each time with the wonderful reception we received. I think Sainabou enjoyed a certain status, too.

On one occasion a hospital driver/orderly drove me to a village to follow up with a baby who had been hospitalized. Sainabou wasn't at work that day and I felt my Mandinka was good enough for one-on-one discussions, though I was still a little intimidated about making a Mandinka speech to a crowd.

After my visit, in which I found the baby thriving, a young boy came to the hut where I visited and asked me to come with him. He waited patiently outside while I said my goodbyes.

He took me to his family's compound where his mother ironed outside at a rickety table. Her iron, perhaps five inches tall, was filled with hot charcoal. She set down the iron and after very brief greetings told me that I was doing important work and that all the mothers needed to hear what I had to say. Would I come back to their village and talk?

I found it interesting that even though these people had limited experience in anything outside their daily living and surroundings, some stood out among the others. This woman was one of those exceptions, the little boy who frequently visited us, Alieu, another. This woman was obviously a natural leader. We set a date and time, well, as close as Gambians ever get to time. The women would be ready, she said, to learn from me.

Talk about heady experiences! In the business world, this would be called a career high.

There were a few places I could reach by walking without having to depend on the availability of a driver. I began on my own, leaving from home, visiting women to whom I had spoken at the hospital. I mentioned it to Peggy, thinking she might want to go with me, but she didn't seem interested. These home visits weren't planned in advance like our group meetings. Upon entering a village, I asked someone where the Alkala's hut was and they usually walked with me or sent one of their children, who often hung around to see why I was there.

I became friendly with several families. In one family in particular, the woman, Aisa, probably in her forties, had many children. Her little girl who had been admitted to the hospital for malnourishment, was a twin. It was obvious to me that the rest of her children were healthy. The little girl no doubt had other issues that caused her health problems. The woman introduced me to her mother, a tiny wrinkled lady who smoked a pipe. We sat by her fire and talked for a long time.

From time to time I called on my new friend, Aisa. On one visit, I saw the little twin boy running around, but I didn't see the girl. I asked Aisa about her.

"A bunta." She is gone.

Unfortunately the word for dead and gone are the same. I held my hand over my heart. *"A bunta?"*

Yes, dead.

Though it may happen frequently, African mothers grieve as much as any mother when her child dies. I told her that I could see how well she cared for her family, that her children looked healthy. I told her I wasn't a doctor, but I believed that this child had other problems that weren't the mother's fault.

She seemed relieved, maybe just because I felt that she was a good mother.

One late afternoon, I sat in my hut reading and heard my name sung out. I stepped outside and opened the gate. A woman I had counseled and then had gone to their home to follow up, smiled at me. She reminded me that her name was Sibo and that I had visited her at her compound. Sibo carried a basin on her head containing a parcel wrapped in cloth.

When woman went to market, or made a formal visit to one another, they dressed up for the occasion. In this case, Sibo wore a nice top with a matching wrap-around skirt, and matching head scarf. I found their clothes attractive. Most tubobs I knew couldn't manage a wrap-around skirt, we just couldn't keep it secure without buttons, zippers or pins.

I invited Sibo into our house. As she lowered her load to the table, I offered her water, which she accepted. She had walked a distance. Her village was well beyond the Health Centre.

After taking a swallow of water, she opened the cloth to reveal perhaps five pounds of rice. Her family had grown and harvested the rice, she said, and it was a gift to me for caring. I was stunned. This was a gift of sacrifice, representing back-breaking work. Not only was the gift wonderful, but she'd walked miles in the hot sun to deliver it. I barely had the Mandinka vocabulary to express my appreciation. *"Abaraka,"* I said, with my hand over my heart. Thank you from the bottom of my heart. Repeated several times, it was about the best I could manage. I brought out my enamel bowl and she poured the rice from her cloth into the bowl, not spilling a kernel.

We chatted for awhile, she looked at our wall hangings, snapshots of our family, a U.S. map and a world map. I showed her our home state, then showed her where she lived. She obviously had never seen a map before. I invited her to see my kitchen and she marveled. By American standards it would be primitive, but to her it was luxury. She surprised me by saying my kitchen was good because I didn't have time to prepare food the way they do, over an open fire.

I heard a motorcycle putter up to our compound, idle while the driver opened the gate, then a quiet rumble as he rode the motorcycle to our door. Many volunteers who lived in outlying areas were issued small motorcycles, some more like motor scooters. The rule was they were to use them only within a fifty mile radius. Dave lived in Fatoto at the eastern tip of the country and often stopped by when in our area. He was in Peggy's group, six months ahead of us, and like Peggy, was a health worker. After I introduced them, he launched comfortably into Mandinka with Sibo.

After a short while, Sibo said she must return to her home to prepare dinner for her family. Dave offered to give her a ride on his motorcycle, but she declined, laughing. When I said, "Sibo, why don't you? It would be so much faster," she hesitated. Dave turned his motorcycle around and said, "Na." Come. Much to our amazement, she hiked up her skirt to climb on, covering her legs as best she could. Dave indicated that she had to hang onto him. She stood her basin on end between them, then hung on and they took off at a sedate speed. She grinned back at me. What a sight.

Gambian rice has a rich, nutty flavor and takes a bit longer to cook than our processed rice. We ate it soon because it had limited shelf life. I didn't want this precious gift to become chicken feed.

* * *

An inconvenience became a welcomed short-cut for me. For two days I had red, itchy eyes and when I awoke in the mornings, my eyelids stuck together. I found the bright sunshine very irritating. When I arrived at work one morning, Sister Roberts immediately diagnosed it as conjunctivitis, or pink eye, gave me medication and sent me home. Pink eye is highly contagious. She suggested I remain in a darkened hut for a day or so.

I mentioned to Sister that I had no idea how I'd picked it up. In my calls I hadn't seen any evidence of this condition. She said germs were all over, especially in dust.

"I walk to work and to the market on the dusty road, so I guess I'm always exposed to these germs."

"You walk on the road? Why don't you go the back way?"

"The back way?"

She told me to go behind the hospital, past the laundry/cook hut, and there I'd find a path. "It's the way I always come to work. I never use that road."

Oh, my! It was wonderful. The lovely meandering path skirted all the dirt, honking and traffic of the road. The path led me through millet fields, behind the police department, and behind the row of government officials' houses. I learned I could go that way to market, that it reached beyond the Health Centre. That was my route from then on.

The pink eye cleared up in a couple of days and now I had a great way to walk to work, to the market, and home again.

* * *

One particularly hot Sunday we decided to cool off in The Gambia River. Beyond the marketplace, the river was probably two miles from home. Hot when we arrived, we stripped off our outside clothes to our swimsuits and made our way through dark sticky sand to wade in.

We longed for our two-person kayak, currently being stored at Bruce's parents' home. What a joy it would be to paddle the river. Overhanging trees and brush provided shade along the shore. Just being on the water seemed cool and refreshing.

Once in the water, it was glorious. Unfortunately, we drew a crowd. Gambians really never swam in the river. They fished in it, paddled their dug-out canoes in it, but never swam for pleasure.

One man waved frantically. "There are crocodiles in the river!"

Another man warned, "I've seen hippopotamus in there!" Actually, I had to look that Mankinda word up when I got home. All I knew at that time was that it must be something bad.

After walking that distance in 100-degree heat, we really didn't care what we shared the river with. It was cool and we luxuriated in it. At that point, the river was about two hundred feet across. We swam out to get into relatively clean water.

Even so, we made every effort to keep our mouths closed, knowing the water would be polluted.

Although it was wonderful while it lasted, all cooling effects were gone by the time we reached home again, leaving only a pleasant memory.

* * *

Mr. Lopi, a superintendent of the UN well digging project, returned upriver to his home and workplace about a month after Bruce started. Apparently he had been working downriver for the last several weeks. Bruce, totally uninterested in the politics of the project, just wanted to get the job done. Mr. Lopi, on the other hand, lived in The Gambia and had become a man of stature. He had a job of importance and leadership, bringing water to areas desperate for this precious commodity. Mr. Lopi had two wives and seventeen children. Amazingly, his salary after working for his government for about twenty years was equal to Bruce's modest monthly living allowance, a sum many single volunteers found inadequate.

I marveled that Gambians managed at all. Of course, most didn't pay rent, didn't pay utilities because there weren't any, didn't have cars of their own, and medical attention was paid by the government. Still, they bought clothing and what food they didn't grow.

I found Mr. Lopi appealing. Tall, he had that amazing African male physique. My association with him was very different than Bruce's. Although they managed a cordial relationship, Bruce often felt frustration that Mr. Lopi's decisions were often based on political advantage rather than public need.

One evening Mr. Lopi invited us on a wild boar hunt. Muslims wouldn't eat "the filthy swine," so we weren't sure what we would do if we got one, but we went along for the adventure. Of the four of us, Mr. Lopi was the only one carrying a gun, a big, old single-shot shotgun. We loved the adventure, tramping around in an area we hadn't seen. I followed Mr. Lopi, Bruce followed me and the other Gambian brought up the rear on a rough path through scrub forest, sort of like a safari. We didn't find our boar but it was a fun adventure. Outings like this helped make our stay memorable and, I felt, closer to the people.

Bruce and Mary enjoy cool ocean breezes in Bakau

Chapter 12

*P*eter Moore came into our lives after we'd lived in Mansajang for a few months. Peter had heard we were living in the UN compound and called on us. He had been in Africa with British Medical Research Council (MRC) for twenty-three years and in The Gambia for about a year. He had project homes both in Basse and Bakau and split his time between the two.

Peter's wife and two daughters lived in England. On some assignments his family accompanied him, but his daughters were students and it was important for them to be in England at this time with their mother. Peter managed to get home to England occasionally.

Our association with Peter was a beacon in our lives. With a droll sense of humor and great British clip, he'd entertain us with his stories of Africa. Peter was currently studying the effects of the mosquito that caused malaria. His initial visit was to invite me to join him on trek to call on a village with reported heavy incidence of malaria. It was my great pleasure to do so, and to my satisfaction I found I could be useful as an interpreter.

As a result of decades living in sub-Saharan Africa, Peter spoke a very effective "pidgin English" and always seemed to manage to make himself understood, but often couldn't understand replies. Interestingly, I could understand him, too. His language seemed to be made of a combination of English and words and phrases used all over Africa. It takes years of living in several different countries to be able to do that.

Peter, seasoned in African ways, was the perfect person to know. We invited him to dinner and he raved about the catfish and the creamed potatoes and onions I had prepared. He couldn't get enough of our salad of sprouts, onion and tomatoes.

He chided Peace Corps in general, how we tried to live like Africans. "You can't, you know, live like them. You might as well live comfortably, it's still tough enough even so. That you walk everyplace you go is really ridiculous." But Peter agreed that we had struck a good compromise, considering the limited allowance we lived on. He was lavish in his praise about how we managed...considering.

Peter invited us to dinner at his home and we were impressed. On the waterfront, it was the nicest house in Basse with ceiling fans and breezes from the river. The cool house was pure luxury: nicely furnished with tropical rattan furniture, a real bathroom and a kitchen with running water. Not only that, but Peter was an excellent cook. He hired a housekeeper, but he did all his own shopping and cooking. After living those many years in Africa, he found he could maintain his health and strength by adhering to his own diet. He did incorporate local foods and taught me how to cook okra, a vegetable not grown in America's northwest.

We mentioned to Peter that we occasionally swam in the river, but it wasn't entirely satisfactory because we always drew a crowd, and getting into the water was unpleasant with the sticky riverbank.

"Come over here. Come in through my gate and swim from my beach, whether I'm home or not." We took him up on his offer. Not only did we have privacy after that, he had a nice little beach with a way to get into the water without getting our feet gooey.

We managed to see Peter often and he was always a delight. Over the course of time, through Peter we met other British MRC researchers and formed wonderful friendships.

* * *

We planted a few vegetable beds. The soil, mostly sand, needed a great deal of enhancement. Animals--cows, goats, donkeys and sheep--roamed freely just outside our compound. Fences in The Gambia were to keep animals out, where usually in the States we have fences to keep them in. Bruce and I gathered animal droppings and mixed the manure and kitchen scraps into the soil. We quickly found that our chickens would peck at anything green that popped out of the ground. Bruce built raised beds and covered them with netting to protect our budding garden from chickens and other birds..

Our moderately successful beds grew small tomatoes and squash. Beans and lettuce, seeds brought from the U.S. didn't fare well. They'd start out, but soon succumb to local conditions. Mung bean and alfalfa sprouts, an indoor project, were some of our main vegetable staples. We had brought an ample supply with us, and Bruce's mom occasionally mailed more seeds to us. We normally had sprouts in two different growing stages at all times, with a bowl in the refrigerator ready to eat. A common salad for us was bean sprouts, tomatoes and onion. When available, we added lettuce.

When volunteers came for dinner they couldn't get enough of our salads, they were so starved for fresh vegetables.

We made an interesting discovery with lettuce. During the season when lettuce was available at the market, we bought many heads. Actually, I would have bought more, but other people were hungry for it and I didn't want to hoard. The leaf lettuce heads were small, no more than five-inches long, with the roots still intact. After awhile, it occurred to us to just use the outer leaves and plant the rest. Then, when the lettuce head took hold, we just picked off the outer leaves, leaving the plant to continue to grow in the soil. We enjoyed lettuce long after it was available in the market.

One time, as I knelt at a garden bed carefully picking lettuce leaves, Tombong came to visit. "Just pull 'em out," he advised.

"If we do it this way, the plant will keep growing."

"Oh, fine."

As much as I shared our little discoveries, I never saw much change in the local way of doing things. To our African neighbors, there seemed to be the tubob way and their way. They stuck to their way.

* * *

Although we loved having company, it soon got out of hand with uninvited guests. Volunteers dying for a home cooked meal often came konk-konking at our door. Sometimes it was fun; usually it meant extra work for us.

Volunteers understood the concept of bucket baths, but many of them took their supply of water for granted. In Peggy's case, a woman in her compound brought her a bucket of water every day, common among volunteers. But in our case, we hauled our own water from the UN well, seventy-five feet from our compound.

Our rule was to always have filled water buckets in the kitchen and in the bathing area when we went to bed. We never knew when the well's foot pump might go out; it happened every once in awhile. Running out of water could be serious, or at least inconvenient. I often had to remind guests to refill the buckets when they were finished with their baths. Sometimes they complied; often they didn't.

Many volunteers didn't understand how much work it took to acquire food. Their living arrangements were so different from ours and growing, buying and preparing food was done for them. We worked regular hours so our time was limited. Our tiny refrigerator only held a few supplies. Volunteers from other areas often dropped in, around dinner time, and pretty much expected to be taken care of. This meant dinner and the next morning's breakfast, since evening company meant overnight company if they lived a distance away.

No one goes any distance in The Gambia without need to spend the night at their destination. Night travel isn't safe, not because of human harm, but if the vehicle has a break-down, more common than you'd think, you're stuck until someone comes by. Then, there's always the possibility of wild animals and that's not a comforting thought. If you leave the vehicle, by the time you get back you're apt to find the vehicle stripped of tires, batteries, and other items that could be resold. So, with the exception of those who lived very close, company meant overnight guests.

Sometimes volunteers came to the Basse area on business, as did the fisheries people on a regular basis. Fisheries volunteers scouted the country for places to build ponds in which to breed and grow tilapia. Perry, from our training group, always asked in advance if they could stay with us. Without fail the fisheries guys pitched in to wash the dishes afterward (rare among volunteers) and if they were there for more than one night, they treated us to dinner at Jobot's All Necessary Foods. They were often a group of at least three and sometimes six if they had out-of-country fisheries volunteers. In the course of two years, they visited several times and were always a joy.

The word of a good tubob place to stay spread even farther. One night as we finished dinner a fellow came to the door. He stepped in and shrugged off his big backpack. He mopped his sweaty face. "Are you the Trimbles?"

"Yes, we are." It was hard to keep the incredulity from our voices.

He eyed our dinner leftovers of meat sauce over rice and a salad. "Some folks in Senegal told me about you. Mind if I have some of that rice?"

Gary stayed four days, but I admit he was one of our better guests. A journalist, he'd traveled over much of Africa. He fit into our household like he'd always been a part of it. He was gone during the day, doing his investigative business. He often walked me to work, then went on with his own projects. "Can I pick up something from the market for you?" He was perfectly willing to pay his own way. He always filled the water buckets when he finished his bath, he helped with the dishes, and on the last night he treated us to dinner at Jobot's.

But many guests were not as thoughtful. One couple from United States Agency for International Development (USAID), in their mid-thirties, wanted to see "the bush" and decided to stay with us, unannounced. As it happened, the USAID people consistently had the best housing situation in The Gambia with household help, yard help, guards at their front gates and the only automatic washers in the country. Although we did know several USAID staffers, we didn't know Paul and Jan. They just appeared.

From the start, I could see Paul was game to try anything, but Jan was hesitant on almost every count. She was fairly horrified that her bath would be a bucket bath and I had to show her how to do it. I explained that after she was finished, she'd need to refill the buckets for the next person. She was further shocked when she learned the water wouldn't be heated. I explained that the water from the ground was refreshingly cool but not cold.

I showed her the well and she watched as one of the local women used the foot pedal.

"Why do you do that work?" She nodded toward Mosalif whom they'd met upon their arrival and who happened to be walking by. "Why don't you have him get your water?"

"Mosalif doesn't work for us, he's a mechanic at the UN shop." I went on to explain, "We do everything for ourselves, except I hire a woman, Mosalif's wife, to do our laundry."

She reluctantly went to our shower area and took her bath, probably cringing the whole time. After her bath she came back into the house. I noticed she hadn't filled the water buckets.

"It's so much hotter here than in Bakau. How can you stand it?" she asked.

"It is hot. I don't know if anyone really does get used to it. When I walk to work in the morning, it's cooler, but by the time I come home, it's often the hottest time of day."

Her jaw dropped. "You walk to work? Whatever for?"

"We don't have transportation. Some volunteers have motorcycles, but I work at the hospital, about a mile away, and don't have a vehicle. A driver takes me to villages if it's too far to walk."

Jan shrugged. "I can't imagine."

"Do you work?"

"Oh, no, Paul works for USAID. I don't work."

"What do you do?" I knew she had her housework, cooking and laundry done for her. There was always shopping, I supposed.

"Oh..." her voice trailed off. Paul and Bruce came in after Bruce had shown him the UN project next door.

"Boy, it's hot," Paul said. "Is it all right if I take a bath?"

"Sure, it's a bucket bath."

"Okay, that's great."

Soon he returned. "Where do you get the water?"

"Oh, oh. I guess the last person to take a bath didn't refill the buckets." I tried not to sound judgmental, but I was irritated.

Paul gave his wife a disgusted look. I showed Paul where to get the water. After his bath he dutifully filled the buckets.

Most guests gave no thought to using our sheets and towels, many didn't even ask if we had that work done for us. I was glad we amply paid Binta, because some days she had a large load of laundry.

Drop-ins most often didn't bring food of any kind, but just took it for granted that they'd be fed.

Not all USAID people were like this. We had good friends, a doctor, Harry Hull and his wife, a nurse, Suz Henricks, who were always welcomed. Suzi had stopped by our Jenoi training camp and we had struck up a friendship. When they came, they pitched in, always doing their share and often bringing something from downriver that we couldn't buy in Basse.

Another joy to have visit was Charlie, an agricultural advisor. Charlie, originally from Scotland, stopped by from time to time, always bringing something with him, usually processed milk because he knew we couldn't get anything but powered or condensed milk in Basse. He loved Bruce's oatmeal and we enjoyed the milk he brought with our breakfast oatmeal. Charlie, affable and easy to talk to, became a regular and welcomed guest.

Peggy loved having company, but it didn't really mean extra work for her. The women in her compound brought her water, and cooked all the meals. Company was just a nice diversion for her. A few times, though, she had more company than she could handle and we got the overflow. A little of that goes a long way.

Peggy and Nathaniel's birthdays were close to the same date. On one of her frequent downriver visits, she invited many people upriver for a party to celebrate the joint birthdays. The result of that was that we had four over-night guests, plus the whole crowd for breakfast.

Of course, we expected to have company from the people who worked for the UN project. That's why we were given the house and hut to live in, so that visiting UN people would have a place to stay. Henri, a Frenchman, on UN business, often stayed with us. He was a nice fellow, but couldn't speak more than a few words of English and I didn't speak French. Many Gambians can speak French and Bruce gets by amazingly well, so they managed to get their work done. The company Henri worked for sold the foot pumps for the UN wells throughout Africa. When Henri was in country he spent most of his time in the bush checking equipment, returning in the evening for dinner and to spend the night. He would often be there for two or three days.

Henri and I had card playing in common and we played a variety of games, some he showed me and some that I taught him. Bruce doesn't care for cards, so he'd either read or play his guitar and sing. They were fun evenings.

One time, rather late in the evening, though it was still light, we heard a long series of car honks. Gambians don't usually give a little toot, they keep blasting away until something happens. Bruce went to our porch and looked out over the fence. A woman stood on the running board of the Land Cruiser in which she was the passenger.

"Will you open that gate!" she ordered, with an impatient British clip.

I could see Bruce stiffen. "Who are you?" he asked in his best puzzled voice.

She mentioned her name. "I'm going to be staying here."

We'd just had visitors after visitors. We needed to be alone.

"I think you have the wrong place," Bruce said "This is our home. Maybe you could try the hotel in Basse or the government rest house." Neither place would be appealing, but it simply wasn't our problem. We didn't join the Peace Corps to entertain tubobs.

* * *

Villagers stopped by just to greet us and stay a few minutes. I always offered them cold water, or sometimes I made tea. I enjoyed these casual visits. One young man, Arjana, spoke excellent English. Arjana wasn't originally from The Gambia, but was currently living with his uncle in Mansajang.

"Do you have anything to read?" he asked. "I would like to read magazines or books in English." Arjana spoke Wolof, English and French.

Indeed, it was rare for local people to have reading material. Newspapers, magazines or books were rarely seen in homes.

As it happened, we had a lot of reading material. Newsweek furnished complimentary copies of their international edition to Peace Corps volunteers and the magazine was often included in our mail when someone brought it upriver. In addition, the Peace Corps office had a book exchange program. No one kept track of the books taken or received; a section of the building was simply set aside for our "library." George had sent up a large box of books for the upriver volunteers and we stored it in our spare bedroom. Local volunteers often stopped by to donate books and select others to take home.

I gave Arjana a copy of Newsweek that we had read and offered to let him borrow a book from our upriver library. "You may keep the magazine, but after you have read the book, you must return it and then you may select another to borrow."

He was delighted. He returned a week later. "I have come for another book."

"Where is the book you borrowed?"

"I gave it to my uncle."

"But these are not my books, I am only storing them. Remember, I told you to bring that one back when you finished it and then you can pick out another."

"I gave it to my uncle."

"As soon as you bring it back, then you can have another." I knew it sounded stingy, but they weren't really my books to give away and I thought it a good lesson on "library borrowing."

We chatted awhile and he left.

* * *

Even before we arrived in Africa, Bruce and I cut each other's hair, although at home I occasionally had mine cut by a professional. It had been years since Bruce stepped into a barbershop. Not only was it a time-saver, it was economical. We normally cut each other's hair in one session. Bruce had cut mine and I was in the process of cutting his on our porch when Perry, our fisheries volunteer friend, stopped by. He was on his way home after being in Banjul and brought mail for us.

His eyes lit up when he saw what I was doing. "Could you give me a haircut? I don't want to go to these local guys. I'm afraid they'll shave my head!" Although the practice was to shave little kids' heads, some adult men also shaved theirs.

Word spread and I became the official tubob hair trimmer for the upriver guys. I didn't mind and I knew how much better they felt having trimmed hair. My equipment was merely a pair of scissors and a disposable razor to trim the neck. Although some of the guys let their hair grow, most of them preferred short hair because of the heat.

* * *

After we had been at our posts for two months, we decided it was time to go to Banjul. Most volunteers went at least once a month, some much more often. Peggy normally went once or twice a month, often staying for a week.

We both had business to take care of in the capital city and could combine it with a couple days of rest and relaxation over the weekend. There was always a need for a shop vehicle to go downriver for supplies. Bruce had sent word he was coming and made an appointment to talk to the project director.

Bruce had been downriver on a few business trips and had stayed at the Bakau apartment, but I had yet to stay there and looked forward to it. After checking with Nathaniel that neither he nor Norman needed to use the apartment, we set our date. To clear it at my workplace was no problem at all. Going downriver was a common occurrence among the senior staff.

A driver drove the Land Rover and we left only an hour or two later than we'd planned. It was a long, tedious drive.

At that time much of the way was a rutted dirt road except for the last 120 miles of paved road. The driver dropped us off at the apartment.

What a wonderful investment that apartment turned out to be. Although the fellows left it looking like a bachelor pad, I quickly straightened the two tiny rooms to make it "home" for a few days. Later Norman joked that he loved it when we stayed there because we always left it so tidy.

Near the ocean, the weather was noticeably cooler in Bakau, the apartment quite comfortable. We enjoyed running water showers and treated ourselves to dinner at one of the local hotels. Sitting on a hotel patio overlooking the ocean, we grinned at one another. We often had to remind ourselves that we were really doing this, living in Africa. We ordered our meal in Mandinka, much to the pleasure of our waiter.

The next day, Sunday, we walked to the American Chargé d'Affair's, about a twenty minute walk, and enjoyed a swim in the ocean. That evening we ate at LaPizza, joining friends who lived nearby.

On Monday we took the bus into Banjul. Bruce went on to the Yundum shop and I walked to the Health Department to see Sister M'Boge. Sister expressed her appreciation for my monthly reports. Much to my surprise, she said I was the only upriver volunteer who submitted reports to her.

Sister wasn't a particularly friendly woman. Unlike most Gambians, she was extremely businesslike. I think this was probably a reflection of her British education. Some found her intimidating, but I appreciated being able to talk business with her and the fact that she treated me as though I had something to contribute.

Her next comment left me reeling. "I would like you to organize a training program for the auxiliary nurses."

I stared at her. I wasn't a medical person, she knew that. I couldn't imagine how I would tackle such a project.

"Think about it," she said. "You'll find a way."

Bruce met with the usual frustrations at Yundum. People he had planned to meet weren't there. Supplies they'd ordered either weren't available or had been sent, but not received. Things had a way of disappearing in The Gambia, mysteries that were never solved. He would return Tuesday to see if he could take care of at least some of his business.

We met at the Peace Corps office to check in with George and to pick up mail. Once in the country, Bruce had decided to grow a beard. He'd long had a mustache. I grew used to his beard, seeing him every day, but for some it was always a surprise. George took hold of Bruce's beard, as though he were measuring it. "Ummmm, it's been that long since we've seen you. You guys need to come down more often."

I was always amazed how word spread. Harry and Suzi, our USAID doctor and nurse friends heard we were downriver and she stopped by the apartment to invite us for Tuesday dinner. It was a treat visiting a real house. Although they had much of their work done, Harry and Suzi preferred to do their own cooking. They gave us a standing invitation that whenever we were downriver, we were invited to dinner.

"If for some reason, your apartment is being used, plan to stay here. You're always welcome." What a great offer.

Early in the morning we heard tiny, weak mewling. It was a sad sound and we both feared the source. At first light we went into the alley in back of the apartment and verified what we'd dreaded. Someone had dumped about six little newborn kittens there. The alley of sorts was apparently a place people used as a dump, another litter issue that bothered us, but live kittens were another matter. They were almost dead. Their little teeth were falling out. The humane thing to do would be to put them down. Bruce saw no other choice but to do it himself. A Gambian wandered by and saw the sad scene and watched as Bruce hit them on the head with a board and killed them, one by one.

Afterward, the man said, "This is not good, leave small animals here. Thank you." I think he remained out of respect for what Bruce had to do. And it was Bruce, I don't think I could have done it.

We needed to get Christmas packages in the mail if our families were to receive them in time. We shopped at

GamCo and bought several locally made items: batik wall-hangings, tie-dyed tee-shirts for the kids, and two copies of a book, The Gambia, beautifully illustrated and published in France, to give to my sister and Bruce's folks.

We set out in the morning for the post office. Crowds of people pushed and shoved, mostly men. Women rarely handled that kind of business. Bruce and I split up our packages and each fought our way to a different window. We found that the local people had difficulty adding too many items. By splitting up, each clerk would only have two or three numbers to add.

When I got close enough I could see many, many boxes of incoming mail to be sorted. No wonder our mail was so sporadic. I also saw several people asleep, sprawled over boxes, typewriters, anyplace to lay their heads.

I finally made it to the grilled window, pushed my parcels toward the clerk, and so that I wouldn't get shoved aside, hung on to each side of the grill while I conducted my business. Nevertheless, a man attempted to shove me aside and at the same time began talking to the clerk at the counter.

"Batu doman ding!" Wait just a minute! I snapped at him.

He registered such surprise that the clerk behind the counter laughed.

When Bruce and I completed our business we compared shipping prices for the books, wrapped identically in individual packages. We were charged different prices for the same items, both going to the Seattle area.

At the end of our downriver visit, no project vehicle was returning to Mansajang, so Bruce and I took a bush taxi home, an adventure in itself. To take a taxi in Banjul, one goes to the taxi stand. Normally, the first leg of the trip only goes to Serrekunda. That taxi was a regular car, packed with four people in the front seat, four in the back, the trunk stuffed with packages and baggage and what wouldn't fit there, rode on our laps. It was a miserable one-hour ride. We found Serekunda a depressing place, sort of an overflow of

Banjul with corrugated tin pounded out flat for fencing, and piles of garbage on street corners.

Then another taxi ride to Soma with similar crowded conditions. After a short wait, we caught the typical bush taxi, a small Peugeot truck with the canvas-covered back. In this small space, seventeen people, several carrying chickens, crammed in, our goods stowed by our feet. We rode this way on the rough, dusty dirt road for about four hours, watching the countryside through the open back of the truck. We were let off in Basse, then, climbing out of the truck stiff and weary, walked the mile and a half home with our packs on our backs, carrying packages.

Mosalif met us as we entered the compound. Two nights earlier, he'd heard a noise and thought it was the wind. When he heard it again he got up to investigate, just in time to see someone escape over the back fence. Someone had broken the door padlock (which was probably the first noise) and had stolen our radio/cassette player. Nothing else was missing, but our radio was a major loss to us, our link to world news and a source of our favorite music.

Mosalif was distraught, nearly in tears. We assured him it wasn't his fault, but agreed that when we left we should hire someone to guard the house. We had a bed on the porch that we used as a place to sit outside and read. Our friend Tombong became our guard when we both needed to be gone. He would sleep on the porch and watch our house and hut for us. No one would bother it with Tombong there. It was a great arrangement and gave us a reason to occasionally hire our good friend.

I felt perfectly safe upriver. I never feared a personal attack. Property was something else. Stealing, even among themselves, does happen. But to steal from a tubob seemed fair game. Not true of all Gambians, of course, but to a few. Many volunteers had items stolen.

One night while we slept, I awoke to a strange noise. I woke Bruce up. What was that? We heard drumming, not rhythm drumming like what we were used to hearing in the evenings, and not the talking drum, but a constant steady ominous beat. Then a roar from a crowd, then the drumming resumed. This pattern continued for many minutes.

The next morning I asked Mosalif about it. He hadn't left the compound, so I assumed he'd learned about it through the talking drums. Someone had stolen earrings from a family hut while the occupants slept. The man who lived in the hut heard a slight noise and actually saw the thief come in and grab the wife's earrings. The husband cried out and very quickly men surrounded the village. They formed a circle, a human barrier, and slowly, slowly closed in on the fellow. The occasional roar was when they stepped forward. Finally surrounded, the thief was captured and beaten within an inch of his life. Then, they sent for the police. Gambian stealing from Gambians certainly had more serious consequences than stealing from tubobs.

* * *

Early Sunday mornings we often enjoyed walks to distant villages. Leaving early allowed us to walk in the relative morning coolness. The Gambia is very flat, but occasionally we found a slight rise, barely what we considered a hill. We often hiked to the top for another perspective of our host country.

The Gambia/Senegal boarder lay about six miles from Mansajang and we sometimes made the border-crossing sign our destination. The sign had French on the Senegal side, English on The Gambia side. We carried water, a snack and our snake-bite kit for the twelve-mile hike. After awhile it wasn't unusual for people to call out to us, people who recognized us from our work. Occasionally, we stopped at a village, paid our respects to the chief, then continued our trek..

I often recalled how much I suffered in Banjul without being able to take long walks and felt so thankful we could walk here in safety.

We normally walked on regular dirt roads, but there were roads of sorts between villages, too, many deeply rutted. When Bruce went to the bush to check on a well digging team, he often marveled at how drivers, when they went on these back roads, knew when to abruptly turn to go to a specific village. There were no signs, nothing that Bruce could recognize as a landmark.

Nathaniel visited Mali and he told us that they traveled for hours in the desert when suddenly the driver made a right turn. Nathaniel said there didn't appear to be anything like a landmark in any direction. But they reached their exact destination without any navigational equipment.

Africa would remain a mystery to many of us, no matter how long we stayed.

Alieu's mother and siblings

Chapter 13

One early evening Arjana, the book borrower, called on me again. We chatted for a few minutes and I knew he was about to ask for another book, though he didn't have the originally borrowed book in hand.

As was his practice when we had guests, Mosalif walked over from his family hut to greet Arjana. I knew immediately something was wrong. Mosalif could have a dark look about him, a warning. I'd seen it before and I knew enough to pay attention. Mosalif greeted my guest stiffly, but then stood off to one side, watching, rather than going about his business.

Suddenly I knew. Arjana was the thief who had broken into our home. He would have seen the radio when he'd selected his first book.

Not only that, I could see by Arjana's expression, that he knew Mosalif knew—his eyes kept darting toward Mosalif. He said something about just wanting to say hello and quickly left.

Watching Arjana leave, Mosalif's expression remained dark. After the young man was out of sight, Mosalif said that he hadn't gotten a close look, but he was pretty sure Arjana was the thief.

Arjana never returned, nor did I ever get that original book back.

* * *

The Upper River Division's Commissioner called a community meeting, inviting representatives from the area's many agencies, village chiefs, etc., to attend and speak. Doctor Ceesay asked me to represent the Health Centre.

Gulp! Give a public speech? I'd spoken to women, but to speak to the leaders of the whole community?

"Mariama, our official language is English. Just talk about your work in English, especially your nutrition counseling."

I was impressed with the event and the preparation made by the Commissioner's office. A row of three speakers' tables stood on a raised platform. I was equally impressed with the vast crowd. Representatives from many organizations attended: the schools, the Agriculture Department, Police Department, the Health Inspector (Peggy's counterpart), religious leaders, Planned Parenthood, Catholic Charities, and me from the Health Centre. Most of the local village chiefs were present, all dressed up in their flowing robes and skull caps. A few Gambian women attended the event, those who had government positions, beautifully dressed with matching head attire, top and skirt. I was the only tubob and wore my tailor-made swearing-in dress.

We speakers rotated, stepping up to the platform and seating ourselves at one of three tables, two to a table. Speakers gave their talk, then stepped down and the next speaker stepped up. After about four people had spoken, I stepped up to the platform, sat at a table and awaited my turn to speak.

The woman who sat beside me continually spat. Gambians don't brush their teeth as we do with tooth brush and tooth paste. They use a twig of soft wood, preferably from the lemon tree, with which they vigorously scrub their teeth. The process involves spitting the little wood fragments. The woman sitting next to me, a representative from the Area Council, vigorously cleaned her teeth, frequently spitting–all perfectly acceptable behavior.

It was my turn to speak. A high school principal, Mr. Sanjung, offered to translate for those who didn't understand English. I spoke two or three sentences which he translated into Mandinka, Wolof and Fula. We got into a rhythm and my talk went amazingly well.

A day or so later, Mr. Sanjung called on us. Bruce happened to be home and we had a delightful visit. Mr. Sanjung had attended college in England. He'd gone on a scholarship with the promise that he would return to The Gambia to teach. Cheerfully, he told us what a drastic change it had been to go to England.

"But that was easy to get used to. Coming home was more difficult. To have my wife bring me a bucket of water to take a bath was so different than stepping into a shower. When I first came home we had no electricity and I couldn't read in the evenings. My wife still cooks on an open fire. I've offered to get her a stove, but she refuses."

It's hard to imagine the challenges Mr. Sanjung endured when he returned to a third-world country. I admired this man of honor who worked so hard to improve his country. I mentioned to him the term "brain drain." He'd never heard the expression, but knew the concept. "But look at you people," he said. "You come here to help us. The least we can do is help ourselves."

He moved on to the reason for his visit. "Mariama, I would like you to come to the high school and talk about health. Come at least three times. We'll make a schedule."

Flattered, I readily accepted. We set the dates that day. My nutrition talks were basic, but I had attentive audiences and the students asked good questions. "How do you know what vitamins are in what food?" "How do you know that eggs won't make us stupid?"

"I eat eggs," I said. They all laughed. I didn't know if that was good or bad.

Amazingly, Mansajang had a Catholic church and boys' and girls' schools. The best schools in our area, virtually the only schools other than the local Arabic schools, were run by the Catholics. It was part of their world charity work, though in the schools they could not utter one word about Christianity in this strongly Muslim country.

When we first arrived, the Church seemed to be between priests. I had met the previous priest, whom we unkindly called Father Freako, but not to his face, of course. When I introduced myself to him, he looked as though he wanted to escape, as though he was scared to death. When the new priest, Father Fagan, arrived, he told us that the former priest had actually had a nervous breakdown and had extreme anxiety around people. The man had spent his entire priesthood in Africa.

Father Fagan had with him a sort of intern priest, Collum. Both were from Ireland and we immediately struck up a lasting friendship. We attended Mass on a regular basis. Again, we observed the African habit of crowding into small places. The tiny church had a pretty little altar and about twelve pews. The building had a ceiling fan but could still get quite hot. Only a handful of Africans in Mansajang were Catholic. Those Africans, about eight of them, crowded into a pew designed for five people. Peggy happened to be Catholic, too, so there were often the three of us, the teaching nuns, plus those few Africans in attendance.

We learned that Collum played the guitar and sang and we invited them to dinner, asking Collum to bring his guitar. It was as though Bruce and Collum had known each other for years, the way they played guitar and sang together. Bruce learned some songs from Collum and vise versa. They had a Gambian cook so were always delighted with our tubob food.

Collum liked to cook and they occasionally had us over for his specialty, Irish stew. The nuns from the school often joined us. Those were fun evenings.

The holy Muslim day of Tobaski approached. Tobaski, the feast of sacrifice, is marked by the ritual of slaughtering sheep. We learned that it can be a stressful time for men because they feel duty-bound to buy a sheep, even if they have to borrow money. Bruce and I discussed it and decided to give Mosalif and Binta a gift of money.

About a week before the event, when he came for his morning greetings, we gave Molsalif one hundred dalasi and told him it was for their Tobaski. Overwhelmed, he hardly knew what to say. We heard him call "Binta!" when he returned to his hut.

Close to the time of Tobaski, Bruce saw a string of men leading sheep to the river for the traditional washing of animals before the slaughter.

On Tobaski, Mosalif, Binta and the girls stopped by, all looking resplendent with new clothes. They were sharing Tobaski with Binta's cousin who lived in Basse and Mosalif had helped purchase the sheep and other food for their feast.

The next day, the Health Centre staff had a dinner party with Tobaski leftovers. The cook made a wonderful stew and served it over millet. Orderlies carried two tables outside where they set up the feast. The men brought the food out on a board and set it on the table.

I wasn't prepared for the sudden rush to the table, nor was I sure what to do with myself. It was though these people hadn't eaten for days and had finally found food. An orderly saw my confusion and took me under his protective wing. I was touched by his concern.

"Mariama, I will help you. You have to learn to act quickly or the food will be gone!" Many ate from a common bowl, but a few plates had been set on the table, together with spoons.

He handed me a full plate. I thanked him, found a place to sit and enjoyed the marvelous food. One of the orderlies fished the sheep skull out of the stew pot. While we ate, the skull sat on the table, dripping broth and grinning.

After the meal, one of the guys grabbed the skull and threw it to another orderly and off they went, playing with it like it was a football. Everyone laughed. Although I thought it ghoulish, I couldn't help but laugh, too.

Bruce had gone downriver on business and would be gone two days. I had arrived at the party in the late afternoon. Darkness had settled in and the staff sat around the table talking, then the party broke up. I knew where a few of the staff lived, but to my knowledge no one lived near me in Mansajang. This time, rather than use the back path that would be very dark, I walked down the road. Small groups milled around and several people greeted me by name. I felt quite safe.

As I opened the gate at our compound, Mosalif met me and I got quite a lecture. I had failed to let him know where I was going. Since Mistah Bruce was gone, Mosalif felt responsible for me and how could he do his job if he didn't know where I was? He had been worried. He'd asked Peggy, and she didn't know where I was. I apologized. It had been really thoughtless of me. Lesson learned. After that night, when Bruce was gone, I always checked in with Mosalif or Binta to let them know where I was going and when I'd be back. Day or night, I checked in with them.

* * *

I continued to go on trek, sometimes with Sainabou or other auxiliary nurses, sometimes alone. An orderly/driver took me to a distant village where a family lived whose child had been hospitalized. As was so often the case, several people crowded around the Land Rover as we arrived, all talking loudly and extending their hands to greet us. A man, a leper with badly deformed hands and feet, greeted me. He extended his stub of a hand and I felt no choice but to shake it, quickly realizing, at least hoping, that he was no longer contagious. As I grasped his hand, I saw in his eyes a warmth toward me, a look that I'll always remember.

A man standing near us left and returned, carrying a live chicken and gave it to me. *"Abaraka."* Thank you, he said quietly. I wondered if this man was the leper's relative.

Binta had shown me how to carry a chicken in the crook of my arm and I did so now as I made my follow-up call. No one blinks an eye when someone carries a live chicken, not even the chicken. We named her Blue, for her color.

We'd heard the expression "pecking order" without realizing its full significance. Mosalif had bought our first four birds all at the same time, so if there was any adjustment, it wasn't obvious. But when I arrived home from trek and could finally set Blue down, I couldn't believe the ruckus. The other chickens flew at her, pecking at the poor thing. She defended herself as best she could. Feathers flew, the noise was unbelievable. By nighttime they seemed to have it all sorted out and Blue filed in with the rest of them, at the end of the line, and the next morning it was as though she'd lived there all her life.

* * *

In November, the weather was noticeably cooler, especially at night. It actually dipped to 52 degrees and we had to dig our sweaters out of the trunk. Blankets appeared in the market and at night we used a sheet and blanket. We had been told it got cold, but we could hardly believe it and had looked forward to our first shiver.

One early morning, Bruce, hunched up, bundled up in a sweater, hands in the pockets of his long trousers, said, "Damn, I'm really cold."

During the day it soared to the low 90's, but after feeling so cold during the night and early morning, it didn't seem that hot to us. For a few weeks, we spent our evenings inside reading, or sometimes I talked Bruce into playing cards.

* * *

Bruce's job continued to be one frustration after another. He described it as "running a business on promises." Getting supplies in a timely fashion was challenging. Many trips downriver could have been avoided if the upriver crew could have depended on routine supplies, such as motor oil, fuel and spark plugs. As it happened, they had been unable to change oil in the vehicles for some time because they couldn't get enough oil to perform this task. They could only top up the oil when it was desperately needed. The disregard for vehicle maintenance grated on Bruce.

Sometimes equipment would go into the bush, only to break down and have to be rescued. Bruce knew many of these breakdowns could have been avoided with consistent maintenance. It was expensive for yet another vehicle to go into the bush to rescue the first, change a tire because there was no spare, take fuel which should have been filled before they left. The time and resources wasted slowed down the operation and raised expenses.

To help alleviate needless trips, Bruce made an itemized list of things that needed to be checked off before the Land Rovers and trucks left for the bush. Bruce instructed the lead mechanic to pick up the list before a vehicle left on a job and check off the items as they were performed.

__ Tires checked
__ Spare tire checked
__ Radiator Level Checked

__ Oil changed, if needed (see schedule)
__ Check battery
__ Check brakes

A truck was about to depart and Karafa, the head mechanic, handed the to-do list to Bruce, with all items dutifully checked.

Bruce looked over the form. "Karafa, you've checked off 'Oil Changed.'"

"Yes."

"But we're out of oil."

"Yes."

"How could you check this off then, if we don't have oil?"

"We must check this off before we go to the bush."

"But you couldn't change the oil."

"Isn't it."

Isn't it. We heard that phrase many times and it never seemed to fit the situation.

Even the best-laid plans don't always work. Later Bruce learned that Karafa, as well as most of the men in the shop, couldn't read. But they could check off items on a list.

* * *

Sitting at my table at work entering figures from the previous day's antenatal clinic, I noticed two women enter the hospital. One woman, hugely pregnant, walked stooped over and the other seemed to be assisting her.

I found the nurse mid-wife and they ushered the pregnant woman into the operating theatre.

About an hour later, the exhausted nurse mid-wife came out and collapsed into the spare chair at my table. "I just can't get that baby out."

I looked up. She was talking to me. "You can't get it out?"

"No. It's stuck there. Come look."

Alarm ran down my spine when I saw the scene. The woman lay on the table, feet in stirrups, her baby's arm and part of a shoulder hanging out of her.

"Have you sent for Doctor Ceesay?"

"No, not yet."

"I think we should do that right away." I told an auxiliary nurse to send an orderly for Doctor.

Amazingly, the pregnant woman greeted me and we exchanged pleasantries. I couldn't imagine the pain she was in. Yet in all my time at the hospital, I never heard a Gambian woman cry out in childbirth. Those women were amazingly stoic.

I asked the nurse mid-wife if she knew how long the woman had been in childbirth.

"Long time. There is no more fluid. The baby is dead."

Doctor Ceesay came within a very few minutes. Wearing street clothes, he donned a rubber apron, still bloody from the last patient.

He struggled and tried several different ways to discharge the baby but all attempts failed. Then, as a last resort, he administered a small amount of anesthesia. "Enough to make her muscles relax." With this assistance, he delivered the dead baby and sent the woman back to her village. Doctor hung the apron back on the hook behind the door and returned home.

* * *

A boil developed in Bruce's left armpit. He showed it to me, though he wasn't too concerned. I suggested he apply hot packs, which he did on and off for a couple of days

One morning we awoke to a terrible stench. The boil had ruptured. He drained an amazing amount of pus from it, leaving quite a hole.

"I guess I'll take my chances with your Health Centre," he said. "I need to get some antibiotics."

"I dunno...remember what Ann said."

"There's no way I'm going to go all the way downriver to get something I could get right here." So, with that Bruce walked with me to work that morning.

Doctor Ceesay happened to be in and looked at the boil and prescribed an injection of penicillin and tetracycline tablets. As instructed, Bruce left for the dresser dispensers, right next door.

Bruce got his injection and tablets, but then the dresser dispenser insisted on cleaning the area. Bruce considered the whole episode a nightmare. "Their cotton is just one giant ball and they tear off a piece from that. I didn't even see the fellow wash his hands after seeing the last patient. There was already a bowl of stuff on the table.I think it was watered down Phisohex, though it was kind of brownish. The dresser dispenser picked up the scissors, probably already used on another patient, and trimmed the hair around my sore, then dabbed the cotton in the bowl and cleaned the area under my arm. He cut a piece off of a roll of bandages (with the same scissors) and applied it. Every ounce of me was screaming 'Get out of here!'"

When he got home, there was a note on the door from two tubobs we knew from Banjul. They had told us they would be coming up on the riverboat, Lady Chilel, and staying for a couple of days. But when they got to Basse, they found it just too hot and decided to turn around and go back downriver on the boat.

Bruce nodded. "They should try it during the hot season."

The boil healed with no complications. Bruce credits that to the antibiotics, not the dresser dispenser's treatment.

* * *

Thanksgiving was almost upon us. Even though it wasn't a locally celebrated holiday, we intended to make it a special day and invited Nathaniel and Kevin for dinner. Peggy would be going downriver.

Our chickens were all producing eggs, so we didn't want to slaughter one of them. I decided to buy a chicken.

At work, I asked Sister Roberts if chickens were always available at the market.

Sister was familiar with our Thanksgiving. "You'll want a big bird, Mariama, so you should buy a rooster. But you must leave now or they'll all be gone. People buy birds early in the morning."

"Leave now? But I have this work to do."

"That work can wait. You need to get your Thanksgiving bird."

So I left the Centre and walked to the market. Sure enough, the few birds for sale were going fast. I found a large rooster and bought him, probably paying more than I should have. I'd forgotten to ask Sister Roberts what it would cost.

It was big and I had my hands full of flapping wings before I could settle him into the crook of my arm.

Planning to put him in our chicken coop, I stopped by the hospital to tell Sister I'd purchased my bird and I'd be back as soon as I took him home and walked back again.

"Why walk all the way home and back again? Here, give him to me."

She opened a supply closet door, put the rooster on the floor and closed the door.

Once in awhile that day we'd hear a muffled cock-a-doodle-doo coming from the hospital closet. No one seemed to think it strange at all.

At the end of the day I picked up my bird and carried him home.

We had yet to slaughter our first chicken. I'd put the rooster in our chicken coop, so he was easy to catch. After the rooster put up a good fight with frantic scrambling and wings flapping, Bruce managed to cut off its head. The rest of the body ran around the compound. It was awful. The bird finally gave up and we put him in a basin and poured hot water over him so that the feathers were easier to remove.

A chicken, especially a big rooster, has more feathers than I would have imagined. In America, most of us get our chickens from a supermarket, all nicely dressed and cleaned. Preparing this rooster took hours. Granted, we weren't very adept. It was a huge chore.

The next day, Thanksgiving, Bruce mounted the bird on a spit over a charcoal cooker we had recently acquired. From time to time, we rotated it so that it was a nice even golden brown.

In the meantime, I prepared a pudding made of squash, sort of an imitation pumpkin pie without the crust. At times like this I missed an oven. Still, with sugar, eggs and cinnamon, our pudding was delicious. We wouldn't have gravy, but I creamed potatoes and made a salad. The bird was pretty tough and we decided after that experience, we would stew chickens. Even with the tough bird, our Thanksgiving was a welcomed treat and provided a little taste of home. I know Nathaniel and Kevin appreciated sharing this holiday meal with friends in this place so far from their homes.

* * *

Bruce tired of the men at the shop continually asking for money. "Mistah Bruce, help me one dalasi." Sometimes he wondered if they were serious or just trying to make conversation. He knew better than to just give money away; he couldn't start a precedent like that.

But often, near the end of the month, many seriously asked for a loan of money. Not all of them asked. Mosalif and a few others never did, but enough asked that it became a frustration. Finally, Bruce settled on a routine. If someone borrowed money, Bruce wrote down in a little notebook he carried the amount of money being lent. He did this in front of the borrower. On payday, the men often came to him to repay their loan, but if they didn't, he'd go to them. Bruce would scratch out the debt in front of the borrower. Almost always he was repaid.

Another frustration was the constant use of project vehicles for personal use. Sometimes they asked permission to use a project vehicle when they made a large purchase, such as a bed. Bruce usually consented. There was simply no way to haul goods back and forth within the villages except by animal cart or a motor vehicle. Bruce could see the necessity.

One day Bruce and a driver took a Land Rover into the bush to check on the progress of a well digging job. They came upon their own dump truck, filled with about 30 women, all dressed up and carrying shopping bags, obviously on their way to market.

Bruce told his driver to signal the driver of the dump truck to stop, which he did. The truck driver climbed out of the cab and hurried over to where Bruce stood. The driver had his back to the truck in an obvious attempt to obscure Bruce's view of the passengers.

"What are you doing with that truck?" Bruce demanded.

"What truck?"

"That truck with all those women in it!"

"What women?"

It was so absurd, Bruce had to laugh. It was not only a violation to use a truck in that manner, the man had probably charged them all money, so he was also making a profit.

"Take those women back to their village and get the truck back to the job!"

"Okay, Mistah Bruce," the man replied cheerfully. Bruce was never called his Gambian name, Dawda Kinteh, by these men, it was always Mistah Bruce. Many called me Mariama, but a few called me Missus Bruce.

Using vehicles inappropriately went on all the time. People didn't seem to realize that they were stealing from themselves, from the good of all.

Men working on pile of peanuts

Chapter 14

*D*espite the fact that Christmas is a Christian holiday, it is observed in The Gambia, no doubt a hangover from British colonial days. We knew that the community wouldn't observe it with decorations or holiday fare, but at least it would be a holiday from work. We invited Nathaniel for Christmas Eve and Christmas Day and he expressed relief. He dreaded being away from home and family on Christmas. Even in college, he always had made it home for the holidays. Peggy planned to go downriver to observe the holiday with volunteers from her group.

We hoped the gifts we sent to our families would arrive in time, but were sure our gifts from them would not. Mail was so slow and sporadic. We'd been to the post office enough times to know that much of the delay was right in The Gambia. They would be hard-pressed to handle Christmas-time mail.

Basse had a post office, but it was pretty hopeless. Once I discovered it, a small building tucked behind the Commissioner's office, I was delighted that I'd found a source of postage stamps. I didn't trust the service enough to actually mail letters there. In any event, we normally knew of someone going downriver who would take our mail. This was a common practice among Peace Corps people. But we did like to have our letters ready to mail with the correct postage.

On my way to market, I swung by the post office to buy stamps. Although the hours were posted and it should have been open, it was closed. I went on to the market to do my shopping. Our friend Charlie was coming to dinner and I thought I'd serve catfish.

I approached the fishmonger and bought a fish, then asked him to remove the head. He slipped the remaining fish into the bag I held out, I paid him and went on my way. Soon I heard a loud argument. Two ladies fought over the fish head! I learned from that experience. The next time I wanted to buy a fish, I looked around for someone I knew at the market and asked her if she wanted a fish head. They always did. They could serve their family's dinner with that. I'd have her go with me, ask for the fish, pay for it and tell the fish monger to give the head to my friend.

My favorite peanut butter lady and I had a fun on-going game. One of us would spot the other, but step out of sight and stare. I'd get the feeling that someone was looking at me, I'd turn around quickly and "catch" her. I always made my peanut butter purchase last, letting the game gain momentum. Sometimes I played it on her and she'd "catch" me. We'd always burst out laughing while the other vendors watched, amused.

After finishing my shopping, I returned to the post office. The post mistress was just unlocking the door. No apologies, no excuses. After all that, she was out of stamps. "When will you have more?" She didn't know, maybe later that day.

* * *

Bruce had given me an early Christmas present. On his way home from one of his downriver trips, he'd stopped at the village of Jarreng, the village where he'd bought our bed, and purchased a nice chair. Made of reed-like material with a back and arms, it was quite large. We had a tailor make pillows for it from fabric I had on hand and foam rubber from an old mattress we'd found at the house. So I finally had a comfortable chair to sit in while reading.

One evening I accompanied Bruce when he ran an errand to the weather station, hoping to use their radio to call Yundum headquarters. Afterward, we swung by the "blue store" to pick up a case of The Gambia's own JulBrew, a very good locally made beer, and a case of their equally good soft drink, Bitter Lemon. After returning the Land Rover, we walked by the guard's station and greeted an old Gambian, Mohamed, who worked as a night guard. We watched as he wrote out a verse from the Koran on a flat, very smooth piece of wood. His pen was a bamboo stick, dipped into a dye made from charcoal. He taught children the Koran and was writing the next lesson on the board.

The next evening while Bruce took his bucket bath, I went to the guard's station and ordered a board for Bruce for Christmas. I told Mohamed it was my Christmas present to Bruce and the old man seemed surprised, but pleased. He had no idea what to charge, so I offered twenty-five dalasi. He seemed delighted. I thought it a very fitting ecumenical gift.

The day before Christmas, Nathaniel arrived early in the morning and we explored areas around Basse. We found an old cemetery, both Muslim and Christian. Although Basse is quite flat, we did find a small hill and hiked to the top for another prospective of our "town." Though close to Christmas, the daytime temperatures were in the high 90's and we stopped at Pa Peacock's White House Fuladu East Bar for a cold beer for the fellows, Bitter Lemon for me. Just like any bar, there were regulars, the same people we saw each time.

We'd been gone for some time with no chance to relieve ourselves. The guys went behind the building. When they returned, I asked Bruce to go back out with me, so he could stand guard. There was no latrine at all, just smelly dirt surrounded by a woven krinting fence. I made it quick.

Just as we returned home from our hike, another volunteer, Chris, came along. The Peace Corps friend she was to meet, a fellow from the other side of the river, didn't show, so she joined us for Christmas Eve. We had thought there would be the three of us, Nathaniel, Bruce and I, but it turned out to be four for dinner. Our menu of grilled hamburgers cooked on our charcoal grill could stretch. We had ground the meat, and I spiced it up with chopped onions. We topped the hamburgers with tomatoes and sprouts we'd grown and the "buns" were the good French baguettes always available.

Christmas morning I presented Bruce with the Koran verse board and he was so pleased. In addition to the chair, he gave me a quart thermos and I also gave him a dish of hard candy I'd bought in Banjul and saved for the occasion. We enjoyed our unique and simple Christmas.

Mid-Christmas day, we had another surprise. The Danish owners of LaPizza, Fleming and Englise, where we often enjoyed pizza while in Bakau, walked from Basse to the UN compound. Their car had broken down on the way to Senegal. They'd found a mechanic and then spent that first night in Basse's only hotel and found it unclean and crawling with insects.

As planned, Nathaniel joined us for Christmas dinner, but Chris continued on to the village of her friend. Even the LaPizza people, professional cooks, seemed to enjoy our holiday meal of canned Danish ham, creamed potatoes and onions, mashed squash, a fruit salad, and I'd made no-bake bar cookies from Rice Krispies bought at CFAO, the tubob store in Bakau. Our LaPizza guests furnished the wine for dinner and champaign later on in the evening. I thought it fitting and Christmas-like that we could "take in" others who needed a place to stay.

As it turned out, Fleming and Englise's car repair took four days and they gratefully spent three nights with us.

The weather turned Christmas-like, windy with a tendency toward rain. It was probably as cool as we would ever experience in The Gambia. Rain that time of year was rare, and not welcomed. The peanuts as well as millet were drying in the fields and rain could cause them to mold.

The Gambia's national product was peanuts, but since they didn't have proper drying facilities, many countries including the United States, refused to buy from them. It's too bad and it didn't seem like it would be that difficult to improve the storage situation by erecting a roof and building a platform to keep the peanuts off the ground to prevent molding.

That next week, Bruce and I trekked with Nathaniel to a place where they store peanuts for the country's use. Bruce took a picture of men standing on a mountain of peanuts. When I saw them, I wondered how many peanut shells were being broken by their weight.

Nathaniel was going to Banjul for meetings and offered to take our empty butane bottle to have it filled since there was no butane source in Basse. Luckily, we had another full bottle. The first bottle lasted us almost three months of pretty steady cooking. Nathaniel normally had a project car and driver when he attended his monthly meetings.

Other than Peace Corps volunteers, I didn't know anyone in our area who used butane to cook. The local people cooked with open fires and burned either wood or charcoal. Cooking was one of the most time-consuming efforts in The Gambia, though much of that work was shared. In a traditional compound of six or seven related families, perhaps two women cooked for the entire compound, two washed clothes, and others worked in the fields. Often, the grandmother took care of small children, those who had been weaned from their mothers' breasts.

Before the end of December, I needed to complete a report due for Peace Corps, a three-month projection of my activities. Nathaniel would take my report to the Peace Corps office. Apparently, I was one of the few who sent in this mandatory report.

Almost everywhere we went, Bruce took his camera, a gift from his dad and brother. There was no place to have the 35-millimeter slide film processed in-country, so Bruce mailed the exposed film directly to Kodak with instructions for them to mail the slides to his parents to view and critique for us. One of Dad's suggestions was to get more light on Gambian subjects. Most local people didn't mind having their picture taken, some even asked Bruce to take their pictures. But people were not going to stand around in the sun, they'd seek shade. Their dark skin combined with shade, resulted in a picture showing just teeth. Having critique from the folks allowed Bruce to take some very good images.

We enjoyed New Years Eve by ourselves. Most volunteers we knew were downriver for the holidays. Nathaniel left to have New Years Eve in Bakau, then would attend their monthly small business advisor meeting. Peggy seemed to spend all holidays downriver. We enjoyed just having each other for company, bringing in the New Year in our own quiet way. Having each other for entertainment was definitely an advantage. Volunteers who were the only tubob in a village longed for English conversation and companionship.

After a long delay, we finally received two decent mail calls when volunteers returned to their posts after having been in Banjul for the holidays. Some were letters and a few Christmas cards. None of the Christmas packages we were expecting arrived.

* * *

I noticed the hospital had no calendar. I wondered how people kept track of days, but soon learned they really didn't. It worried me that the correct dates weren't always noted on medical records. More, I worried that instructions for administering medications weren't being followed with an accurate indicator of days.

I had asked Bruce's mom to send me a calendar for the hospital in our Christmas package. Luckily she had air-mailed two calendars, one for the hospital and one for us. It was a good thing since we still hadn't received our Christmas packages.

Proudly, I hung up the pretty calendar and showed everyone at the hospital where it was. "Now we can keep a little better track of time."

The next day it was gone and no doubt hung in someone's hut.

I hated to do it, but I donated our own to the hospital. It, too, disappeared.

That night, at home, I drew two blank monthly calendars on typing paper, using carbon paper to duplicate. I filled in the dates for both the hospital and home. Not surprisingly, no one took my home-made calendar home. At least now the nurses had a way to keep track of dates. I did that each month.

* * *

Early one evening we heard wailing from Mansajang. Traditionally, when someone dies the women scream and wail. We walked over to see if it was anyone we knew. I recognized the family. The mother had been admitted to the hospital to give birth to twins. One baby died, but the surviving twin, though tiny, looked as though he would live. Mother and child were released but the mother hemorrhaged and died. That had been her thirteenth childbirth in almost that many years. Although she appeared to be a strong woman, a body just can't recover that rapidly from repeated childbirth. Bruce knew the man from the shop. He sat on a bench, elbows on knees, his hands locked behind his head, the traditional mourning pose for men.

About the same time, another woman died at the hospital, this time a mother of one of the auxiliary nurses. I heard a loud, shrill scream, and a nurse-midwife who happened to be standing near me said, "Faatu's mother must have died." Others began to wail, something I didn't expect from nurses, especially at a hospital.

* * *

Much to our surprise, wrestling was popular in Africa. We attended a match in Mansajang which drew many spectators, some from Senegal who traveled with their team. The wrestlers' attire seemed odd to us, and inconvenient. They covered their lower trunk with cloths tied with rope. Some wore pieces of fabric wound around and around making a loose rope, and tied it to their lower trunk. Drummers from both sides kept things at a frenzied pace. Unfortunately, although the drumming was very good, it was often accompanied by whistles, like a police whistle, which we found irritating. Wrestlers stepped out in time with the drums and began their match. They don't have wrestling pin holds as in the United States, but rather the winner of a match has thrown his opponent to the ground. Holding on to costumes is considered fair. The games started Friday night, continued all day Saturday and ended around two Sunday morning. We stayed a couple of hours but heard the drumming all through the nights.

* * *

This seemed to be the season for snake sightings. We had two snake bite incidents at the hospital, both men, and one died, his snake-bitten leg gray and puffy. I heard reports of more snake-bites, but the victims didn't come to the hospital.

Over a three-day period, snakes caused a bit of excitement at the UN shop yard next door. During the night the guards killed a 70-inch snake they identified as a spitting cobra. The next night they killed another, this one 48-inches long. They left the snakes for Bruce to see in the morning.

Black with a white stripe around the neck, their spit can temporarily blind a predator, but the spitting cobra rarely bites. If its venom gets into the bloodstream, however, it is highly toxic. Obviously, Gambians have a healthy respect for snakes.

At work, I asked Dr. Ceesay if the hospital had snake-bite treatments and learned that although the hospital does carry some antivenin, they don't always know the type of snake the patient has encountered.

* * *

We increased our chicken flock by two that week. A young girl came to our door with a strange looking chicken in her arms, asking if I wanted to buy it. I did, always happy to increase our flock. We'd seen this kind of chicken and now we had one of our own. We named the hen (black with disorganized, wild head feathers) Yvonne, after our Peace Corps Director.

On Wednesday, as a follow-up call for a child who had been hospitalized, I visited a village near Demba Kunda whose residents had the predominant name of Manneh, my Gambian surname. In recognition of my "family name," I was given a young rooster, which was quite an honor. The rooster was the most awkward bird I had ever seen. Its wings had been clipped, not uncommon, but they had done a poor, uneven job. The bird had a strange gate, as though its legs were too long. When he pecked at food on the ground, he seemed to bend his knees. We called the gangly bird George, after our very tall Assistant Peace Corps Director.

I'd always thought that roosters automatically knew how to crow, but I learned differently from our rooster, George. First thing in the morning, Binta's rooster crowed a sharp, clear "cock-a-doodle-doo." George tried it, but all that came out was a pathetic garble. He tried again and again, each time getting closer to the real sound. Finally, after several more practice days he proudly greeted us each morning with a glorious crow.

* * *

George Scharffenberger had sent word that he and "The Gambia Desk" person from Peace Corps Washington, D.C. would be calling on us and spending the night. They arrived, bringing our mail and Christmas packages. Along the way they had visited other volunteers. Terry, the Washington, D.C. lady, was impressed with our living situation. She became less enthusiastic when I told her how much work it was to keep up. She wondered why we didn't have household help.

"We could," I said, "but we would sacrifice privacy." I didn't go on to say how much company we had and how we seemed to fight for every moment of privacy we did have.

George and Terry sat at our dining room table, rehydrating with our clean well water after a long day's travel. Nathaniel and Peggy would be joining us for dinner.

George faced the yard. "You've acquired a few more chickens, I see."

"Yes, one of them is named after you, George, our only rooster."

Two chickens walked by, including the black one with the wild head feathers. "What a weird chicken," George observed. "That black one with the messy head feathers."

"That's Yvonne."

Terry and George howled in laughter. George wagged his finger at me. "You guys are terrible. I'm going to tell Yvonne!"

Then our rooster walked by. George leaned forward to look at the peculiar gangly bird, then sat back. "Oh, no."

"Yep. That's George."

"You guys are terrible."

I knew George well enough to know he'd see the humor in this.

I'd prepared a big beef stew and served it over rice. I'd discovered a product at the blue store, Bird's Custard Powder, from England, that I often used to satisfy our craving for sweets. I began to add different flavors–chocolate powder, also available at the blue store, peanut butter, which was not that successful, bananas when available. For this dinner I used chocolate. Peggy and Nathaniel, at least, were thrilled. We could only buy the unsweetened chocolate, but mixed with sugar, it satisfied our craving.

It was getting hot again. We'd been down to one bucket bath a day, but as the temperature rose, so did the need for increasing the number of daily baths, if only to cool off. Soon we'd be back to three baths a day. I explained the water-hauling procedure and Terry became even less enthusiastic about our living situation. When he could see we weren't going to, George offered to haul water for her.

We celebrated Christmas again that day, February 28th, with the packages from home our guests brought. George suggested we go ahead and open our gifts, but we only opened one package in their presence, wanting to savor the other packages by ourselves. The package we opened from Bruce's folks contained hard candy, which we shared, several packages of different flavored Jello and a folk-song book.

After Peggy and Nathaniel left and we'd settled our guests down for the night, Bruce and I retired to our hut and opened the other two packages. One was from my family, more hard candy, dates, sesame snacks, foot-long cheese, real Yuban coffee (our first ground coffee since we'd been in The Gambia), two kinds of tea with a tea strainer, dried soup, all wonderful treats. Also special in that package was a Noel banner that the girls had made. Even though it was after Christmas, we would enjoy that as a wall hanging for many Christmases to come.

My sister also sent a nice package with a three-foot plastic Christmas tree. We didn't take it out of the package that year, but it would be a welcome decoration for our next

Christmas in Africa. Also in the box was a Monopoly game, checkers, cribbage board and two decks of cards, hard candy, Frisbees, and a small tinned ham, a can of yams and a can of cranberry sauce. She intended the food to be our Christmas dinner. Maybe it would be Easter dinner.

That night we had a harmattan, a huge sand storm. After we went to bed the wind really blew, "a real honker," Bruce called it. During the night we awoke, hot and gritty.

"Now I know what a sugar cookie feels like," I said.

We got up, swept off our bed as well as we could, knowing it would just get dirty again. By morning, a thick coat of sandy dust covered everything. We had to wash all our dishes, silverware and cooking pots before we prepared breakfast. I could see our guests becoming less and less enchanted with our place. Where George lived, in Bakau, there wasn't much sand, and coming from Washington, D.C., Terry had never experienced such weather.

Before they left, George said that Yvonne Jackson, our current Peace Corps Director would be finishing her contract within a few months and he would become the new Director. Meri Aimes, whom we met in Philadelphia, would be the new Assistant Director and would be in charge of the health workers and therefore would be my adviser. A new fellow would come, another Assistant Director, Doc, and he would be Bruce's adviser and oversee other Peace Corps projects. At that point, health workers constituted about half the Peace Corps population in The Gambia.

George asked and we agreed to have trainees spend three days with us, as did Peggy. The new trainees were in that phase of their training as we were when we first visited Mansajang.

The trainees arrived the next Sunday afternoon. We had two, a young man, Charles, and a young woman, Judy. Although they wouldn't be assigned to Mansajang, it was a good opportunity for them to see how volunteers live. Peggy had two women trainees.

Bruce was especially interested in Charles' project, appropriate technology. Judy would work in the health field, as would Peggy's two guests. We agreed to pool our resources and show these four around as a group.

On Monday, I took the four trainees to the hospital with me and showed them the kind of work I do and explained the necessity for good record keeping to ensure a steady supply of needed medications and vaccines. They seemed appropriately grossed out by the hospital, but, surprising myself, I defended it. I also showed them where laundry was done, by hand I pointed out, and where hospital meals were prepared over an open fire.

Later, Bruce met us at the hospital and I joined him to take the group into Basse so they could see the market, local businesses, and the river. We bought a few things at the market so they could see how it was done. I had fun showing off my Mandinka and was also pleased when the vendors called us by name. Sometimes it was difficult for us to see how far we had come. Seeing ourselves through the eyes of new volunteers was enlightening.

Peggy took the group on trek with the Catholic Relief Services, an international humanitarian agency. CRS had just begun its operation in The Gambia in 1979 with its main focus on health, clean water, education and livelihoods. As any emerging organization here, progress had been slow, but their efforts admirable.

Our two trainees seemed to enjoy our home-cooked meals, but Peggy said her two didn't like her compound's food and could hardly eat it. So the next day we had the whole gang for dinner at our place, including Peggy. By this time the guests were fairly overwhelmed with the strangeness of it all.

Bruce intended to take the group into the bush so they could see a well-digging operation, but the only Land Rover left at the shop broke down so he couldn't take them. Still, he explained quite a bit of their operation right there at the shop.

On the last night we all ate dinner at Jobot's All Necessary Foods. We decided not to show them the kitchen.

Bruce and I needed to get away. So much of our energy was spent entertaining others. We needed a break.

We would accompany the trainees, at least part way, by boat, on the Lady Chilel. We had talked about doing this for some time and were a bit disappointed that we wouldn't be doing it alone. However, it would be a way for the trainees to get back to their group and the boat ride would give them a different prospective of The Gambia.

Mary working foot pump at the well. UN shop in background.

Chapter 15

*I*t was a fine March day when we boarded the Lady Chilel, named after one of the President's wives. The boat made the journey upriver once a week in dry season, twice a month in the wet season. By local standards, the 175-foot boat seemed quite spiffy. Its three decks were clean and a dining area was open to all passengers, though many people brought their own food and ate on the deck, or below decks. There were several cabins, but the cost was considerably more, about eighty-five dalasi for each passenger, and only fifteen dalasi each to sleep on the deck. For the price difference we gladly chose the deck.

Travel by boat offered a calm, smooth ride, so much nicer than bumping along in a Land Rover. Throughout the cruise, the boat stopped at a dozen villages along the way. Vendors paddled out to sell passengers fruits and vegetables, crafts, even clay pots of all sizes.

Monkeys swung from tree to tree, but we saw no hippos or crocodiles. We did see many colorful birds, much to the pleasure of the tourists aboard. At dusk, a British fellow pointed to a long-winged bird, "Look, a nightjar!" and binoculars turned to where he pointed.

During training, Bruce and I bought lengths of cloth to use as a ground cover at the beach and we used these to spread out on the deck at night. Those cloths, which I had hemmed by hand, were so handy. We'd brought sheets to cover us, thinking that mosquitoes might be a problem. We slept in a group with the trainees, piling our packs in the middle. By early morning, my hips complained of a hard deck, but we were glad to be sleeping under the stars on our moving island rather than in a stuffy cabin.

George had suggested that we stop with Charles and Judy at Jenoi to meet the other trainees. Jenoi, about half way to Banjul, was a good stopping place for us. At most stops, the boat didn't have a dock, nor did they in Jenoi, so we were taken ashore, four at a time, in a small skiff.

Bruce and I managed to talk to all fourteen trainees. We knew just what they were going through and how important it was for them to talk to people who were doing what they were being trained to do. We were so glad we'd stopped. Peace Corps encourages "old-timers" to talk to trainees.

Although we'd planned to take a bush taxi to Bakau, we were able to get a ride with a Peace Corps driver right to our apartment door.

The next morning we caught the bus into Banjul to pick up our mail, check in with the Peace Corps staff, and, as instructed by nurse Ann Saar, get inoculated against meningitis because of a recent outbreak. Although it was past opening time, no staff had arrived yet. The night guard recognized us and let us in.

We could access the Peace Corps mail boxes, sorted by geographic division, and we pulled our mail out of the Upper River Division box. Before we left for home, we'd pick up any mail in there and deliver it to people upriver.

As we sat reading our mail, the phone rang. And rang. Bruce muttered, "Well, I might as well get it."

Afterward, he told me the conversation. "Hello?"

"Who's this?"

"Bruce Trimble."

"Bruce! This is Yvonne. What are you doing here?" This spoken with an edge to her voice.

"We came down for business, Mary's attending a medical conference, I have business at Yundum, Ann Saar needs to give us shots, and we're taking time for some R&R."

"But my mother and I are leaving today to go upriver and we'd planned to stay with you!"

"Sorry, we're not there."

Bruce was disgusted with the whole thing. George had encouraged us to take more time off, to come downriver more often. Bruce was also irritated that Yvonne and her mother planned to stay with us, unannounced. "You'd think a director would have more sense than to just drop in," Bruce said, shaking his head. We were so glad to be downriver and not entertaining more company.

The next day, we took a bus from Bakau into Banjul. Bruce spent his time at the Yundum shop and I called on Sister M'Boge. She expressed approval of my work so far and asked if I'd given thought to an in-service training program for the auxiliary nurses. Luckily while I lay awake on the Lady Chilel I'd had an inspiration.

"I have, and wondered what you thought about my inviting guest speakers to talk to the nurses, people like Catholic Relief Services, Planned Parenthood, the Health Inspector, just to let the nurses know what others are doing."

"That is a very good idea, Mariama. Have you discussed it with Sister Roberts?

"Not yet."

"You'll need her permission. She will like your plan."

I soared out of Sister M'Boge office, so relieved I had a plan. The information for the nurses didn't have to come from me. It would come from our guest speakers, many of whom would be knowledgeable Africans, successful in their fields, and good examples for the auxiliary nurses. Yes! I mentally punched the air.

All volunteer health workers were asked to attend a 4-day seminar and we had worked that into our stay downriver.

Bruce was able to get a project vehicle to take several of us health workers to Yundum, where the conference would be held. We both attended an opening dinner, then Bruce left for the Bakau apartment and I stayed at Yundum in a dormitory, much like Jenoi. Bruce used the time to meet with UN people to see what they could do about supply shortages.

Chris, who had been with us Christmas Eve, and I signed up to be roommates. I admired her work in Bansang and found her to be fun and friendly.

David Werner, author of *Where There is No Doctor*, was the featured speaker for the seminar and was excellent. Although crippled with arthritis, Dr. Werner was a bundle of energy. The sessions started at 8:00 a.m. and often didn't end until 10:00 at night, taking short breaks for lunch and dinner. I didn't know how the man could keep up that pace. Ours was just one stop on his busy itinerary teaching in many African countries.

Dr. Werner had accomplished wonders in remote Mexico. His specialty was working with people who couldn't read, creating visual aids that showed them how to diagnose and treat many diseases and how to respond to emergency medical situations. We saw movies and slides of his work in Mexico and held discussions on problems and attitudes we encountered.

One of the things Dr. Werner emphasized was that materials were often right at hand, materials that would make life so much easier for those afflicted. For instance, in developing countries, a cripple is often seen using a walking stick, hanging on to it with both hands, thereby handicapping him even more. "Find a forked stick and put another stick across the top, like a crutch. Wrap the cross piece with rags for comfort. That will free up one arm." It's so simple, yet unless a person has seen a crutch, it's hard to imagine its benefit. His book, which had been issued to all of us in training, had illustrations of many of his suggestions.

At another session we discussed diarrhea and dysentery. I really hadn't known the difference, but learned that while diarrhea was loose, watery stools, dysentery had blood and mucus in the stool.

Diarrhea can be caused by many conditions including poor nutrition, a viral infection, food poisoning, and malaria. Babies may get diarrhea by trying to digest foods that are new to them.

A well-nourished child is less likely to have diarrhea, but if he does, he usually recovers quickly. A malnourished child is more likely to get diarrhea, and there is a much greater chance he will die from it.

Most children who die from diarhhea do so because of dehydration. At the first sign of diarhhea, we learned, a rehydration drink should be given: To one liter of boiled water, add 2 teaspoons of honey (preferred) or sugar, one-quarter teaspoon of salt, one-quarter teaspoon of bicarbonate of soda (if no soda is available, increase salt to one-half teaspoon). Actually, I hadn't seen measuring spoons since I'd arrived in the country, but I knew I could demonstrate the approximant amounts, which would be better than nothing.

The information I gained from this conference could save lives. The key would be passing the information on to the villagers.

I liked spending the little free time we had with Chris. We thought alike on so many issues. Except housekeeping. I prefer to keep things simple and in order. The sparsely furnished room had two single beds, a shared open closet to hang clothes, with two built-in shelves.

I have a habit of making my bed each morning. I simply like the looks of a made bed. Chris doesn't worry about it. Nor did she worry about putting things away.

When Bruce and I traveled downriver, we often put our clothes in a box or in a pack. We didn't have a traveling suitcase, just our large trunks and day packs. So I'd unpacked my clothes from a box and put them in the closet. I'd also brought a pillowcase for my dirty clothes. Chris and I returned to our room from time to time to leave material gathered in class. I put my classroom information in the box. It was a lot of stuff: samples of visual aids, pamphlets, etc.

Chris simply dumped hers where ever she found an empty space.

Soon Chris' belongings were spread all over and began to spill onto my side. "Chris," I said. "I really don't want to be picky, but I think I'll just move your stuff to your side of the room."

"Oh! I'm sorry."

"No problem. What's on your side doesn't bother me. I just like to keep my side tidy."

The next morning, two volunteers stopped by to walk with us to the dining hall for breakfast. They laughed when they saw our room. "Wow!" Amber said, "You can see which is Chris' side." It was a rather stark contrast. Chris' unmade bed had clothes from the last two days strung over it, papers were strewn around her side of the room. Her opened makeup kit sprouted bottles, tubes and jars, some things spilling out onto the bed.

My side had a made bed, all my papers in a box, my clothes either hung up or on the shelf, my laundry bag in a corner of the closet, my travel kit on the shelf.

The conference ended at noon on the fourth day. As we finished lunch, a UN driver stopped by and approached me. "Mariama, Mistah Bruce asked me to pick you up. We will meet him at the Peace Corps office."

"Okay. When?"

He looked apologetic. "Right now. I must get the Land Rover back to the shop."

"I'll be ready in five minutes." I turned to Chris. "Do you want a ride back to Banjul? We have to leave right away."

"I'd love to, but I can't be ready that soon. It'll take me at least an hour to pack up my stuff."

The Gambian shook his head.

"Sorry," I said, "we've got to leave now." Another advantage of being organized; you can move quickly.

Bruce and I met at the Peace Corps office and, loaded to the gills with my stuff, we caught a bus to our Bakau apartment. The conference had been fast-paced but I felt so privileged to attend. It would take me awhile to sort out all the materials Dr. Werner had shared with us.

The glorious three days of R&R in Bakau were spent at the beach, visiting our USAID friends Harry and Suzi, even sailing with them on a boat they co-owned with other USAID people. The weather, noticeably cooler, offered a welcomed break.

As part of his USAID epidemiologist job, Harry worked toward a better medical record keeping system for the whole country and asked if I would look at his proposed system to see if I thought it workable at the Basse Health Centre. It looked like a good system, but I worried that it wouldn't be carried out. "I can't even get them to tally things in groups of five."

He planned to come upriver and asked if he could stay with us. "Of course, you are always welcome."

Harry would check out the record keeping there and then conduct a polio survey in neighboring villages. "Maybe you would help me?" I readily agreed.

Before leaving for home, we stopped at the bank to get cash from our account and were again infuriated by the rude, sloppy service. We found it inconceivable that people could keep jobs, the way bank employees shuffled to the counter, acted bored, kept people waiting. Multiply this attitude throughout the country and it wasn't surprising that things didn't get done.

In the few days we had been downriver, Bruce made three attempts to see the Project Director. "I can get up, shower, eat breakfast, catch a bus into Banjul, another bus to Yundum and be there before the Director. The Director, of course, had a vehicle at his disposal and lived a short distance from the Yundum shop. The Director wasn't a Gambian, but he seemed to have adopted the local habit of lateness or not showing up at all.

Bruce had yet to receive any truck or Land Rover parts that he had ordered. Supplies like oil were usually on hand, but trucks that needed repair parts were usually made operational by robbing one vehicle of parts to use in another.

We took a bush taxi back home to Mansajang. As usual, the first leg was in a regular car taxi going from Banjul to Serekunda, then another taxi to Soma, then Soma to

Bansang where we transferred to a Peugeot truck taxi where nearly twenty adults and children squeezed together. The ride was interminable, fraught with breakdowns. The rear left springs frequently collapsed, and the driver wired a piece of wood between the springs. Sometimes we made only a couple of miles before he would have to do it again. The clutch gave out, so the driver had to catch another taxi and go all the way back to Soma, where we had left about a half hour before, to get parts for the clutch. On and on it went. We were very late getting home.

One of our parcels was an electric table fan Bruce had bought at CFAO, the tubob store in Bakau. What a joy! When the electricity was on, that fan gave us hours of pleasure. We moved the fan from the house to the hut as needed. The fan helped us sleep so much better at night.

The next morning we saw that some of our garden squash had been gnawed by animals.. When Mosalif came for his morning greetings, he said sheep had gotten into the compound. We found it strange that when we were present, animals didn't get into the compound. We were more conscientious about securely fastening the gate closed. That squash had been almost ready to eat. As hard as we worked to grow vegetables in our garden, hand-hauling water, babying them along in harsh conditions, only to lose them at the last moment was discouraging.

The next day Bruce went back to work, but I stayed home to organize my materials and make my lesson plans for the auxiliary nurses training. The nurses would keep their counts while I was gone, then I'd officially record them when I returned. I had created an "in-box" in which they put all their counts.

When I spoke to Sister Roberts about my intentions for the Auxiliary Nurses Training, she was very enthusiastic. "Yes, Mariama, start this right away. Doctor Ceesay is leaving to work for a few weeks in Banjul. Start with him. Then later, you can have his substitute speak, that Polish man."

Sister Roberts had news. She was pregnant with her first child and would only be working two or three more months. Sister was in her thirties, much older than normal to be having her first child. Sister was Christian and her husband's only wife.

After rounds with Doctor Ceesay, I explained my project plans and asked him to speak to the nurses that next Thursday as my first guest speaker for the training sessions. He enthusiastically agreed. Sister and I had set the dates up, every Thursday morning, a day when they didn't go on trek.

* * *

As I recorded the many tallies that had accumulated in my absence, an automobile accident victim was carried into the hospital on a stretcher. I hadn't been aware of an accident. Sirens were never used upriver, though I had heard them in the Banjul area. The orderlies carried him straight into the operating theatre. After briefly evaluation the situation, the dresser dispenser left to get the doctor from his home.

Suddenly a rush of about twenty men burst into the operating theatre, all in their street clothes, of course, creating unbelievable noise. I peeked in and couldn't believe the confusion of all these men surrounding the poor victim and not one medical person in the room. The victim apparently had a broken leg. We later found out both the upper and lower leg bones were broken. Although fully awake, the patient didn't utter a sound.

One man attempted to raise the victim's legs and several yelled at him, including me. "Don't touch him!"

Sister Roberts had left for the day, so I looked for the next in charge, the nurse mid-wife, but just then Doctor Ceesay stormed in, kicked everyone out of the room except the nurse mid-wife. I helped usher people out of the hospital. In the meantime, many people had started to gather at the door, pushing and shoving. Just as Doctor Ceesay began his examination, three very well-dressed ladies, possibly his wives, came screaming and wailing in and rushed into the theatre. Nurses pulled the ladies out, still carrying on as though the fellow had died.

I tried to resume my work, but the window above my table was darkened by a crowd of bodies. The electricity was off at the time, so we had to depend on daylight through windows to see inside the dark building. The orderlies demanded the crowd get off the porch. They trickled off, but gradually filtered back.

The dresser-dispenser, who was assisting Doctor Ceesay, came out and announced they needed to find something they could use as a splint. I would have thought a hospital would have basic splints. But, no. Someone rummaged around and found a jagged piece of wall board, left over from a recent renovation and they broke that up for a splint.

In the midst of this confusion, two policemen came into the hospital, wanting to get a statement from the victim, but Doctor Ceesay said they must wait until after the examination and emergency treatment.

Apparently, to avoid the crowd, after the examination and initial treatment, the orderlies carried the patient on a stretcher through another door to take him to the Land Rover/ambulance, but someone saw them and the crowd ran over, got in the way of the orderlies, some even touching the patient. The patient would be driven to the nearest large hospital equipped with x-rays and casting material, facilities that the Basse Health Centre lacked.

The Land Rover rushed off with their patient. The two policemen stood in the street. They'd never had their chance to talk to him.

Later that day I called on Planned Parenthood. Apparently Muslims had no problem with Planned Parenthood, though abstinence didn't seem to go over well. They were okay with the women taking the pill, but with the supply chain being chancy, it sometimes caused more problems than it solved. The tubob I spoke with said that in one case, many women in a village had taken the pill, but when the supply ran out, many became pregnant, all in the same month!

Planned Parenthood was mostly concerned with the
mother's health after multiple births in relatively few years.
They invited me to go on trek with them the next day, which I
did gladly. I also signed them up for my in-service training
program.

On Monday, Harry joined us for dinner, as planned. The
next day, I joined him on his polio survey for children eleven
years and younger. The survey was long, hot work. I could
only volunteer for one day because of my other duties at the
hospital, but Harry and his team worked seven days. The
survey showed that the Upper River Division had many
occurrences of polio, particularly among children three years
and younger. That seemed surprising since polio
immunizations were routinely administered. Apparently,
many children weren't brought into the clinic.

The heat became oppressive, climbing to the high
nineties, sometimes over one hundred degrees. We'd
brought a thermometer and sometimes I think that made
things worse, knowing how hot it really was.

Usually, we were both home during the heat of the day.
Nothing was going on at either of our work places. We
couldn't bear to take naps as many did. To wake up in a
puddle of sweat just wasn't appealing to us. We tried to forge
on. We often read by our new fan, but wearied of that, too. In
the heat of the day the fan simply blasted hot air at us.
Sometimes we puttered in the garden, other times headed
into Basse to visit Peter, or to swim in the river.

* * *

Suzi sent word that she and her mother would be stopping
by. Suzi and Harry had been so generous with us. I knew
Suzi hoped they could spend the night and we were eager to
have them. I wrote back inviting them to stay with us,
appreciating the advance notice.

Suzi's mother was one of the few people who didn't
complain about the weather. She was from Florida and I

guess The Gambia didn't seem that hot to her. She was an amazingly good sport.

They took their bucket baths together. We could hear them giggling at the novelty. Suzi was so grateful to stay with us. "I wanted Mom to see how you guys lived. Harry and I are just staying in Africa, but you guys are really living here."

"You two must be campers," Suzi's mom said.

"Yes, we are."

"This must seem like one long camping trip."

"Really long," Bruce said, which made everyone laugh.

"Yes, I suppose it seems long when you're also working. Well, I admire you both for what you're doing."

* * *

When I first arrived in Mansajang, women often asked me where my "hat" was, meaning head-scarf. I couldn't imagine wearing one more thing. The women actually wrapped a length of cloth artfully around their head. Binta tried to put one on me, but with my slippery hair, it wouldn't stay on. I had a scrap of material leftover from having a dress made and I fashioned a triangular piece of cloth into a scarf that I could tie in the back. I couldn't believe how much cooler I felt not to have the sun beating down on my head. Now, on these extremely hot days, I sometimes soaked the scarf in water before wearing it and that cooled me even more, though it quickly evaporated.

I understood why so much didn't get done. It was impossible to work in that heat. If it wasn't the heat, we still couldn't always work because of the lack of supplies. At the UN shop, shortages prevented projects from completion. At the Health Centre, I often couldn't visit villages because they only had enough fuel to go on scheduled clinic treks.

Needs were so great, but at times I felt overwhelmed with the little I could do. I expressed my discouragement to Bruce. His job was actually far more frustrating than mine. Talking about it helped and each time we came to the same conclusion: all we could do was give it our best. We both knew our best wasn't enough.

Fuel-efficient stove Bruce built for Binta

Chapter 16

$\mathcal{A}$ mother and her daughter, perhaps ten years old, came into the hospital led by the dresser dispenser. He spoke with Sister Roberts. The four of them went into the treatment room and the dresser dispenser left.

I heard a piercing scream and much to my amazement, saw Sister Roberts, still screaming, run out of the room, hands flapping by her head. I left my table and rushed in, just in time to see whitish pink roundworms pouring out of the girls mouth and nose. The girl continually gagged while the mother held her daughter's head, steadying her.

Apparently, this wasn't the first episode and was the reason the mother brought the girl in. The girl, crying, stopped gagging for the moment. About the time I entered the room, one of the nurse mid-wives also came in. I admired her calmness; it was a terrible sight. She asked me to stay while she talked to the dresser dispenser. I gingerly patted the girls back, speaking soothingly, but all the while terrified that she would have another episode. The nurse soon returned with piperazine tablets the dresser dispenser had packaged. The nurse gave the girl six tablets, together with water. Only this one treatment would be necessary.

The nurse explained to the mother that worms could be prevented by washing hands often, especially after using the latrine. Although this sounds pretty basic, it's sometimes a challenge when there is no running water.

When I returned to my working station, Sister came back into the room and apologized to me. "I'm sorry, Mariama, that was terrible of me. It was just so awful. I'm already queasy with my pregnancy and..." Her voice trailed off.

I tried acting nonchalant. "I've never seen anything like that. Just one treatment will take care of the worms? That's impressive."

"Yes, just one treatment. I hope my child never does that. But if she does, I will not scream and run away. Not again."

* * *

Men in The Gambia often blew their noses without the benefit of a handkerchief. "Farmer style," Bruce called it. I never could get used to that and cringed every time. Another habit I saw among men was vigorously picking their nose. I couldn't help but turn away or I'd gag. I kept thinking I'd get used to these two habits—I certainly saw them enough—but I never did. It bothered me every single time.

One day I ran into Sean, a male nurse and volunteer who lived in a remote village on the other side of the river. He was a nice guy and I enjoyed talking to him. "It's my birthday," he announced, "and I'm taking the day off."

"Your birthday! I'll buy you a cup of coffee." We found a little outdoor eatery, 'chop shop' as it was called locally.

A man sitting at the next table blew his nose farmer style and Sean closed his eyes."I'll never get used to that."

Sean was fun, and full of stories. We finished our coffee and Sean mentioned he was going over to Nathaniel's.

"I'm finished with my marketing, I'll walk with you. It's on my way home." Bruce had left that morning for Yundum and wouldn't be home until the next evening.

As we arrived at Nathaniel's, I had an idea. "Hey, why don't you guys come over and we'll have a birthday dinner for Sean. Sean's eyes lit up and we set a time.

At home, I made a little top-of-the-stove cake. At times like this, I did miss having an oven. Gambians didn't really have desserts, especially in rural areas, so buying something readymade wasn't an option. Although the cake looked more like a pancake, I knew Sean would appreciate the effort.

The fellows arrived and I made a Spanish omelette and a salad.

"I don't know when I've enjoyed a better birthday dinner," Sean said. I'm sure the gesture meant more than the meal, but I was pleased with his reaction.

As usual, Mosalif came over to greet my guests. He knew Nathaniel, of course, but I introduced him to Sean. Mosalif looked a little concerned and as he turned to leave he spoke Mandinka to me in a very quiet voice. "Will they sleep here?"

"No," I answered, "dinner only." Neither of the guys realized what we were saying, but I could see Mosalif's relief. He was supposed to look after things and he would have been upset if men spent the night in Bruce's absence.

* * *

On March 11, we celebrated our second wedding anniversary. We walked into Basse and enjoyed dinner at Jobot's All Necessary Foods. Afterwards we stopped by Pa Peacock's White House Fuladu East Bar for a beer. While there, Pa expressed concern to Bruce about his son's school work. "He does not know his numbers. I cannot help him anymore. Would you work with him? I will pay you."

"I'll be glad to work with him, Pa. But no pay. Have him stop by after school."

A few times a week Pa's son, Lamin, stopped by. He was very shy and Bruce had to really work with him to discover how he could help. Lamin had brought his school books and he and Bruce went over the math homework. This went on for several sessions, until Lamin felt he had a grasp of it. Bruce encouraged him to come back if he needed more help.

Some time later, Pa Peacock, who spoke English to us, asked Bruce if he thought Lamin was "sensitive." It took us both a minute to realize he meant "sensible," which really wasn't the correct word either. Bruce replied, "I think Lamin has good sense and can figure things out."

Pa nodded, obviously pleased.

* * *

Father Fagan and Collum invited us for a Saint Patrick's Day celebration. Never mind that it fell during Lent, the Irish celebrate this big holiday regardless. They invited all the expatriates in the area: all the Upper River Division Peace Corps volunteers, the nuns, as well as Peter Moore and his new live-in working partner, Keith. Bruce offered to bring a case of beer, which they gladly accepted. The case of beer turned out to be a drop in the bucket.

We'd never been to an Irish St. Patrick's Day party and it was an all-out, pull-out-the-stops event. Collum prepared Irish stew and soda bread. To the Irish, this is an important holiday and we had so much fun enjoying the occasion with them. Beer and hard liquor flowed.

* * *

That spring, Peggy's mother and three sisters came for a visit. They spent much of their time downriver, staying in staff homes. Peggy had thought the conditions upriver might be difficult for them, crowded in her hut, the heat and no running water, but they were in Mansajang for three nights.

I was impressed with the family. Peggy's mother and the girls were enthusiastic and Peggy's African family treated them like royalty. The guests came loaded with gifts for the people of the compound.

We offered to have two of them spend the nights with us, alternating so that over the short period, they all spent at least one night with us. At one point we had them all for dinner and another time had them all for breakfast. They appreciated the hospitality and certainly did their share of hauling water, and helping when they could..

* * *

The Sahara Desert creeps closer to The Gambia each year. The need for firewood for cooking, plus drought conditions have created a scarcity of trees. Women and children often walk great distances to gather enough wood for fires.

The local people often used charcoal to cook, which is a waste. Precious heat is wasted making the charcoal. Charcoal isn't in the neat little briquettes we buy in bags, but irregular pieces from wood that the charcoal maker burns. He then sells it in burlap bags. Binta's fire was most often fueled by charcoal.

Bruce longed for projects where he could feel more productive, without the frustrations that he so often experienced. In reading about alternative energy at the Peace Corps library, Bruce learned about building a stove which would use less fuel than an open fire.

Along the meandering path we used to go into Basse, we passed a place where men made mud-bricks. The soil had to be the right mixture of clay and sand to make usable bricks. We watched as they dug up the clay mixture and patted it into molds, and left it to dry in the sun. Many things were made from these bricks such as huts and smaller structures for grain and peanut storage. The bricks would eventually melt or crack, but their lives could be extended if covered with a thin layer of concrete.

Bruce bought a supply of the bricks and they were delivered by a donkey-pulled cart. He had talked to Mosalif and Binta about his project and discussed where in the compound a good place would be to build the stove. The firebox was about three feet long, eighteen inches wide. Bruce borrowed Binta's two cooking pots so that he could make openings in the top to exactly fit her pots.

It was our hope that this idea would catch on and others would make this simple stove. The firebox, closed on three sides and sealed on top with the cooking pots, required far less fuel than an open fire. A small chimney directed smoke away from the cook's eyes.

Days went by, but Binta didn't use her new stove. Finally, Bruce asked Mosalif why.

"I need to build a house around it," Mosalif replied. The Fula, apparently, don't cook in the open. We were aware that there were covered cooking areas, but we had also seen many Mandinka and Wolof cooking in the open, though not the Fula. Binta's current cooking area was the space between walls of her hut, where, in our hut, was our bathing area.

Many times I had called on Binta and sat in that space while she cooked. It was unbelievably hot and I was nearly blinded by smoke. The next weekend Mosalif gathered the materials, grass for thatched roofing, and krinting, such as used for fencing, for the walls. A couple of his friends helped him build the cook hut.

Finally, the day came when Binta cooked her first meal on the stove. They were impressed with how much less fuel it took. Although a few people did come to look at it, the idea never caught on.

The day after Binta first used her stove, Mosalif gave us two identical chickens he bought in the bush. He wouldn't take money, wanting to give them to us in appreciation of the stove. We graciously accepted this generous gift, really thrilled to add two more hens to our flock. We called them Sisters because we couldn't tell them apart.

About that time, I had an idea that would benefit both Binta and me. About once a week I gave her money so that she could include us in her family's meal. I can't imagine why I hadn't thought of it earlier. It was wonderful not to have to worry about cooking dinner that night. I'm sure with the extra money Binta had an especially nice dinner for her family, too. She was a wonderful cook. She brought the food to us in a bowl and we ate it in our own home. We liked our food hot, while they let theirs cool so they could eat in their traditional way with their fingers.

* * *

Mara, a Peace Corps volunteer in the group after ours, had arrived in Mansajang and was a science teacher at the high school. A friendly, open person, she was an effective, dedicated volunteer. She had found a good compound and seemed to fit in nicely.

Mara had been upriver only a few weeks when she suffered a serious setback. Reading at night by candlelight, she did what she had done many times, just let the stub of a candle die out by itself while she drifted off to sleep. The next thing she knew, her hut was on fire. The candle wax had apparently burned through its thin metal holder, onto papers it sat on, which ignited her mosquito net. Very quickly the thatched roof was ablaze.

She awoke with a terrifying start and screamed "Demba!" Fire! Her water bucket was empty. In any event, she probably couldn't have put out the fast-spreading fire with a single bucket of water.

It isn't unusual for a fire to destroy a whole compound, even much of a village. The men in this compound were amazingly efficient, especially considering it was in the middle of night. Several men, using poles, lifted the roofs of the surrounding huts, tilting them away from the burning hut. While this was being done, other men tore down the fencing in back of her hut, to save the krinting surrounding the entire compound from catching on fire. Someone reached in and pulled Mara's trunk out of the hut, thereby saving her clothes.

It was surprising how damaged the hut was. Even the mud brick was destroyed, cracked from the intense heat.

In the confusion, two hundred fifty dalasi was stolen from the trunk, another blow to Mara, but still, she felt gratitude that no one was injured and that no other huts were damaged.

We heard of Mara's fire when a fellow came to our house with a message that the priests wanted to see me. I hurried over to the rectory where Mara's compound family had taken her during the night. She was understandably still shaken. The priests didn't have to ask–I invited her to stay with us until they could rebuild her hut.

Mara was the perfect guest. She had the bedroom in the house to herself. She pitched in and washed and dried the dishes every night. She admittedly wasn't a cook, but certainly did her part by cleaning up afterward. I know she felt she was intruding, but we made every effort to dispel that fear. If anything, Mara's being there preempted having other uninvited guests. A few people came asking to stay and it was good to be able to say, "Sorry we already have a house guest."

I imagine the Peace Corps helped with the cost of a new hut. Locally made mud bricks, thatching and cement all cost money. Within a few weeks, Mara had a lovely new hut, complete with designs on the freshly cemented walls.

* * *

It seemed much of our time and effort at home went into food. The chickens created some work. Using a flashlight at night, when the chickens were subdued and didn't seem to mind being turned upside down, we examined their cloacae. If it appeared dry and unyielding, the chicken was likely past producing eggs. She would soon be in the stew pot.

Bruce tried several slaughtering methods, none worked very satisfactorily. Cutting off their heads left a chicken running around, getting sand in the carcass. Bruce heard that if you held a chicken by its head, gave it a quick jerk, the neck would break, thereby killing the bird, but keeping the body intact, avoiding the macabre running around. I watched as he tried it, watched the chicken again run across the compound without a head. This wasn't how it was supposed to work. Bruce opened his hand and looked at the head with a startled little face looking up at him.

Bruce finally found a good way to slaughter a bird. He held the chicken, gently stroking her neck, speaking softly and once the hen was lulled, he would quickly slice the neck. It made us sad each and every time, but if the chicken was through giving us eggs, we needed to slaughter her. We couldn't afford to do otherwise.

Preparing a chicken for cooking is a chore: Gutting, de-feathering, and cutting up the bird, all without the benefit of running water, and then making the stew. These chickens were too tough for frying.

A hen will lay an egg without a rooster's input, so to speak. In order to have chicks, of course, a male has to fertilize an egg. Chickens ovulate every day, but a rooster's sperm lasts several days so that eggs are fertilized as they are formed. Mating can take place every seven to ten days in order to maintain fertilized eggs.

George, our lone rooster, took his role very seriously. Every afternoon when we opened the chickens' gate to let them forage, George crowded ahead, knocking the hens aside. He then stood at the exit, blocking the way, and nailed each chicken as she tried to emerge. It was a noisy business with indignant clucking and lots of flying feathers.

Our other big food effort was growing vegetables. We had fair success with gardening, but that also required a lot of work and constant watering, which meant hand-hauling water from the well. It all took time and energy.

* * *

In my quest for in-service training speakers, I found many interesting agencies in the Basse area. Once I went with Bruce to the hydro-meteorological office, a weather monitoring station, so that Bruce could use their short-wave radio to call Yundum headquarters to order, or try to order, necessary supplies. The hydro-met supervisor, happy with our interest in what he did, showed us around. They measured rainfall, when it infrequently happened, evaporation and temperature. They had about 15 different thermometers, some measuring air temperature, soil surface temperatures, and several at various depths in the soil. We were surprised to see that it was 85 degrees four feet underground. No wonder our well water felt so warm.

Once I encountered a policeman on my way to market and asked if I could visit the police station. Delighted with my request, he showed me around. Stepping inside, the two desks were stacked with papers. The room itself was relatively comfortable with ceiling fans. Since he currently had no prisoners, he asked if I would like to see the jail. I agreed and he opened a heavy door to a hot, stuffy room with four cells. The place smelled of urine and sweat. If there was ever an incentive to stay on the right side of the law, that place was it.

The policeman took a long time with me, discussing his various duties. As I left, he said, "Mariama, if you ever have trouble, come to see me. I will take care of it." I didn't doubt him for a minute.

The Catholic Relief Services was pleased to be asked to speak at my in-service training and I set a date for that. They were good about gearing their talk to make it clear they were supplementing what the Health Center did, not acting as competition.

Doctor Ceesay left as planned and in his place came Doctor Tom Wochjakowski. Dr. Tom graciously suggested his name rhymed with "where's your house key." From Poland, Doctor Tom worked for the Health Department and was on loan until Doctor Ceesay returned. Many things at the health centre disturbed him and he went about changing as much as he could. But, as he told me, he had no illusions that things wouldn't go right back to the way they were before he came.

A young boy was admitted with an aggressive skin infection. Doctor Tom prescribed a medication to be applied every four hours throughout the day and night. The next day, he was furious when we saw his orders had not been followed and that the medication had been applied only during the daytime. The infection had bored a hole right through the boy's cheek.

Notations on hospitalized patients' health records often lacked any real diagnosis. "Failure to thrive" was a common notation for children dying for whatever reason -- malnourishment, an infection, perhaps a heart condition.

I talked to Doctor Tom about reusing needles and he merely shrugged. "I know, it's not a good thing. But doing something about it is almost impossible. There isn't the money or the time to remedy that."

We enjoyed having Doctor Tom for dinner a few times during his short stay. His life in Poland had been difficult. He had hoped to practice medicine in the United States, but to do so would require additional training. He was in no financial position to support himself while going back to school. He felt he was in a sort of limbo at the time.

* * *

The Gambia's President, Sir Dawda Jawara, was scheduled to tour the country and spend time in the Upper River Division. Much preparation was being made to spiff up the area for the impending visit.

The government rest house in Basse underwent a major cleaning and painting. We had known a person or two who had stayed there before and the report wasn't good. Now, apparently, the rest house would be more habitable.

Also in preparation of Sir Dawda's visit, all tree trunks and posts were painted white from ground level to about four feet. Large rocks along the road also got the white paint treatment. Bruce joked, "Don't stand around too long or you'll have white legs." Roads close to Basse were cleaned up, trash cleared. The place looked nice.

Typical of The Gambia, he didn't come when scheduled. When he did come a few weeks later, the visit was regal. We went into Basse and joined the throngs of people there to see him. Bruce found a good place to take pictures, although a distance away. We couldn't hear what was being said, but we felt the excitement of the crowd and enjoyed being a part of the moment with our African friends.

* * *

A group of young people from the philanthropic group Crossroads Africa arrived in The Gambia. Volunteers pay a sum of money, in this case $1,700 to make a six-week trip like this. Their first destinations had been Nigeria, but at the last minute were denied visas, so the group came to The Gambia. USAID, specifically Harry, had only two days to design a worthwhile program for the fifty-eight volunteers, ten of whom would be assigned to Basse. Steve Fitzgerald, an officer with the Expanded Program of Immunization of The Gambia stopped by on Tuesday and asked if I would go with the group to the large village of Garawol on Wednesday to help them with immunizations. I accepted, pleased to be asked.

Wednesday at Garawol was an interesting experience for me. Garawol, a Serahule village, was among the wealthiest tribes in The Gambia. Much of their wealth came from the gem market and from cattle. I never knew of a Peace Corps volunteer living in a Serahule village, but I had seen Serahule women with their children at the Friday well-baby clinics.

As usual, we first called on the Alkala. The Serahule are known to be reclusive and the Alkala did not particularly welcome the intrusion of our medical team. I think he felt put on the spot. If he said no, we couldn't conduct an immunization program in his village, he would appear uncaring. The chief reluctantly agreed and we set up our tables and began immunizing children and even a few adults. My job was to keep track of the immunizations given and to supply an individual, written record to each family. We'd gotten off to a slow start, but picked up speed during the day. Although it was a grueling, hot and noisy day, we accomplished what we'd set out to do. We worked until 6:00, then packed up and returned to Mansajang, hot, tired and hungry.

Thursday we trekked to another, smaller village, Missera, The day went by pleasantly with shade to work in, and people who seemed more cooperative than the day before. We put in a full day, but by this time had found our stride and discovered what worked and what didn't. Still, it was a long day.

I found the Crossroads workers a nice group of young people, hard working and goal oriented.

* * *

Fridays were often grueling. Although I liked to be busy, the Well Baby Clinic was often frantic. With a room full of people, the clinic was often stuffy and hot. Many Fridays we saw two hundred or more children, sometimes closer to three hundred. This particular Friday we saw three hundred five children who received vaccines, and in some cases, health consultations.

As I walked home, exhausted, I longed for a drink of cool water, sitting down to a quiet lunch, and reading either in the shade of our porch or in the hut with a fan, whichever seemed cooler. Most of all, I couldn't wait to have peace and quiet and time to myself.

As I approached our krinting gate, I saw a project vehicle awaiting me. My heart sank. So much for a quiet afternoon. As I approached, Celeste, a former volunteer climbed out of her vehicle. She was in the area on Agriculture Department business with the USAID, her new employer. Five minutes later, Bruce's big boss, Denis Fernandopoulle, the UNICEF project manager for the entire country and his driver arrived. Next came Mr. Lopi. Mosalif came to greet the guests, followed by Binta and the girls. Tombong stopped by to say hello to everyone. Two fellows from Celeste's group stopped by, then her Basse group director. He left but within a minute the assistant director drove up. Finally, everyone left except Celeste and Denis, who stayed for dinner and for the night. Denis slept in the bedroom; we set up a bed for Celeste in the kitchen. In the midst of all this coming and going I put together a beef stew which I served over rice, along with a sprout salad.

Celeste left right after breakfast and Bruce and Denis left for a day in the bush. I was blissfully alone for a few hours.

Jobot's All Necessary Foods had moved. Apparently the old place was closed down by the Health Department. The new restaurant was spiffy by comparison, with matching furniture and tablecloths. We had been awhile with no restaurant in town during the transition and I had sorely missed having a place to go if I didn't feel like cooking or when we had spur-of-the-moment guests and not enough food in the house. But now we had a decent place to go and Denis treated Bruce and me to dinner that evening.

After dinner we returned home and just the three of us sat out under the stars and talked. Denis, originally from Sri Lanka, had several big projects under his belt and was an interesting person. Bruce felt encouraged by the new leadership and hoped the project would now accomplish more.

All this time, wells had been dug and completed, but not at the rate they might have been had supplies arrived on time to keep the equipment in repair.

We welcomed a quiet Sunday. My sister had sent newspapers in her Christmas box which Bruce and I had saved for a special occasion. This was the perfect day to lose ourselves in these treasured bearers of news.

* * *

On Monday, a tragedy happened at a well digging site near Yorobowal. Foday, one of the project's best workers, a family man with several children, went to work early that morning. Alone, he apparently decided to go ahead and start digging. To lower himself into the well in progress, he stepped into the bucket which is controlled by a pulley. He must have grabbed the wrong cable, plunging the bucket twenty-seven feet down to the bottom, impaling himself in the abdomen on a rebar reinforcing rod attached to the next section of concrete lining.

When the rest of the team arrived at 8:30, Foday was still alive. They took him to the Yorobowal Clinic, he was then transferred to Basse, and then on to the next largest hospital in Bansang where he died, twenty hours after the accident.

The unfortunate accident was a blow to all who knew this fine man. According to Muslim custom, Foday was buried within twenty-four hours of this death.

* * *

The following Thursday I had a chance to again work with the Crossroads people, this time on a Nutrition Survey that Harry lined up for them. They conducted what they called a "random survey." It gave me a new understanding of "random." If I were to pick apples randomly, I would select one here, one there. But the scientific term, in this case, meant to begin with a selected village, then, as protocol demands, go to the Alkala's compound, explaining our mission to him. We began with his children by weighing, measuring for height, and measuring the upper arm, a good measuring place to detect malnourishment.

Next came the random part. The group leader took out a one dalasi bill and read the last serial number. If the number was between one and four, it was used as the basis; if not, one worked backwards until a number between one and four was found. Then, facing east toward Mecca and working clockwise, number one was east, number two south, number three west, number four north. After leaving the Alkala's compound, the group followed the number going the direction as dictated by the number on the dalasi.

Then, the next number on the dalasi determines where you stop. If it was a three, the group stopped at the third compound and took the measurements of the children there. We continued to follow this formula, eventually getting the measurements of thirty children. The word "random" will forever have that memory for me.

The reason for the random survey is that it's so easy to be swayed. People see malnourished children and take their measurements to confirm their suspicions, or see healthy children and want to "reward" the parents by measuring those children. The random survey produces a fair sampling without local influences.

I think as a group, these people accomplished more in six weeks than many Peace Corps volunteers do in a two-year hitch. Of course, part of the reason for that is that people like Harry planned their projects to good advantage.

We were again "companied out," too many visitors in too short a time. We were ready for a break. Also, it had been some time since we'd received mail. Downriver people coming up often forget to check to see if there was mail. I don't think they could appreciate how much it meant to us and how irregular delivery was. Not hearing from home was depressing and made us both anxious.

Peggy planned to leave the next day for four days in Banjul and stopped by to see if we had mail to go downriver. We did, a stack of it.

"I think it's time we had a party up here," Perry said. "I'm going to spread the word when I'm downriver."

"Ah, who's we?"

"Well, all of us up here."

"Peggy, we're burned out. We've had a steady string of company."

She shrugged. I honestly think she couldn't comprehend the work involved in our having overnight visitors. To her, having company meant something entirely different, since she didn't go to any work. "Well, see you Thursday."

Mosalif with his family

Chapter 17

*B*ruce had projects at the shop that needed a few days to resolve. I had been on trek with the Crossroads people, so felt I should spend the next few days at the Health Centre to catch up. But we were both desperate to get away.

"I really don't like to miss well-baby clinic on Friday," I said, looking at our home-made calendar.

"Okay, let's leave Saturday morning. I'll try to arrange some kind of transportation."

We expected the rainy season to start any time. Once it started, much of the equipment would be taken downriver and Bruce would be busy with overseeing that and trying to keep the shop running upriver.

During this month of May we'd had a few thunderstorms but no sign of real moisture, except the sweat running in rivulets down our bodies. We looked forward to the sea breezes downriver.

Peggy returned on Thursday as planned and brought several letters. She didn't mention any party plans, nor did we. I hoped she'd gotten the hint and given up on the idea.

We eagerly opened letters from the kids, from Bruce's parents and my sister. Our families were so faithful about writing. We'd asked everyone to save our letters. I thought of our letters home as our journal. I wondered how our ramblings seemed to them.

Friday's clinic was interminable. At the end of the day I had just enough energy left to pack for our trip. We couldn't wait to go. When Tombong stopped by that morning, we made arrangements for him to stay during the nights as our night guard. Daytimes, with all the coming and going, were not a concern.

Bruce had arranged for a driver and had made a list of supplies to get and things to do while downriver. I planned to see Sister M'Boge and also try to find visual aids to use on trek. Our trips downriver never seemed to be only for pleasure, but at least they were a pleasant break in routine and climate. The driver, a couple hours late, picked us up and we were on our way.

After only a few miles, the driver, Bubacar, said, "Mistah Bruce, we need fuel."

"Why didn't you get fuel before we left?"

"I forgot."

We'd gone too far to go back. "Okay," Bruce said, resigned, "let's stop at Bansang."

Government vehicles fueled at designated supply centers. Fuel for the UN well digging project was in either Basse or downriver at Yundum. So Bansang, although they had fuel, was not a regular supply outlet for the UN vehicles.

Running on fumes, we pulled into Bansang's government supply yard. We all climbed out. Sitting in a parked car in that heat is impossible. Bubacar and the mechanic at the shop launched into a heated argument.

I don't think either of them realized that we understood much of what they said, since they were speaking in Mandinka.

The Bansang fellow said words to the effect that there was a fuel shortage and he could only give fuel to their own vehicles.

Bubacar responded that he had to take Mistah and Missus Bruce downriver, so he had to have fuel.

The man repeated what he'd said earlier.

We almost laughed when Bubacar said, "Don't you understand Mandinka?" in the same tone we would say, "Don't you understand English?"

The man repeated he couldn't give fuel for this car unless he had his boss's permission and he wouldn't be there until the next day.

Bubacar thumped his finger on the mechanic's chest. "Do you want to take these tubobs home with you to spend the night? We can't leave without fuel."

With that, the man filled our tank.

We were on our way again with a full tank, having only lost an hour.

I sat in the middle of the front seat and dozed, welcoming an escape from the hot Peugeot pickup's bumpy ride.

Suddenly I heard a shattering noise and felt pelting from hundreds of little pieces of windshield.

A truck had passed us on the gravel road and its wheel threw a rock, hitting our windshield and shattering it.. Bubacar had a cut on his forehead; in fact, the small piece of glass still protruded. Bruce and I were not injured, but glass was everywhere. Bubacar pulled off to the side of the road. Bruce plucked the shard from the driver's forehead and from the kit we always carried, cleaned the wound and bandaged it.

We shook glass out of our clothes and brushed it off the seat and out of the truck and continued on our way. Driving without a windshield is very nerve wracking. Wind rushed in, along with flying insects and gravel. Every time we encountered a vehicle, I held up a magazine to protect Bruce's and my head. Bubacar drove without any protection. After we got onto the paved road, it wasn't so bad and we drove the remaining one hundred twenty miles without incident, though the howling wind in our faces became tiring.

As we arrived in Banjul, we passed another volunteer and I waved through where the windshield should be. The fellow looked so surprised and we all laughed.

Bubacar dropped us off at the apartment. I could never really enjoy myself until I straightened it up, washed the dishes, which always seemed to be left in the dishpan, put a clean sheet on the bed and made the apartment "home."

Following our usual routine, we took showers and then walked to a nearby hotel for dinner. We shook our heads over the journey down. Couldn't a trip ever be just normal?

The sea-breezes were everything we'd hoped for and we began to relax. The next morning we stopped at the nearby open market to buy groceries for the next few days.

Bruce managed to get some work done at Yundum. I called on Sister M'Boge who, in her reserved way, praised me for the job I was doing, especially the in-service training program. We checked in with the Peace Corps staff. George Scharffenberger was now Country Director. My new advisor was Meri Aimes, Assistant Director, much to my great pleasure. She, like George, was a former Peace Corps volunteer and had spent four years in Nigeria. Meri had good, practical ideas and I enjoyed talking to her. She showed appreciation for what I had been able to accomplish.

We'd had both a productive and relaxing four days downriver, with the majority of the time spent at Bakau. We were ready to return to our post. When I showered the morning we were scheduled to leave, I noticed a centralized swelling on my vulva. Although I wasn't alarmed, we thought it best that I have it checked out with nurse Ann Saar before heading upriver.

After examining me, Ann said, "I think it's just a cyst, but I want you to have this checked out by a doctor before you head back upriver. I can send you to Dakar, or, if you wouldn't mind, you could go to the Queen Victoria here in Banjul."

"Aren't there USAID doctors?"

"Yes, there are, but they're assigned to projects and don't see individual patients."

Neither going to Dakar nor to Queen Victoria was appealing, but I wanted to get it over with. "I'll go to the Queen Victoria."

Queen Victoria hospital was quite large, so Ann saved me time by describing just where I'd go as an out-patient to see a gynecologist. She would call ahead to make arrangements.

Bruce walked me to the hospital. We shuddered as we walked down the sidewalk with the open drainage ditch running from the hospital along the walkway. The smell was enough to gag a maggot. I suggested to Bruce that I'd meet him back at the Peace Corps office. I expected this would take some time and there was no point in having him sit in the waiting room. Relieved, I'm sure; he left me at the hospital.

The waiting room was filled with about fifty women, all Africans. So many times, in crowds of people, on buses and now here, I learned what it was like to be a minority.

I had brought our complimentary copy of Newsweek and resigned myself to a long wait. I heard British voices and looked up to see three British women, obviously touring the building. One seemed to be showing the others around. They spotted me as I looked up from my reading. They stopped talking and looked at me in amazement.

Suddenly, the tour guide stood in front of me. "Excuse me."

I looked up. "Yes?"

"What are you doing here?"

"I'm waiting to see a doctor."

"But why? Why would you come here?"

I was taken aback by her rude question, but I suppose it did seem odd to have a solitary white women among a room full of Africans.

"Because this is the closest doctor and I don't want to take the time to go all the way to Dakar."

"You're an American? With the Peace Corps?

"Yes."

She was stunned. "Well."

I smiled and went back to my reading.

I know I was called ahead of others who had waited longer, but I didn't argue the point. The doctor examined me and said, "I agree with Ann Saar. This isn't serious, I'm sure it's just a cyst. However, you shouldn't travel for a few days. It would not be good to have this rupture when you're traveling. It is important you keep this area clean and you can't do that on the road. If this should become infected, it could be very serious.

"This cyst may go away on its own, or it may rupture. Give it about five days. If it gets larger, come see me. If it ruptures, keep it very clean. I'll give you a supply of gauze. I will also prescribe antibiotics. Before you go upriver, see Ann Saar."

I agreed to his directions, accepted a supply of gauze and a paper packet of antibiotics and made my way back to the Peace Corps office. I found Bruce rearranging books at the Peace Corps library. I checked in with Ann Saar and we headed back to Bakau. Actually, having five more days in Bakau was an unexpected treat. I wasn't suffering with my "condition," so to us it was a delightful bonus.

During that period of time, Bruce and I were in Banjul on our way to a museum we'd heard about when we ran into Al, one of the fellows in our training group.

"Hey," he said, "what are you guys doing here? I thought you were having a big party."

"Party?" we said, the reality slowly dawning.

"Yeah, Peggy said you guys up there were having a big party tomorrow night. Lots of guys are heading up your way."

Bruce could hardly keep from laughing. "Peggy didn't tell us about a party. I guess just Peggy is having it. Mary can't travel, doctor's orders."

Al looked concerned.

"Oh, no," I assured him. "Nothing serious. Just a cyst. I spared him the details.

"We'll be going back up in three days. Are you going to the party?"

"Yeah, I'm heading up now. I'll tell Peggy you won't be coming."

So Peggy was having a party! Our not wanting more company, not wanting to participate in a party was of little concern to her. Well, she'd have the whole thing by herself. Nathaniel was there, but his place was very small, as was Mara's. We were just glad we'd escaped another bunch of overnighters and preparing a mass breakfast. We were weary of Peggy inviting company and our doing the work.

The cyst healed on its own and we were on our way home, five days after our original date of departure. Bubacar had gotten the windshield fixed. The back was filled with barrels of oil and other supplies, plus our stuff. It was a pleasure to not have to take a bush taxi. We both felt rested after our extended stay. Life was good.

Tombong greeted us as we entered the gate and helped carry our things into the house.

I could tell he was concerned about something.

"I don't know if I did the right thing," he said.

"Why, what happened?" Bruce asked.

"That Peggy had a big party. Many people. She come here and want me to open your house so party could be here."

"What did you say?"

"I said no, no one could come to your house. You were not here."

"Tombong," Bruce shook his hand, "that's exactly right. You did the right thing."

He looked relieved, but still worried. "She was very mad. She went to Mosalif."

"What did he say?" I asked.

"He said I was boss. I was the guard."

"That's right. That's why we hired you."

Bruce paid him, and gave him an extra five dalasi. "Thank you, Tombong. I know it was hard for you to refuse her, but you did the right thing."

After we put things away, we went to Peggy and Mara's to deliver their mail.

We walked to Peggy's first.

"Hi, Peggy," I said. "We have mail for you." I handed her two letters. "We ran into Al in Banjul and he said he was on his way up here for a big party. I guess we missed it."

"I thought you said you'd be home by Wednesday."

I explained the situation. "So, how was the party?"

"It was a party with no place to go. That Tombong wouldn't let us use your house."

Bruce nodded. "He was guarding the house and following our orders."

"But I told him you wouldn't mind."

Bruce shook his head. "He was just doing his job." He nodded to me. "Let's deliver Mara's mail and go home. I'm beat."

* * *

There were always flies. We never got used to them, but in Africa flies were a fact of life. Over the two years, I spoke to many an African while a fly ran along the rim of an eye and they barely flinched, they were so used to it. We never acquired that acceptance.

When we drank anything out of a bottle, we automatically kept our hand over the opening to keep out flies. Woven straw fans were as much for batting away flies and mosquitoes as for stirring up a breeze. But the day we forever after called "fly-day" was unbelievably terrible.

It happened on a Sunday so we were home all day. Conditions must have been just right, or just wrong, to create the "perfect storm" of flies. Our screened hut remained relatively fly free, other than those who sneaked in when we entered, but we could control those few. On that day, the house was another story. Flies were on every surface. There must have been three hundred flies on the overhead electrical wire that reached between the kitchen and the dining/living room, where we ate breakfast. We couldn't bring a bite of food to our mouths without flies landing on it. In the old days we might have thrown out the food, but you'd starve if you did that every time a fly landed on your food in Africa. But this day that scenario was magnified a thousand times.

A video of us would have revealed people who appeared to have delusions with arm waving, hands suddenly going to our ears, nose and eyes. It was a nightmare.

"Whose idea was this?" Bruce asked, using Newsweek as a fly swatter, nailing three at one time.

I laughed. "Not mine! I think coming here was your idea."

As soon as we could after eating breakfast we retreated to our hut, to spend the day hiding out, reading, and writing letters.

We had to brace ourselves to leave the hut to prepare meals. We worked like a well-oiled team, swatting and carrying on, then making a dash for the hut with our prepared food.

Fly-day lasted only the one day, to be followed by lots of flies, but not at that level.

* * *

The country was desperate for rain. Blazes of heat lightning and thunder claps teased us with promises, but other than a few scattered raindrops, no real rain. Even Africans complained of the heat and the desperate need for rain.

Nathaniel invited his colleague Norman to Basse for a work related meeting, and invited us to join them for dinner at Jobot's All Necessary Foods. The walk into Basse was unusually humid, hot and sticky. I could almost feel rain in the air.

I grumbled to Bruce. "I couldn't feel any wetter if it actually rained."

He agreed. "I'll bet before the end of this evening, we'll have rain."

It couldn't be too soon for us.

We had our usual great dinner at Jobot's, making a big effort to ignore the heat. We headed over to Pa Peacock's White House Fuladu East Bar for a cold drink. We'd been there for only a few minutes when it started to rain, a few tentative drops, and then a deluge.

Bruce and I stepped outside and stood in the rain, laughing and getting soaked to the skin. Most Gambians don't like to get wet and will take great steps to avoid it. Nathaniel and Norman stood in the doorway watching us, amused. An African fellow watched with them and said to Nathaniel, "What's wrong with those people?"

"They're from Seattle," Nathaniel replied.

Woman at market carrying load on her head

Chapter 18

*M*ango season was upon us and we couldn't get enough of them, we were so starved for fresh fruit.

We'd been eyeing the large mango tree close to us in Mansajang, watching its fleshy fruit ripen. People often came to our door to sell us eggs and other food. Mamadou, from the UN shop, who made Bruce's Christmas present, the prayer board, called on us with a bucket full of mangoes, asking if we'd like to buy some. Would we! I bought the whole bucketful. After that first bucket, he simply gave us mangoes, refusing to accept money. His gesture made us feel accepted and part of the community.

The Gambians had a way of eating mangoes that, unlike ours, was so tidy. I couldn't eat a mango without the juice running down my chin and arms. Gambians made a little hole and seemed to suck out the goodness of the fruit. Their system never worked for us.

Scattered all over the ground during mango season were the large mango pits. As we approached them on the ground, they appeared as something brown or black, but walking closer, we recognized an orange mango pit covered with flies. As we passed by, flies rose up in a cloud. I learned to automatically shake my skirt to keep them from flying up my dress.

People worked diligently in the fields now. Most villages had a "farm," a section of land where they ran cooperative farms. Some farming is done by men, such as groundnuts (peanuts), millet and the care of goats, sheep and cattle. Women cultivate the produce, such as garden vegetables. Rice is grown almost exclusively by women, though men helped with the harvest. Women take care of the chickens.

Binta didn't go to a farm to work, but ours wasn't really a "family" compound. She did grow cassava along the fence during the season. But women in Peggy's compound had a farm and they invited her to go along to see what they do. She mentioned it to me, excited at the prospect of seeing the process. I would have asked her if I could tag along, but it was clinic day at the hospital and I needed to be there.

The next day I ran into her and asked, "How was your visit to the farm?"

She shrugged. "I didn't go. No one brought water to me that morning, so I couldn't take my bath."

Stunned, I asked, "Couldn't you get your own pail of water? I think being able to go to the farm and watch would be so interesting."

Peggy shrugged again. "It's just easier if somebody brings it to me. By the way, I'm going downriver for spring break. I'll be gone for a week."

Spring break. Still the college mentality. I wondered how it would be for some of these volunteers once they got regular jobs.

One day, during our walk, we happened to pass a group of women working in a field. We were surprised when we saw their primitive tools. Bruce remarked, "We should go back to that museum in Banjul and take pictures of the 'ancient' tools.' It's what they're still using today."

Before we left for Africa, we had shared Thanksgiving with my sister. By this time we knew we were going into the Peace Corps and knew we would be assigned to The Gambia. We watched on television one of the educational channels that featured a segment on African peanut growers, comparing them with farmers in President Carter's home state of Georgia.

The film had been an eye-opener. First they showed automated planting of the peanuts in Georgia, then the two-man planting by hand done in Senegal, the country that surrounds The Gambia on three sides. Later, huge combines worked the Georgia peanut fields; then switched to Africans using sticks to shake the peanuts off the plant. Every step of the procedures was shown, comparing modern Georgia with modern Africa, so primitive by comparison. At the end it showed a Georgia farm family sitting down to a Thanksgiving dinner, the table magnificent with turkey and many scrumptious side dishes. Then the camera showed a Senegalese family, sitting on a dirt floor around a common bowl, eating with their fingers.

At the time we saw the television program, we could hardly believe it, but by this time we had been in-country long enough to have seen, in fact been a part of, that very African scene.

* * *

One Saturday morning while Bruce worked, I walked to the market. On my way home, going past the Health Centre, I noticed tables set up outside and stopped by to see what was going on. Regular clinics or treks weren't scheduled on weekends, so I figured something special was happening.

The staff, many there just for the special occasion, were gathered and sitting down to a party. I hadn't been invited.

I found myself in an awkward situation.

"Forgive us. We forgot to mention it to you," one of the nurses said.

"That's fine," I replied. I knew that, especially for informal occasions, the nurses and orderlies felt more comfortable talking in their own dialect. Unless it was pure Mandinka, I couldn't always understand what was being said, and they had to interpret for me. But, nevertheless, my feelings were hurt to have been left out.

I just smiled and said, "Have a good time," and turned to leave.

"You can stay, Mariama. We'll eat soon."

"No, that's fine. Bruce is expecting me." I found the situation very uncomfortable. I certainly didn't want to impose on them.

I realized I wasn't one of them, nor would I ever be. Still, it hurt to not be included.

* * *

Bruce seemed more encouraged about his project. The new project director seemed to be a go-getter and it looked as though funds would be available to buy equipment. Bruce said he'd believe it when trucks rolled through the gates, but at least it looked like relief was on the way.

The head UN storekeeper in Basse was caught putting UN gas in a private vehicle. Bruce had often suspected that happened because they were so frequently running out of gas, but this time the guy was caught. The problem was, it was almost impossible for anyone to get fired. People stuck up for their friends, and getting to the bottom of things proved impossible, even with obvious transgressions.

Nathaniel was equally disturbed with an incident that happened within their small business organization. Apparently one of his colleagues, a Gambian, misappropriated fifteen hundred dalasi, a huge sum of money. Nathaniel couldn't believe it when he learned the fellow wouldn't lose his job, he was only required to pay it back. Of course, there's no way he could repay that sum, so it was simply considered a loss. That money represented dues that small businesses paid into a co-operative fund, so it was a loss to every small business client involved.

* * *

The rain didn't last. We'd had a few "frog stranglers" as Bruce called them, but not nearly enough to get some of the local crops toward healthy growth.

After work one afternoon, as I made my way home on the path, I came across a man, also walking toward his village. We exchanged greetings and walked together.

The dirt path wound through a field of thin, withering millet. Although this staple grain towered above our heads, it wouldn't produce much this year.

"This field is dry," I commented in Mandinka. My walking companion nodded, his black face glistening with sweat. "Yes, we need more rain."

Although the nights had been cool, daytime temperatures were again climbing. I tried not to think about the heat, now soaring close to 100 degrees. My dress stuck to my back, the long skirt caught at my legs. "It's too bad we can't get ... water ..." I groped for the correct Mandinka word.

"Irrigation," he prompted.

"Yes, irrigation."

"It is too far from the river to irrigate, Mariama."

We stopped at a snake's twisting track, its thick impression in the sandy soil still fresh. The Gambian held out his arm, holding me back until he determined we were out of harm's way.

We resumed our trek. The trail narrowed and I automatically stepped behind my companion. "Couldn't water from the river be piped in?"

"But how? Irrigation systems need motors and fuel and they are expensive."

We reached a fork in the footpath. From the village at the right, pungent smoke from cooking fires greeted us. Voices and laughter drifted from behind woven fences.

My new friend gestured to the right. "I will go this way now."

"Yes. Thank you for walking with me."

"Mariama," he called over his shoulder. "Your Mandinka is very good."

Highly complimented, it was only then I realized my entire conversation had been in Mandinka; his had been in English. Without my realizing it, we had been practicing each other's language.

* * *

A malnourished child had been admitted to the hospital and was released about a week later. Concerned about the little boy, Sister asked me to follow up with the family. The village was a distance away, so one of the orderlies took me in the Land Rover. I went alone this time, as the auxiliary nurses needed to stay for the antenatal clinic.

We found the compound and I visited with the family. The little boy had improved and seemed to be gaining weight. I had taken my posters and talked with them about what the boy could eat now at his age. Another compound sent word for me and I called on them. One thing led to another and I found myself running out of drinking water. I always carried a supply of our own, safe water.

I felt desperate, tired and hot. Someone offered me a cup of water and I accepted it. I had no choice; I was terribly thirsty and wouldn't be home for some time. Before the end of the day, I'd accepted two or three cups of their local water.

Later that evening, I began to get stomach cramps and by the middle of the night had made numerous trips to the latrine. By morning, I not only had diarrhea, but I also had a fever and vomited. When Bruce left for work, he left water by my bedside, urging me to take a swallow each time I either vomited or had diarrhea.

Walking the two hundred feet to the latrine in that heat was almost more than I could handle. I counted twenty trips to the latrine with diarrhea in one day. The vomiting had stopped, but by then I could hardly eat anything anyway. That night, I was too exhausted to climb out of bed, stoop under the overhanging roof, and walk to the latrine. Bruce moved a bed outside to help save my energy. He bathed my hot skin frequently and urged me to drink a rehydration solution he'd made for me.

We remembered what Ann Saar had said: "Don't go to the local hospital, try to get to Banjul." The problem was, we knew I could never make it that distance. I was desperately ill and weak. The mere thought of even trying to make that trip in a bumpy Land Rover was more than I could bear.

"Whose idea was this?" I croaked to Bruce.

He chuckled. "Yours, it was your idea to come here."

Slowly, slowly I recovered, but it took days. I missed about ten days work. When I did get to work, I told Doctor Ceesay my story. When I mentioned I'd had such frequent diarrhea, he was shocked that I hadn't come to the Health Centre. "You could have died, Mariama." I didn't tell him that was the very reason I didn't go to the hospital.

* * *

Ramadan was again upon us. This time it didn't seem as difficult as when we were in Banjul. Bruce and I noticed that people at work were under pressure to observe the fasting rules of Ramaden. Bruce had an even more difficult time than usual getting the men at the shop to keep at their jobs. But at least in Mansajang he didn't have to go to their compounds and round them up.

Sister Roberts took a leave of absence because of her pregnancy, and in her place Sister Ruth arrived. I liked her very much, though I was sorry to see Sister Roberts leave. Sister Ruth was a Gambian, but happened to be Christian.

I often found the nurses short-tempered during Ramadan. One time a huge argument broke out. One of the nurses, a devout Muslim, insisted on wearing a head scarf.

The others complained that it wasn't part of the uniform. The yelling escalated to an unbelievable level, especially in a hospital. It sounded as though it might turn to blows. Finally, Sister Ruth stepped in. She agreed with the majority. A head scarf was not part of the uniform and shouldn't be worn. She told me later than she hesitated interfering in the argument, not being Muslim, but needed to put a stop to the disturbance.

"During Ramadan," she said, "everyone is on edge."

"I'll be glad when it's over," I said.

Sister merely rolled her eyes.

Finally, the end of Ramadan was at hand. Noticing a shortage of auxiliary nurses, I gathered some had slipped out so they could go to the market.

Toward the end of the morning, I had occasion to go into the supply room. I noticed all the vaccines and medication that were supposed to be in the refrigerator were on the table. Alarmed, I opened the refrigerator and it was full of meat!

I thought I should mention it to Sister Ruth, but couldn't find her at the moment. I managed to cram the meat onto one shelf, medications on the other.

A short time later while at my table recording counts, Doctor Ceesay rushed up to me. "I need your help."

"Sure, what can I do for you?"

He gestured to the Operating Theatre.

"In there? You need me in there?" Incredulous, I looked around for one of the nurses.

"Mariama, they've all gone home to prepare for the holy day. Come, I need you."

While my mind screamed, "No! No!" I followed him. A young girl, about twelve lay on the operating table. A serious infection had set in after her circumcision. She was in tremendous pain, but fought the doctor's efforts to help her.

"What can I do?" I whispered.

"I need to get in there and clean this out. Hold her down."

The girl was strong and fought my every effort. She even tried to bite me.

The doctor stopped what he was doing and yelled something at her to the effect she wouldn't get better if he couldn't see the wound and clean it up. Unfortunately, he didn't administer pain medication of any kind.

She calmed down a bit and let me hold her down but her body heaved so violently I couldn't imagine how the doctor could treat her.

Finally, it was over. The girl had come to the hospital alone. He wanted to keep her in the hospital, but she refused. He walked over to the dresser-dispenser with her to get antibiotics.

When he came back, he stopped at my table and thanked me for the help. He went on to say that hers happened to be a botched circumcision. "Sometimes the procedure causes women's bladders to permanently leak and then no one will marry them. Some get serious infections and are unable to bear children. Female circumcision is against the law, you know, but these people don't pay any attention to that."

The phrase "these people" was often used, even though they might be talking about their own people. "This is not Muslim practice, this is tribal," he continued. "I have seen too much go wrong. Most of the time the instrument isn't clean, sometimes not even very sharp." He shook his head. "It is wrong."

Circumcision is usually performed on girls between the ages of five to ten, though the girl just treated was older than that, probably closer to twelve. A group from a village would be taken into the bush, or sometimes it is done at home by an aunt or grandmother. In The Gambia, female circumcision isn't as drastic as in some African countries. Normally, only the girl's clitoris is removed. The idea is that if they remove the source of pleasure of sex, they remove the chance of promiscuity. Still, generation after generation of women consent to have this procedure done on their daughters. It was a subject we weren't to discuss, but I often wondered if it was the fathers who insisted on it and the women didn't have a say.

I guess the word got out that I'd helped Doctor Ceesay because the next day one of the nurses came up to me. "My family does not do female circumcision. My mother had it done but she said 'no more'."

"Do you know the girl that was here?" I hoped to be able to follow up, learn if she recovered.

"No, I do not know her. Most of them turn out okay but it is still not right."

I remembered Sister M'Boge's comment on the subject and I followed her instructions and didn't discuss it further.

* * *

While Bruce fixed breakfast, I swept the hut. As usual, I swept the bed. Even though we had stretched a cloth as a canopy over the bed, droppings from the grass roof still landed on the bed sheet. As I stooped my way around the room with my short broom, I picked up the laundry bag and stopped, broom suspended. There, tightly coiled, a small snake glared at me.

"Ah, Bruce?" I called.

"Yeah?"

"Would you come here?"

He could tell from my tone that something was up. He bounded over to the hut. I held up my hand in caution, and then pointed to our unwanted guest.

"Oh, boy. I'll be right back."

"Bring a jar."

He came back with a jar and his machete. Sitting the jar a distance away from either of us, he carefully slid the flat side of the machete under the snake and slipped it into the jar, then leaped over and screwed on the lid. After poking holes in the lid, we admired our catch.

Mosalif stopped by and viewed the snake from a distance.

"Can you get word to Peter Moore to come here?" Bruce asked him. "We don't know what kind of snake this is, do you?"

Mosalif shook his head and hurried off to get someone to tell Peter Moore we wanted him. I couldn't believe how quickly Peter arrived. Within minutes he pulled up in his Land Cruiser.

He studied our snake. "This is a puff adder. Very deadly. Even though this one is quite young, his bite could kill. What I'm wondering," he said in his dead-pan British clip, "is where are the other dozen or so? This one is too young to be far from his mother and siblings."

Gulp! Several of us scoured the compound's huts and grounds. But ours was the only one found.

Peter asked permission to take the snake home to test it for malaria, as part of his study. He brought it back in a neat little specimen jar, pickled for eternity.

News spreads so quickly in Africa. For the next several days we had a steady stream of people coming to our door, asking to see our pickled puff adder.

* * *

One night we sat outside in the dark talking, waiting for our nine o'clock breeze to bring relief. We heard a little stirring at the gate, then a low growling. Bruce reached for his flashlight and signaled me to come with him.

We crept to the gate and stood on tiptoes to look over. About a dozen sets of eyes reflected back in the flashlight's beam. Wild dogs.

Apparently many people complained of the number of wild dogs. Those dogs can be vicious, to say nothing of the diseases they carry. The next afternoon, the Field Force spread the word to stay in our compounds. For hours we heard gunshots as they systematically killed them. They must have taken the carcasses with them as we didn't see evidence of dead dogs.

* * *

Sean, the volunteer from across the river, loaned us a set of high-powered binoculars. One night we studied the full moon, already appearing almost close enough to touch. It was an amazing sight with its shadows and valleys. We called Mosalif over to see it and he gasped at the sight. Later, he sent Binta over and she marveled at the close-up moon. I doubt if either of them had used binoculars before, and to be exposed to this magnificent sight was rare indeed.

* * *

George Scharffenberger and his Senegalese "brother," Omar, stopped by. Omar was a member of the family with whom George lived when he served with the Peace Corps in Senegal. They had business to take care of and another place to spend the night, but George had mail for us so they stopped by.

"Mary," George said, "how about cooking up some rice for lunch?" And off they went, to return in an hour.

In the first place, I didn't care to cook at noon, it was just too hot. In the second, it wasn't only the rice, it's what you're going to put on it that takes the time and effort. I griped to Bruce. "I just don't feel like cooking something for those guys in the middle of the day."

"Then don't. Why don't we have our regular lunch?"

What a gem of an idea. Bruce walked over to our little store and bought four baguettes. We usually had one item besides peanut butter to put on our simple open-faced sandwiches, but since we had company, I brought out a tiny can of British pâté, canned Danish cheese, a small jar of mayonnaise, jam, and the wonderful Gambian peanut butter. I'd fixed tea, but we also had cold water and Bitter Lemon soft drink.

When they returned, George looked a little surprised,
even dismayed, when he saw our lunch. But Omar's eyes lit
up. Bruce said, "We thought we'd serve a real American
lunch," which George translated to Omar. The Senegalese
was like a little kid, trying everything. We had to stop him
from mixing mayonnaise and jam. It was fun.

When they left, George said, "This was really special for
him. Thank you."

Our favorite tailor Dawda with his wife and child.

Chapter 19

$\mathcal{A}$ nn Saar sent word that everyone in our training group must come to the capital city to have our yearly examination. Actually, it was past time, but the Peace Corps doctor was in-country and it was imperative we have various procedures done at the half-way mark of our tour of duty.

We discussed the situation with Nathaniel. Our small Bakau apartment could hold the four of us, but it would be crowded. Nathaniel and Norman decided to let us stay in the apartment alone, that they had a place where they could crash for a couple of nights. We did have an open invitation to stay with Harry and Suzi, but didn't know if they would be home.

The timing was not good for Bruce to leave. I would just as soon not have gone, either. We weren't due nor felt ready for a break. But, orders are orders.

A UN project vehicle had to go to downriver headquarters anyway. We packed just enough items for a couple of days, and were on our way. This happened to be one of the rare times that Bruce drove and it was just the two of us. Arriving in Banjul, we drove directly to the Peace Corps office. Ann Saar had paperwork for us to complete, questions about health, and then we were told to go to the Queen Victoria Hospital to have chest x-rays, blood tests and stool tests for intestinal worms. It all took longer than we expected.

We had hoped that we could leave for home on the same day the doctor examined us, back at the Peace Corps office. Bruce was called in first and was out in just minutes. "Next," he said.

As the doctor gave me a pelvic check, he frowned. "Are you feeling any discomfort?"

"No."

He probed some more. "Mary, we need to have this checked out. I think you may have a fibroid tumor. If you do, you'll need surgery."

I must have given him a blank look. I just wanted to get back to my village.

He turned to Ann. "Will you get this started? She should go right away."

"Go where?" I asked.

"To Washington, D.C."

"Washington, D.C.? Whatever for?"

"Mary," Ann chimed in, "you don't want to have surgery here."

"I don't want to have surgery anywhere."

The doctor gave me a stern look. "You don't have a choice, Mary. I can't overlook this."

I dressed and Ann invited Bruce into the examining room and they all discussed it while I sat, stupefied. Ann suggested we go talk to my adviser, Meri Aimes. In the meantime, she'd started making medevac plans.

As soon as we were on our own, I said to Bruce, "This is crazy. I don't even have clothes to go to Washington, D.C."

We stepped into Meri's office and told her the news. "I don't even have a regular suitcase!"

Meri nodded. "I have one you can borrow."

Bruce offered to drive back to Mansajang, get my clothes and come back.

"I'll go with you."

"It's better if you stay here. I could get delayed and you might miss your flight."

I made a list of clothes for him to bring, clothes stored in our trunks that had proven to be too warm for The Gambia's climate. Although Meri offered to have me spend the night at her home, I declined, saying I'd spend it at the apartment.

Bruce left immediately, dropping me off in Bakau.

But, as it happened, knowing that we had planned to leave for Mansajang, Nathaniel and Norman had planned to spend the night at the apartment so they could attend a meeting the next day.

Oh, well, no big deal. By this time I knew these guys so well, it didn't bother me at all and they were fine about my staying there. We went to LaPizza for dinner, and then settled into our apartment for the night.

Nathaniel looked at me carefully. "How are you feeling about this? Are you worried?"

I shrugged. "No, I'm not worried. I just think it's a nuisance."

Actually, I worried more about the trip than my actual "condition." I'd never spent time in Washindton, D.C. on my own. I wasn't looking forward to all the logistics involved.

Norman slept on a mattress in the kitchen. Nathaniel slept on one mattress in the bedroom and I slept on the other. It was tight, but we each had our own space.

I fell asleep immediately, as usual.

A man crept in through the window and hovered over me. I lay still for awhile, then, when he made a move toward me, I screamed.

I woke myself and God knows who else, with my own scream. Nathaniel immediately grabbed my arm. "Mary! It's okay. You had a dream."

"Oh, God. I can't believe I did that. I'm so sorry." My heart pounded in my ears.

"So, you're not too worried about this trip, huh?" Nathaniel teased.

I laughed. "Maybe a little."

We settled back down.

"Mary," Norman said from the kitchen, "You can really scream."

We all laughed, marveling that the neighbors didn't come. They probably knew there were three tubobs here and we had our ways...

The next morning I returned to the Peace Corps office to see what arrangements had been made. Flights only left Dakar on Monday and Thursday so it would still be another day before I would fly out.

Ann had made all the arrangements for me and it didn't seem so daunting. Bruce came along mid-day, making the trip in an amazingly short time. He had brought clothes for himself so that he could go with me, but they declined permission, promising that if I had surgery he could join me then.

Meri Aimes insisted we spend the night at her home and she and Bruce would take me to the airport the next day.

The trip went smoothly. They had given me travel money and, as instructed, I went to an apartment complex in Washington, D.C. where Peace Corps maintained a unit for just such emergencies. Another volunteer was staying at the two-bedroom apartment, undergoing treatment for an infection she had contracted in Costa Rica.

The apartment was close to Peace Corps headquarters. Even though I wore clothes too warm for The Gambia, I was freezing in Washington, D.C. in late September. A woman at headquarters took me into a room with racks of clothes and told me to help myself. It was an amazing array of clean, used clothing and I found two outfits I could wear in comfort.

The hospital was within walking distance of the apartment and I reported in the next day. The doctor examined me and shook his head. "I'm not seeing anything." He referred me to another doctor, a specialist, who could see me within an hour. The specialist didn't find anything abnormal, either. They did an ultrasound. Nothing.

As it happened, my period was about to start, so there was some swelling. Both doctors concluded that the Peace Corps doctor, quite young, had seen mostly uteruses of young women, not those of a forty-two year-old who had borne four children.

"There's nothing wrong with you," they both concluded.

"Well, good. Now what?"

"If you have R&R time, why not visit your family? No sense wasting that expensive flight."

And that's exactly what I did. Peace Corps was to call Ann Saar with the test results, get word to Bruce and tell them of my plan. Bruce had thought to bring me our charge card and I proceeded to make arrangements.

I flew to the Seattle area and arrived the day before my youngest daughter's birthday. I had a wonderful three-week visit with family and before I knew it, it was time to go back.

Because it was two months before Christmas, both my family and Bruce's folks sent their Christmas packages with me, remembering that the previous year we didn't get them until well after the holiday. Bruce's dad packed everything into a cardboard box and then made a rope handle, making it more convenient to carry.

I flew directly to New York from Seattle, but we couldn't land due to congested traffic. We circled endlessly. At one point, I counted seventeen circling planes from my small window. I was getting nervous. If I missed my flight, it would be days before Pan American again flew to Senegal. Finally landing, I gathered my suitcase and box and then actually ran the entire distance through the airport, across the way to the international flights building, arriving breathlessly at my gate.

"Relax," said Jim, a USAID fellow I happened to know. "The flight's been delayed." He had been sent home for back surgery and was still not fully recovered. He could only sit for a very limited time.

For hours we waited, Jim pacing, trying to ease his back. I tried reading, but couldn't concentrate.

Finally, our flight took off. Jim took pain medication so he could sleep away the ten-hour flight. I sat squashed in the middle of a five-seat row. We landed in Dakar, Senegal, made our way through Customs, and I prepared to get a flight to The Gambia.

Jim approached me, with another fellow he knew in tow. "You want to ride in a car with us? My back is killing me and I need a seat where I can stretch out. You could sit in the back behind the driver.

"Wonderful! I'll pay a third of the cost."

Jim waved my money away. "Forget it."

At the Senegal/Gambia border, we all piled out of our cars for a Customs inspection. Others were being inspected, too.

My two companions passed through Customs with no problem, but the border guard pointed to my box. He was intimidating, as we so often found uniformed people to be.

"What is in that box?"

"These are Christmas packages." This was one of those times where my naive act might be called for.

"Open that box." He pushed it toward me.

I blinked. "But I am a Christian. These are presents from my family for my husband and me. They are supposed to be a surprise. I can't open them here without my husband!" I must have looked close to tears. Actually, I was close to tears. How awful to have to open these presents all alone, without Bruce, at a stupid border crossing. In front of everyone.

Stunned, the Customs officer started to say something, then clamped his mouth closed.

Other people arrived and he inspected them and let them go through. My ride was on the other side, waiting. I hated to delay them, especially the fellow with the painful back.

Another car approached and the border guard walked toward them.

He turned back to me. "You, Christian, go." He motioned me toward the gate.

I gathered my things, thanked him, crossed over to the other side and climbed into the car.

"I can't believe he let you do that," Jim said.

"Me, neither." I couldn't believe how tense I had been until we pulled away, safely in The Gambia.

They let me off at the Peace Corps office. Bruce had gotten word that I was on my way. As so often happened, Bruce came along just minutes after I arrived. He surprised me with the news that Peter Moore had offered his Bakau house for us to use for a few days.

What a treat! Peter's Bakau home, where we had never visited, was more colonial than the Basse house. A servant was there, but Bruce gave him money and sent him home. He offered to come back and cook, but we just wanted to be alone.

Ceiling fans kept the house cool. The spacious rooms and comfortable furniture were pure luxury. The kitchen, detached from the regular house, colonial style, was quite complete. Bruce had picked up a few things at the store and market. We carried our prepared food from the kitchen into the house since it was much cooler there.

After eating we walked along the beach, then returned and fell into bed, exhausted. The next morning, I opened the Christmas box and extracted apples from the folks' yard that Bruce's dad had carefully wrapped in tissue and packed among wrapped gifts. We enjoyed our fresh Washington apples with cheese Bruce had bought at CFAO, the tubob store. We talked for fourteen straight hours. It was wonderful.

We stayed at Peter's another day, enjoying the typically British gardens with the brilliant red bougainvillea, a pink orchid tree, huge hibiscus, and sweet-smelling white jasmine.

Reluctantly, we left Peter's paradise and returned to Mansajang.

* * *

Nathaniel and Mara joined us for Thanksgiving dinner. We slaughtered two of our chickens and stewed them, making a rich gravy and dumplings.

This would be our last Christmas in The Gambia. There were still things we wanted to get done before we left. One of our goals was a trip to Ziguinchor, in Southern Senegal.

We planned to leave early Saturday morning for Ziguinchor, the first week of December, stay three nights, and return home on the fourth day.

On the Thursday before we left, we had a terrific windstorm. We were both amazed our compound didn't suffer damage except for some sections of our krinting fence. The wind was so strong, we couldn't go out in it for fear of being sand-blasted.

The wind died down a bit while we prepared for bed, but during the night it picked up with a vengeance, waking us. "I can't believe the roof can take this kind of wind," I said.

Just then, I found myself looking at stars. A part of the grass thatched roof had blown off. We feared it might rain, so we cleared everything out of the hut that we could, jamming it into the spare bedroom in the house, and slept in the house the rest of the night.

The hut had been built by Fula tribesman. It had soon become obvious to us that each tribe had their own hut designs. In our opinion, the Fula huts were the best. For one thing, we had the outer wall that gave us additional space for bathing on one side, and our chickens on the other. Plus, the double wall construction kept the hut cooler.

The next morning Mosalif came over and inspected the damage. We kept spare cash in the house for emergencies and Bruce asked Mosalif how much it would cost to reroof the whole hut. It was already a few years old, there was no sense in patching it. Mosalif gave us an estimate and offered to get some Fula tribesmen to do the job.

The day we were to leave for Ziguinchor, a truck came with thatching for the roof, together with about six Fula. About that time Tombong, our Mandinka friend, came over to greet us and to talk about his job of guarding our home while we were away.

He watched the men climb around our roof rafters to remove the old thatching. The Fula are generally small people and, as we could see, agile, as they made their way easily around our pointed roof.

"Why do you have those Fula do that job?" Tombong asked.

"Because it's a Fula hut."

Tombong's eyes narrowed. "I don't trust those little people."

Our trip was well-timed. It was just as well we were out of the way while they were doing that messy job. Mosalif could oversee them and we didn't have to put up with the possibility of Tombong's interference.

We caught a bush taxi and we were off on a four-day pleasure trip. On the way the bush taxi picked up a Senegal volunteer and he told us John Lennon had been killed in New York. John Lennon wasn't a particular favorite of mine, but I hated the violence associated with his death.

Reaching Ziguinchor, we checked into a little upstairs hotel. Bruce's limited French got us around quite well. We planned to do some Christmas shopping, but mostly just wanted to see different sights and taste different food. In our wandering, we learned of a Peace Corps apartment where all volunteers were welcomed to stay, but Senegalese volunteers had first crack at it. The apartment could accommodate eight people.

The first night at the Peace Corps apartment, we were the only volunteers there. I was impressed with how nice the apartment was kept up. The furniture was serviceable, the kitchen well equipped with dishes and cookware. The second-floor apartment had a lovely little deck where we sat and watched the world go by. Bruce found many opportunities to photograph from the deck. We spent hours up there.

The third and last night two more people joined us and we had a good time with them, comparing notes on the two countries. Senegal volunteers usually already knew French but they also learned a tribal language.

The bush taxi ride to Mansajang seemed to go quickly and we were pleased with our fresh looking hut when we arrived home. We had just enough energy to put everything back into the hut before collapsing for the night.

* * *

Our favorite tailor, Dawda, set up his business at the market, in front of a Mauritanian-owned fabric store. He happened to be the first tailor I went to with one of Peggy's dresses to use as a sample. Dawda understood the concept of learning. He always had a spare chair next to him and often invited me to sit and chat. At first he talked slowly so that I could understand and often gave me new words that I could use. He was a wonderful man and very skilled on his treadle sewing machine.

I had brought back from the States a large selection of thread for Dawda and he was thrilled. The thread tailors often used was quite breakable, so he was pleased to have strong polyester thread. He had a scrap of material left over from another project and while we talked, he made a triangular head scarf for me, using his new thread.

By this time we could converse fluently and I asked him about a bulubah for Bruce, a sort of robe. His eyes lit up. "Most tubobs don't even know what a bulubah is," he said.. We went into the fabric store together to find suitable fabric, something that would look good with Dawda's wonderful machine embroidery.

The blue and gold garment would come down to Bruce's ankles, had loose, flowing sleeves and would serve as a bathrobe in the evenings. It would be my Christmas present to him.

Tourist season had started and would continue through February. We occasionally saw tubobs wandering around the market. They were usually so pale, Bruce and I referred to them as "cadavers." Most of them arrived by the boat

Lady Chilel, slept onboard and were gone when the boat headed back downriver the next day.

A couple stood by while Dawda and I talked. "Listen," the woman said, "she's talking their language."

Dawda and I totally ignored them.

Bruce at the shop radio. Finally, good communication!

Chapter 20

B ack in the States, Ronald Reagan had defeated Jimmy Carter in their race for the presidency. I was surprised with how badly many of the local people took the news. "Oh, poor Jimmy Cattah, poor Jimmy Cattah," one of the nurses repeated, anguish showing in her dark face.

"Well, that happens, that's what elections are all about," I said. But, as a matter of fact, it doesn't happen like that in many African countries. Sir Dawda Jawara was first prime minister, then president in 1970 when The Gambia became a republic. Now it was 1980 and he was still president. Although Peace Corps doesn't get involved in local politics, it was our understanding that any opposing party was deemed against the law. Their form of democracy was defined differently than ours. It occurred to me then why the nurse was upset. As so often happens in African countries, when a person in power is replaced, it is often accomplished by assassination.

"Nothing will happen to Jimmy Carter," I assured her. "He will go back to his peanut farm now and will live out his life." The local people related to Jimmy Carter because of his peanut farming background.

She looked at me with relief. "Oh, good. He will not die." Throughout the day, I heard her telling the others the good news.

After work that day I went to the market with a long list of groceries we needed. These days I avoided the meat market altogether. At this point during the sub-Sahara drought, the animals were just skin and bones and too tough to bother with. Our protein came from our own eggs, or chickens, and the local peanut butter.

Later, walking home, my backpack was full but my hands free. The local folks couldn't understand why we didn't put parcels on our heads. They learned to do it as children. I'd seen women walk with large bundles on their heads, a baby on their back, and their hands free. Often, people walked with a single item, like a banana, on their head.

I tried not to think about the heat and began planning Christmas. Who would we invite? We had already invited Nathaniel; Peggy would probably be going downriver. Ah, the fisheries guys. They always enjoyed a home cooked meal. I'd get word to them.

Absorbed in my thoughts, I trudged along the winding path. Suddenly I stopped in my tracks. A large herd, maybe fifty head or so of long-horned cattle, grazed on the scrub grass, completely blocking the path.

To turn around and go back to take the road home would add at least a mile to my walk, not appealing in that heat. I looked around for a Fula herdsman, but didn't see him, though I was sure a herd this size wouldn't be here on its own. Most cattle, especially this many, were owned by the Serahule, but herded by a Fula. Well, I'd just take my chances.

I walked down the dusty path, talking softly so I wouldn't startle them. "Hi, guys," I murmured. "I'm just going to slide right by you here." I kept watching out for those long horns, hoping one wouldn't stick me. Almost as worrisome was being swished by a shitty tail.

"Okay, here I am, just step aside." I kept my voice low key, almost a whisper. A few of the cows mooed at me, some sort of grunted. None were alarmed, though they rolled their huge eyes at me. A few stepped out of my way; others let me step around them. Flies from the cattle landed on me, but I concentrated on not waving them off, trying not to make sudden moves. Churned-up dust settled on my shoulders and hair. I walked perhaps a quarter of a mile through the herd before reaching the other side of them.

At one point along the path, a small hill rose on one side. From the hill I heard, "Abete ata bake, Mariama!" Well done, Mariama!

I looked up and saw the herdsman sitting in the shade. He waved. I waved back. The poor guy probably had held his breath the whole time I wove my way through the cattle, expecting to have to peel me off one of those long horns.

For weeks afterward, I heard about that incident. The word spread like locusts in a maize field. Woman couldn't imagine why I would do such a thing. Men thought I was probably just ignorant of what could have happened to me. I kept telling everyone who questioned me that it was just too hot to turn around and go the long way home.

* * *

The mail situation seemed marginally better. In any event, I'd brought most of the Christmas packages back with me from the States. Mail was still irregular though. We received a Christmas card from a family friend who said her dad was quite ill. Then, a second card was in the same pile of mail. She must have forgotten she'd already sent one, I figured. In this card she talked about the Christmas party she planned and that her dad would be home from a trip in time to attend.

What? A trip? I thought he was ill. I looked at the dates. One card had been en route fourteen months, while the other made it in the usual several weeks time. We received them both in the same mail call. Where had that letter been for a year? Wouldn't it be wonderful to have a way of tracking it?

This year we had more Christmas decorations. We hung the Noel banner the girls had made us, unpacked the little three-foot Christmas tree my sister had sent the previous year. The cute tree had its own miniature decorations. We strung our Christmas cards across a corner of our living/dining room. Our home looked festive.

We decided to have a Christmas party on the twenty-third. The fishery guys would come early and take care of business while in Basse. We invited a British woman we'd met, Hazel, who was doing some sort of survey. Peggy, who would leave for Banjul on Christmas Eve, came along with Nathaniel. Chris came, then would spend the night with Peggy and go downriver with her. Much to our delight, our friend Charlie Frazier stopped by on business and to spend the night. We wished Peter Moore could join us, but he went to England to spend Christmas with his family. The priests came, too, and Collum brought his guitar. I invited the only Christian nurse, Sister Ruth.

We had a delightful party. I decided to have that be our "Binta dinner" and gave her extra money to cook a meal for that crowd. The food was wonderful.

One of the guys said, "Binta's such a great cook, why don't you have her do all your cooking?"

Perry said, "Are you kidding? Then we wouldn't have Mary's home-cooked meals!"

"Oh, right. Forget it."

As usual, the fisheries guys washed the dishes and later we sat around swapping Christmas stories of home. One of our gifts the previous year had been a folk song book and it had a whole section of Christmas carols. I had made copies of the words on my typewriter, two carols to a page, using carbon paper to duplicate copies. We shared sheets of music and, while we sang, Bruce and Collum played along on their guitars, following the chords in the song book.

Sister Ruth knew only one of our carols, "Silent Night," but sang for us several beautiful African carols. It was a memorable night. At the end of the evening, Nathaniel walked Sister Ruth home and Chris went to Peggy's. The fisheries guys slept in the living/dining room, giving Charlie the spare bedroom.

Charlie left the next morning, more enthusiastic than we'd ever seen him. He praised the party, the group we'd had, and was especially impressed with Sister Ruth. He said, "This was one of the most wonderful Christmas celebrations I've ever been to." I was highly flattered.

For Christmas dinner with the fisheries guys and Nathaniel, we enjoyed a canned ham and canned yams my sister had sent. Before they left, one of the guys asked for a haircut, then another and I ended giving all three haircuts. As usual, they treated us to a meal at Jobot's All Necessary Foods and then left for their various villages.

As they had done the previous year, many children came to our door asking for their Christmas, not unlike American children on Halloween. They were after money, but we gave them hard candy.

New Years Eve was quiet, just as we liked it. The night temperature was chilly and we spent the evening playing cards and reading. Unbelievably, before the end of the year, we would be home.

After experiencing the pattern of overnight guests the previous year, I had kept a tally for 1980. In that year, we had 81 overnight guests, several invited, many not only uninvited, but unannounced beforehand. Many of the unexpected guests required two or three meals a day, most of whom never lifted a finger to help shop for the food, prepare the meals or clean up afterward. Many didn't even haul their own water after using the supply they found ready for them.

* * *

Nathaniel came over, excited to announce that his mother was coming to visit. Nathaniel and his mom were obviously close. "Would you give me a haircut?"

My normal hair cutting "station" was in the shade of the front porch where we might pick up a bit of a breeze.

From the porch we had a good view of the well. About a dozen women gathered, outside the rocks as Bruce had instructed, and chatted while they scrubbed mountains of laundry by hand. As they finished the last piece or two, they often slipped off their tops and washed them, too. That left them topless, which we were all used to by now.

"It's long past the thrill value," Nathaniel commented. Occasionally a mother would nurse her child, and then forget to put the breast back, leaving one in, one out. To them it was nothing. Often, around the compound if the women were hard at work perhaps pounding grain, they worked bare-chested.

Now legs, that was something different. Other than in the hospital, I never saw a Gambian woman's bare thighs.

I handed Nathaniel a mirror so he could look at his haircut.

"Great. Thanks. Mary, I'm a little worried about my mom being comfortable at my place."

"Why wouldn't she be? You've got a nice place."

"I wonder if I should buy a mirror."

"You don't have a mirror? How do you comb your hair?"

"I don't have a comb, either." What a character.

Mrs. Jackson, from North Carolina, came within a week and we enjoyed her visit immensely. Of course, we had Nathaniel and his mom over for dinner. She was a professional woman and asked questions about Gambian sociological perspectives. I'd been so caught up in day-to-day events, I hadn't given thought to many of her questions.

She understood that. "Of course, Mary. You're busy just figuring out ways to survive. I'm only an observing outsider."

We sat outside around a small fire, which felt good in the cool evening.

Nathaniel, as a small business advisor, was highly respected among the business community. His clients chipped in and came up with enough money to pay for a traditional drumming in honor of Nathaniel's mother. They also slaughtered a sheep for the feast. It was an amazing show of dedication toward Nathaniel. Knowing Nathaniel, I'm sure he contributed generously to the fund, but he gave all the credit for the event to his colleagues.

On Saturday morning the first of the musicians began to arrive along with two konkorans, Gambian male dancers who pretend they're evil. It was actually the biggest celebration we'd seen, and all for Nathaniel's mother. Although the musicians had been paid to come, those who attended were expected to chip in for the fun occasion. The konkorans, dressed in incredibly uncomfortable-looking outfits made of bark and leaves, leapt around and some of the guests, mostly woman, danced, too. All the tubobs, including Bruce and me, were dragged into the center and expected to dance, which we did, to the roars of laughter of the crowd. The women in Nathaniel's compound prepared the feast and many people attended. It was an amazing party and a touching tribute to Nathaniel and his mother.

We invited the Peace Corps volunteers and Mrs. Jackson for breakfast the next day, and then Nathaniel and his mother left to tour Mali, east of Senegal.

We wished that some of our family could come to The Gambia while we were there, but no one was in a position to do so. Bruce's parents were elderly and we didn't think they were up to the trip. My sister had shown an interest early on until she found out how hot it was. The trip was expensive, too, and many in our family didn't have money to spare for such a journey.

* * *

Bruce's predecessor had ordered a two-way radio for the Basse UN shop. Bruce received word that it had arrived and he could pick it up at Yundum. With no working phones outside of the capital city, what a great thing it would be to have instant communication with downriver headquarters.

Bruce began gathering materials for an antenna tower, not an easy task. No one store would have the materials required, so he acquired scraps here and there. The pipe was from an old well-digging tripod; cable, clamps and pulley came from Hydromet, the weather station. Bruce scrounged around the markets in Banjul and Basse for bolts, wire and rope.

Bruce enlisted a couple of men to dig the hole for the antenna base. They found that all the usable shovels were in the bush at the well digging sites. They did have two shovel heads, but no handles. He asked the blacksmith to make handles. First the man would have to go to the bush to get suitable wood, but there was no vehicle in running condition to take him to find the wood. Progress was slow, or not at all.

Finally, weeks later, they erected the antenna tower, forty-five feet above ground, six feet underground. Then came a long wait for Yundum headquarters to come up with the antenna wire, the feed line, the battery charger. What would have taken three days in Seattle took months to accomplish in The Gambia.

Not wanting to take a chance on something happening to it, Bruce trekked downriver himself to pick up the radio. Returning to Mansajang, he waited until after hours to assemble the radio. Unfortunately, he just couldn't trust the guys enough to do it with them right there. They'd tweak the parts, possibly break something, or walk off with the special tools. Bruce connected all the parts and, joy of joys, the next morning had a conversation with the manager of the downriver UN shop.

Finally, the radio transmitted and received on a regular basis. Bruce was ecstatic. It was probably the single most thrilling and satisfying accomplishment he had made in The Gambia. The radio proved to be a wonderful convenience. As it happened, Bruce, a licensed radioman, was perhaps the only person in the country who had the knowledge necessary to assemble all the parts needed for a working radio station.

Bruce joked to me that he'd created a monster. The shop guys walked around mimicking the calls they heard on the radio. "Basse, Basse, dis is Banjul. Ober," or "Sapu, Georgetown, Ober."

At last, the UN Shop had the convenience of a working radio, of being able to order and know when supplies would be received, know when UN people were going to visit, know when a vehicle was repaired and could be picked up. The radio was an enormous time-saver.

* * *

Word got out that Bruce knew motorcycle maintenance and George requested that he hold seminars for those volunteers who were issued motorcycles. Some of the bikes were two years old and had been driven hard on rough roads. Bruce repaired those motorcycles when he had the spare parts. Of course, many of these volunteers were from a distance away, so when they came to get their bikes repaired or attend a seminar, they normally ended up spending the night with us.

* * *

Nathaniel invited us for dinner and all day I looked forward to not having to cook. We walked along the familiar path to Nathaniel's compound near the Basse Health Centre.

Two men walked toward us and I stepped behind Bruce to make way, and they stepped into single file. As Bruce passed the first fellow, we all exchanged greetings. As I passed the second fellow, he reached out and firmly grasped my breast, then let go. He managed to do so without neither Bruce nor his companion seeing the deed.

To be fair, the fellow didn't know this was the third incident of my being groped, nor did he know my previous encounters had festered within my heart all these months. His act was, unfortunately, the last straw.

Outraged, I lit into him, fists flying. "You son of a bitch!" I yelled. He turned, shocked at my tone. I slugged him in the cheek, then, with the flat of my hands on his chest, pushed him. He staggered backwards. I came at him again. He held up his arms in front of his face. I saw raw fear in his eyes. I stepped forward and hit him again, striking the muscular arm protecting his face. "Who the hell do you think you are, touching me like that?"

In the meantime, Bruce stopped and turned around, astonished. "Geez, Mary, what did he do?"

"He grabbed my breast!"

With that Bruce seemed to swell to twice his normal size and in about three giant strides stood beside me.

The offender's companion, obviously shocked, stepped forward and spoke in English. "This is very bad. I am so sorry." He verbally lit into the other man. They spoke in Wolof.

Bruce stood inches from the man's face. I glanced around. I could see the back of the police station over the man's shoulder. I did not want this to be a police incident. And I did not want Bruce to become involved in a fight.

The interpreter apparently insisted the man apologize, and the offender mumbled something in Wolof to me, not even looking me in the eye.

The interpreter said, "He is sorry for what he did. Please."

I still steamed. "Tell your friend not to do this again. What would he think if some man did this to his wife?" The guilty man's frightened eyes looked from me to Bruce, clearly intimidated. After the translator finished, the man nodded, and mumbled his response.

I touched Bruce's arm. "Let's go." I was satisfied. Actually, I was elated. I hadn't let the incident go unchecked, I had defended myself. We went on our way; they went theirs.

A few days later, the translator in this incident approached me at the market and spoke in English. "Do you remember me?"

"I'm sorry, you look familiar, but I don't remember your name."

"I am Malik. I was with that man when he...touched you."

"Oh, yes. I remember. I was very upset with your friend."

He smiled. "Yes, you were. And rightly so. I want you to know that he was not my friend. I did not even know him. That man was from Senegal and had asked me where the village of Mansajang was and I was taking him there. What he did was wrong."

"Yes, it was. I'm glad he wasn't your friend."

He laughed. "A friend of mine would not do such a thing."

Reedbuck at Niokolo Koba National Park

Chapter 21

I sat at my usual table, recording counts of a well-baby clinic when I heard a ringing, a very strange sound for the Basse hospital. I looked around. It was the telephone, just inches from my elbow!

"Basse Health Centre," I said cautiously.

"Mary! This is Ann Saar."

"Ann, you're the first person who has called on this phone since I've been here. I didn't even know it worked."

"I guess they just got the service running to Basse. Anyway, I want to visit you guys for a couple of days. You two are always so healthy, I want to see what you do, how you live."

From our early days in The Gambia, Ann Saar had been one of our favorite people. We were delighted that she would be our guest. In fact, we'd left a standing invitation, hoping she'd be up our way and stay with us. We set a date and looked forward to her visit.

Ann, one of the few women in The Gambia who drove a car, arrived mid-afternoon. Mosalif came over to greet her and I introduced them. Fluent in Wolof, Ann knew Mandinka greetings, but nothing beyond that. It was obvious that Mosalif knew she was an important person.

Tombong came within minutes of her arrival, though he usually called on us in the morning on his way to work. I greeted Tombong in Mandinka, then introduced him to Ann Saar. He immediately launched into Wolof and they conversed for some time. Here this red-headed Australian lady stood before him: How did he know she spoke Wolof? How did he even know she was here? By this time, I knew better than to ask. I would just get a blank stare and a response something like, "Of course, I knew she was here, Mariama. I spoke Wolof because that is what she speaks."

Although he had stopped by that morning, Alieu came to greet our guest, too, on his way home from school. I invited him to sit and visit. I learned that in addition to Fula, Mandinka and English, this boy of about ten years also spoke Wolof.

We'd slaughtered a chicken the night before and I had fixed a big chicken stew with squash, potatoes and onion. She raved about our sprout and tomato salad and said she'd actually heard about it from other volunteers who had visited us. Ann praised the meal, praised our efforts in gardening, raising chickens, our healthy lifestyle. "Some Peace Corps volunteers try to live like Africans and it just doesn't work. It's a lot of work to do what you two have done."

"But that's part of it," I countered, "there are two of us and we can do it together." She agreed that being a couple makes a difference.

She'd been around The Gambia long enough to understand both sides, the privileged and the common man. Her Gambian husband was a well educated man with a successful business, and she herself was a woman of importance within the Peace Corps and USAID community, but she had many Gambian friends who lived like our neighbors.

At breakfast the next morning, Bruce cooked oatmeal as I prepared a bowl of diced mango, orange and banana, all in season, which in itself was a treat. I mentioned to Ann that I loved mangoes but we found them messy to eat, even to cut up.

"Here, let me show you." She sliced the mango on either side of its wide, flat pit, then scored the flesh into perfect little squares that literally popped off the skin.

I had also learned to make yogurt, using as a starter yogurt we'd bought at the CFAO tubob store in Bakau. I made yogurt about once a week, using previous batches as my starter. Ann raved at its silky texture.

Ann passed on a valuable idea. Because we would return home within the next few months, she suggested we start changing our Gambian dalasi to American dollars. Ann maintained an American checking account so that she could order goods and she offered to write a check for us in American dollars, which would take care of a chunk of our money, about $500. We would settle up as we checked out of the Peace Corps. That was a relief, but we had to make other arrangements for the balance.

After Ann left, we realized that we needed to get busy changing our money. We were on a monthly count-down now. Time was flying by. We knew going to a bank to exchange money would be expensive, plus we'd heard that American dollars were scarce in-country and that the bank didn't always have enough to exchange as people left the country. We had to find another way. We had heard there were money changers around, but had no experience working with them.

One late afternoon we went to the market to inquire about a money changer. We asked the market manager, a man we had met through Peggy. He directed us across the street to a little store. "That man can help you."

We had with us about five hundred dalasi, money we kept on hand for emergencies. We walked into the store, tiny at about ten by twelve feet, and immediately turned around to leave. This couldn't be the place. One man was asleep on the concrete counter, another in a corner on the floor. A Gambian stood behind the counter. Two or three small items were for sale, but otherwise the store looked completely devoid of anything businesslike.

"May I help you?" the man behind the counter asked in English.

"Thank you, but I think we're in the wrong place," Bruce said. We started out the door.

"What are you looking for?"

Bruce hated to say it right out loud, thinking it could be an invitation to robbery, but, on a chance, he said, "We want to exchange money."

With that the man brought out from under the counter a four-inch thick hard briefcase and, placing it on the counter, opened it. The man lying on the counter got up and moved to the other side of the room.

"What kind of money do you want?" he gestured to the contents. There, in the briefcase, we saw Japanese yen, French francs, German marks, Swedish kroner, Chinese yuan, and a huge stack of American dollars. It was an amazing sight. I realized the other men in the store weren't just lounging, they were guards.

Bruce explained that within a few months we would return to the United States and we needed to change our money. The money changer was very accommodating and gave us a rate slightly better than the bank. We asked for twenties or fifties, maybe a few hundreds.

Concerned about receiving counterfeit dollars, Bruce had brought a small magnifying glass and began inspecting the bills the money changer put before him. One after another he scrutinized them, not really knowing exactly what to look for, but hoping he'd spot something out of the ordinary. Satisfied, he nodded.

"Here," the man said "look at these." He pushed a pile of American money toward Bruce. One by one, Bruce went over the stack.

Over the next few months, we visited the money changer. We had lived on one salary all this time, so actually had a bit of money accumulated. Our business relationship was most satisfying. At no time did we feel threatened by the fellows standing around. They didn't seem the slightest bit interested in our money, only in their boss's safety.

But then, what to do with the money? Our house had been broken into already and now even more people knew we had cash. We put the money into a jar, then into a coffee can and buried it in our chicken coop. We told no one.

* * *

We began talking about what we wanted to do once we returned home to the United States. Bruce planned to go back to the marine electronics industry. We had both quit good jobs to join the Peace Corps. I had been the Admissions Director at a professional deep sea diving school in Seattle. The talk now was of computers. Many large businesses used main-frame computers, though small businesses were just beginning to investigate the possibility of word processing and accounting systems, all done by computers.

The more we talked, the more excited I became about attending college. Other than taking a few isolated courses, I had never attended college. We asked Bruce's folks to send us community college brochures and Bruce's mother graciously offered to go to the college to personally enroll me for the fall quarter computer science program.

It seemed impossible that we were close to going home. We would go back to the Seattle home we owned but had rented out. The people renting it planned to buy a home and would move out in time for us to move in when we returned.

* * *

I sat at my table at work, just finishing up recording figures for the antenatal clinic held the day before. Sister Ruth sat at the table with me. It was a quiet day. I glanced out the smudged window and saw Bruce, churning up the path, coming our way. I knew something was wrong. I turned to Sister. "I'll see you tomorrow, Sister."

Thinking nothing of my leaving early, she said, "Fine, Mariama. See you tomorrow."

I met Bruce just as he was turning on the path toward the hospital. He looked like he could bite a baobob tree in half.

"Bruce, what's wrong?" I could hardly keep up. He had barely slowed down when I joined him.

"Karafa," he steamed, "our head mechanic. I told him to put the radio battery on the charger last night. He did, and this morning I had him hook up the charged battery to the radio, something he's done right hundreds of times. Well, he hooked it up backwards, plus to minus." His footfalls churned up red dust.

"And?"

"He blew it up. The components in the radio went up in smoke. The radio is ruined."

I'd never seen Bruce so discouraged. He had been so proud and pleased with setting up the radio and the convenience it brought, and now this.

We were still clipping right along. "Let's go see Peter, tell him about it," I panted, trying to keep up.

Without missing a step, we turned in the direction of Peter's house. Peter, always perceptive, could immediately tell Bruce was upset. "What's up?"

Bruce told him the whole thing, setting up the antenna, radio, etc., the months- long process, finishing with, "...and Karafa blew up the whole damn thing."

After a pause, Peter said, "Well, there you have it."

Bruce's jaw dropped. "That's all you have to say? 'There you have it'?"

"What else is there to say? That's how it is here. Anything that goes right is generally because some tubob does it. There's no understanding of how things work, or what it takes to make things happen." He got up from his chair. "Let me get you guys something cold to drink."

The radio continued to be a lasting disappointment. It had been operational less than three months. There was no hope of getting it repaired before we left. Indeed, none of the vehicle parts Bruce ordered from abroad for the shop would arrive within our two years in The Gambia.

* * *

Bruce and Mr. Lopi planned to go downriver together for a meeting and would be gone two days. The job director had been out of country, supposedly working on funding for the project and had sent for them.

While at the project headquarters, they planned to bring back various supplies. "While we're downriver, we should order extra fuel, in case of tomorrow," Mr. Lopi said.

Mr. Lopi drove the Land Rover and brought along a sheep as a gift for the director. The ram stood behind Bruce in the back and bleated in Bruce's ear "about every fourteen seconds, the whole 252 miles."

Bruce came away from the meeting with serious doubts about the project's future. So much of the success depended upon politics and he worried that power struggles would prevail.

* * *

Nathaniel stopped by with a package he'd picked up at the Peace Corps office in Banjul, a Texas fruitcake from my step-mother. She had mailed it as a Christmas gift in October, 1980 and it arrived, intact, June 16, 1981. It was delicious.

* * *

The Fourth of July was a big event for the Americans in-country and all expatriates were invited to the Ambassador's for a celebration. A few months before, the Chargé d'Affair position had been upgraded to Ambassador and we had not yet met Ambassador Larry Piper, who lived in the same house on the beach in Bakau as had the Chargé d'Affairs.

We were tempted to go downriver, but it was a bad time for Bruce at work and my home visits were picking up, with auxiliary nurses asking to go with me. Their enthusiasm was so encouraging I wanted to support them as much as I could.

We received an invitation from the Catholic nuns to attend a play at St. Joseph Primary School for Girls in Basse and that swung the pendulum for staying upriver. The play, performed by fifth and sixth graders turned out to be impressively well done. The comedy had been a Ugandan school production that one of the nuns adapted for The Gambia.

We all sat outside, in the relative coolness, to watch the play performed on a platform. I estimated about a hundred people were in attendance.

While we waited for the play to start, a fellow sitting in front of us turned around and asked, "Isn't this an American holiday for you? Your independence? I thought you were all going downriver."

"We didn't want to miss this play," I responded, which pleased the people sitting around us.

The man nodded. "How many years have you had your Independence?"

I really hated to answer him. Independence was such a fleeting, and often violent thing in Africa. "Two hundred five years," I answered.

"That is a long time," he acknowledged. The Gambia had been independent at that time only ten years.

The play was extraordinary, with the girls playing all the roles except for minor parts played by two of the men teachers, a king and a warrior. With only two months of rehearsals, these girls put on an amazing production. The lead, a sixth grader, had long passages that she recited beautifully. Many times, the others answered in unison, with perfect timing. That gave more kids a speaking part, but also helped the audience to hear, since there was no amplifying system.

During the course of the production, the girls enacted their normal routines, pounding grain, taking care of little children, drawing water from a well, working in the garden, winnowing grain, sorting rice by throwing out bugs and stones. It was all so realistic. All the speaking parts were in English, also impressive.

African dancing played a major role in the play and a Mansajang kora player and his two wives plus two drummers furnished the music. The dancing itself was delightful. It was truly a quality production.

At intermission, Bruce and I visited with Father Fagan, Collum and Mara. I ventured that I didn't think Gambian boys of the same age could have put on such a production and they all agreed wholeheartedly. Those three also taught and knew the capability of local boys. For one, Mara said, they wouldn't have learned their lines, nor given the production the effort these girls had. "Also," Mara joked, "what would they have been shown doing? Certainly not work!"

During the play, a group of boys outside the fenced-in school yard heckled. One of the men in the audience went outside and yelled at them and the boys scattered. Gambian kids have a healthy respect for adults. If an adult disciplines a kid for good reason, never mind that it isn't his own child, there are no reprisals.

A few minutes later something hard hit me in the head. It was quite a thunk and when I reached up, I could feel a lump forming and felt blood. I assumed one of those boys had thrown a rock over the fence, which surprised me. Kids there didn't seem to do that sort of thing. I mentioned the incident to Bruce. My injury wasn't bad enough to leave the play early, however, and we filed out with the others.

As we were leaving, we saw one of the auxiliary nurses from the Health Centre. "Mariama, how is your head? I saw that bat fly into you."

"It was a bat? I thought one of those boys had thrown a rock."

"No, the bat swooped at your head, then flew away. Does it pain you?"

"It's a little sore, a lump is forming and it's bleeding a bit."

"Come on," Bruce said, "let's get you home and clean it up."

By the time we arrived home the minimal bleeding had stopped, but Bruce thoroughly cleaned the area with disinfectant. The lump was gone within a few days.

* * *

The girls and women appeared to do the majority of the work in The Gambia. Although the men at the shop worked hard when actually digging wells, many of the workers just put in time. Boys are responsible for the livestock, but, other than the Serahule, most compounds only have a few head of goats or sheep. They turn them out in the day and collect them at night, leaving the boys free to play games and loll around. Men work the peanut crop, but that's only for a short period during the year. Most men we observed in Mansajang spent hours lounging and talking under the shade of the baobob tree.

The girls and women garden and toil in rice fields, which is hard work. They do all the cooking, cleaning, washing clothes. They haul the water for men and boys to bathe.

I sat on the porch rereading letters from our girls. They had both written on March 30 and Robin's was received April 14th and Bonnie's on May 12th. The Gambian mail system made no sense at all.

I glanced at the well where three girls scrubbed their families' laundry. One looked up at me and waved, and I waved back. Soon, they walked over to greet me. One of them showed me a blister that had broken and asked if I had a "plaster," their word for bandage. I applied the bandage and they stayed for a few minutes to chat.

The girls were nine, eleven and twelve and were doing that heavy work. The girl to whom I gave the bandage got her blister from pounding grain that morning. I asked what their brothers were doing and they laughed. "Nothing, just playing."

The twelve-year-old would probably be getting married soon. Very often thirteen or fourteen year olds were the second or third wife of an older man. First marriages were usually arranged by parents with the bride and groom approximately the same age. The intended bride's parents establish a price, usually around six hundred dalasi or the equivalent in goods or livestock. Later in the marriage, it was no disgrace for the man to have a girlfriend, and sometimes that person became the second wife and was often much younger. It seemed that the first wife didn't mind a second or third wife. At least she had someone with whom to share the work. But the rule is that the husband must keep things fair among his wives.

Peggy told of an interesting situation in her compound. The younger brother of the head of the compound asked Peggy for six hundred dalasi so that he could acquire another wife. "But," she countered, "you never have enough money, even for one wife and child."

"Yes, that is why I'm asking you for money."

There didn't seem to be any thought to the future. If he's having trouble making ends meet with one wife, doesn't it stand to reason that he'll have trouble keeping two wives? In our minds, yes, but the Gambian looked at things differently.

At the Health Centre I became aware of a recurring situation and one explanation for malnourishment in children. Wives were often in competition with one another, vying for the husband's favor. Often, when feeding their families, wives gave their husband most of the meat, leaving only sauce on rice for the children, a diet seriously lacking in protein.

Another area for competition was seeing who can produce the most children. Thus, many women had more children than their bodies could tolerate, contributing to the high death rate during childbirth.

A girl, Saijo, often visited us with a baby. I assumed it was her little sister. Once when Nathaniel was over, he asked the girl how old she was. Although the older people rarely knew their own age, the younger generation found it important to keep track.

"Fourteen," she answered.

"Is that your little girl?" Nathaniel asked.

"Yes, she is mine."

Saijo was the third wife of a much older husband. From her attitude, I gathered her living situation wasn't ideal. She'd had the child when she was thirteen. Girls develop physically at an earlier age in The Gambia than in the United States. Saijo's situation wasn't uncommon.

We didn't discuss it, but I assumed Saijo had endured female circumcision, so sex didn't offer any pleasure. From what I could tell, women were merely vessels to carry children and strong bodies to do the work. A woman's position wasn't enviable. Still they were mostly good natured and went about their chores cheerfully.

* * *

When we last visited Harry and Suzi in Bakau, we'd discussed going to the famous wild-game reserve, Niokolo Koba National Park in Senegal. They had also planned on taking that trip and suggested we go together. Harry would work on getting one of his project vehicles. We left the timing up to him since he had more complications to overcome with both a vehicle and time off to arrange. They sent word they could leave on Friday but Harry needed to be back at work on Tuesday. Great! That would give us plenty of time.

As it happened, another couple passing through The Gambia joined us, a fellow Harry had known at the Centers for Disease Control in Atlanta. Chad and his girlfriend Kristi, a nurse, had stopped by to see Harry after finishing an assignment studying Lassa fever in Sierra Leone.

The four of them arrived Friday in a nearly new Toyota Land Cruiser that accommodated the six of us and all our equipment. Suzi and I had already worked out the food; the fellows had discussed the other equipment. We borrowed a two-man tent, Suzi and Harry had one as well, and we had enough mosquito netting to fashion another tent.

We served Friday dinner and spent the night at our place, leaving early Saturday morning. Fuel wasn't currently available in Basse, so we stopped just across the Senegalese border. While refueling we noticed a serious tire leak. Luckily, we were in a place where we could have it repaired. So, fueled and repaired, we set out.

In looking at a map, the fellows decided that we could save time by taking a short cut. It may have been shorter in miles, but it took us much longer because of the extremely rough road. That Land Cruiser shook so violently, it made my teeth ache. We could hear our food supplies crashing around and stopped to see if we should rearrange things. I had brought a jar of jam that had broken and the sticky mess leaked over many other food items. Our jar of peanut butter also had broken. We had brought several gallons of drinking water, as we had read we must do, and we distributed our remaining food around the plastic jugs of water.

Upon entering the park mid-afternoon and paying the fees, we were given a detailed brochure with a park map and pictures identifying species of animals residing in the park. The roads smoothed out and we relaxed, ready to see the sights. We immediately began seeing wild game. This was the dry season so there wasn't much in the way of vegetation, which made for bleak scenery, but good animal viewing. We climbed several viewing platforms. We thrilled to see reedbuck, a lioness and a wart hog, known locally as "bush pig." We also saw many animals from the road: several troops of baboon, a buffon cob, waterbuck, bubal, cape bullalo. Although elephants were reportedly in the park, we didn't see any. They were probably in the bush where we couldn't go, since visitors were required to stay on the roads.

Although the weather was hot, hovering around 100 degrees, we didn't use the air-conditioner because we needed to have the windows open to take pictures.

Camping was allowed only in designated areas and we found the camps quite adequate. On our first night, the camp had a round grass-roof hut and a cooking hut with a bench. The hut nicely held four people so Bruce and I elected to pitch our borrowed tent outside.

After getting that hot work done, we couldn't wait to cool off in the river. The six of us rushed in and gave a collective sigh of relief. I heard yelling and looked up to see the park ranger frantically waving for us to get out. "What? Get out? We just got here!"

We didn't want to get into trouble, so we reluctantly climbed out of the river and up the bank, not yet really cooled off. Once he saw us safely out of the water, he pointed upriver. There, we saw a family of hippos, their tiny ears and eyes that reflected red showing just above the surface of the water. Oops. Guess it was the wrong time of day to be cooling off in the river.

It had been a long, tiring day with the flat tire delay and the rough ride. As we climbed into our tent, I said to Bruce, "I don't suppose this little tent is much protection from those hippos."

"There's not room for two more in the hut."

"I suppose we could set the tent up in the cooking hut."

"Forget it. I don't have the steam." With that, he fell sound asleep.

Oh, well, I thought, and immediately drifted off to sleep.

The next morning, we saw dozens of big, flat hippo footprints leading from the river through the campground. Those huge animals had walked within two feet of our little tent, leaving footprints the size of turkey platters.

Bruce fixed oatmeal for breakfast and we were off for another day of adventure.

In the early morning we saw even more animals, many of which we'd never heard of, but identified by our guidebook. One reedbuck, only thirty feet from us, stood stock still for several minutes while we took pictures and studied him with binoculars. About the size of a horse, he had a large head and spiral horns. Bountiful colorful birds chirped and screeched, flapping their wings as we neared their nests.

At one point, we were all out of the vehicle taking pictures and Harry casually said, "There's more stuff over there," in sort of a ho-hum way, vaguely waving his hand toward a family of buffalo. We were getting nonchalant about this fascinating existence!

The second night, Suzi fixed a packaged rice-curry dinner. After the meal we sat outside the huts and listened to the loud roar of hippo and the bark of baboons. I had to keep reminding myself that this was really happening.

Monday morning we headed for home, satisfied that we had accomplished one of our big goals, to see Niokolo Koba National Park.

Our good friend Tombong

Chapter 22

I had an hour before I needed to leave for work for
Friday's well-baby clinic. The previous Friday we'd had a
huge crowd. I smiled, remembering an incident. For some
reason when I took my seat at the table first thing in the
morning, the room was unusually quiet, though every one of
the fifty chairs was taken with mothers and their children. I
looked at the crowd of happy faces and said, "Salaam
Malekum, alle!" Peace be with you, everyone!

In unison they all replied, "Malekum Salaam, Mariama!"
And then we all laughed. They all knew my name, I had met

many of them in person. It was a wonderful feeling of acceptance.

"Konk, konk." Tombong came to our door, breaking my reverie.

Early this morning, he normally stopped by to greet us on his way to work. Bruce went to the door, I at his heels.

After an unusually brief greeting, Tombong said, "Mistah Bruce, you cannot let Mariama go to work today."

Mind you, I was right there, standing next to Bruce. "Why is that, Tombong?" Bruce asked.

"There is much water. It is not safe. You cannot let her go, Mistah Bruce."

I knew we'd had a lot of rain during the night, but at the moment it wasn't raining. I hoped it would hold off until I got to work.

I chimed in. "Tombong, it is not raining now. Why shouldn't I go to work?"

"Come with me, Mariama." He turned, fully expecting me to follow, which, of course, I did.

Side-stepping puddles of water, we walked down the path I used to get to work. After only a short distance I stood, amazed. Where there was once my sedate winding path, now a raging muddy river stormed by, small trees churned past, debris gathering in their wake. The sound of rushing water was so unfamiliar, I just couldn't believe what I saw and heard.

"Oh," I gasped.

"You see, Mariama, you cannot to go work today."

"But it's Friday and I should be there."

"Mariama, no one will be there."

"I can use the road."

He looked at me like I'd lost all sense. "The road is full of water."

"Well, you got here!"

"Yes. I waded into water up to here." He pointed to his mid-thigh, wet, I now noticed.

"Why? Why would you do that?"

"To tell you not to go to work!"

"Oh, my goodness. Tombong, thank you."

"Yes."

He walked me back home, then turned to return to his home. "Tell Mistah Bruce no one will come today."

This time, I believed him.

"I will tell him. Thank you, Tombong."

He nodded and left to ford our new river once again.

Bruce didn't have to wade through water to get to work since the shop and our home next door were on the same level and a distance away from the rushing water. He walked over to see if anything was going on. Sure enough, no one came to work. Only the night guard was there in the little watchman's hut, a fellow who lived on our side of the "river."

They couldn't leave the shop unprotected, but night guard Mamadou said the other guard would be there soon and would take Mamadou's place so he could go home and rest. They had it all worked out.

We stayed home and occupied ourselves inside until mid-afternoon. I had planned to go to the market after work, so asked Bruce if he wanted to go with me. It hadn't rained again, so much of that water should have soaked into the sandy soil.

Again, we were amazed with the surge of water that had covered the area. There were still some fairly good sized puddles, particularly in those areas where the soil contained clay. Where the brickmakers worked, the puddles were deep and wide.

I hesitated to cross at that spot. Bruce walked ahead. "Just step where I step."

I didn't have a lot of confidence in Bruce's plan. Where he stepped, water seeped up. But I followed along behind. At about the fifth step, my foot slipped sideways on the slippery clay and I slid into a puddle. I hollered out and Bruce turned to see me sinking into the puddle, first to my ankles, then knees, then to my waist. I held high my little cloth purse that contained our money.

"Here," I said to Bruce, "take this."

He grabbed my purse, but was laughing so hard, he almost fell in.

I was incensed. "Bruce!"

"I have never seen anyone fall into a mud puddle up to their waist!"

"Just help me out."

It wasn't easy. The slippery area around the puddle made it hard for Bruce to get his footing. Finally, he found a place where he could dig in with his heals and I waded over to him so he could pull me out. I don't know if I could have gotten out without him.

I was a mess of muddy water. We returned home and I washed off at the well and changed my clothes. Cleaned up, we returned to the market by way of the road, which by this time was largely free of standing water.

* * *

Our little neighbor girl, Jariettu, not quite six, walked by with a basin of water on her head. We'd been watching her progress. The pan was a shallow basin filled to the top with water. Just months ago, with the same basin, the little girl had spilled much of the water, but that morning she made the whole trip from the well without spilling a drop. Children learn this skill at a very young age. No wonder Africans have such wonderful posture.

* * *

When we first arrived in The Gambia, I wasn't impressed with most of the huts I entered. But after awhile I could see individuality and beauty. Binta's hut was immaculate and bright with colorful sheets on the neatly made bed and bright pillows on the bed and floor. Black and white photographs of her family decorated the mud-brick walls. The single chair had colorful cushions on the seat, a rarity. Chairs that I had seen were flat wood and a straight back.

In the many huts I entered, pictures were only of people. I never saw scenery or artwork.

Bruce's folks frequently sent us several developed prints made from Bruce's slides. We didn't see the slides ourselves, since we had them sent from Kodak directly to the folks. It was always wonderful to see our pictures. Normally those prints his parents sent were some of the best ones that they thought we should see. In some cases, we'd asked them to send us extra copies so we could give them to our Gambian friends.

The folks sent us an exceptionally good portrait of Tombong, shirtless and muscular. Taken in the evening light, the picture had an unusual golden glow. We decided to have it framed.

We found the Gambian method of picture framing unique. They cut pieces of glass somewhat larger than the picture. In this case, we mounted Tombong's picture on a piece of blank paper. The framer encased the mounted picture between two pieces of glass and then skillfully taped the glass together with red electrical tape. Then, the framer hand painted flowers in each corner, giving the appearance of a frame. As he did this, a crowd gathered to see what the tubobs were doing.

"Tombong," I heard many people murmur. Probably two dozen people had gathered to watch the picture framer at work.

That was at the end of a day. We wondered how long it would be before word got to Tombong.

The next morning I saw him coming our way, his steps very quick. He rarely walked that fast. As we greeted one another, I could see his eyes dart to our walls.

"We have something for you, Tombong."

"Yes." Though old by African standards, Tombong showed the anticipation of a child at Christmas.

Bruce handed him the picture, wrapped in brown paper. I was surprised to see tears spring to Tombong's eyes when he opened the package. "Oh, my. Oh, this is fine. Now I will have something to give to my son. Thank you, thank you." He looked at each of us in turn.

* * *

Just before we arrived in Mansajang almost two years before, Bruce's shop was white-washed. The walls inside and out continued to look clean.

The men at the shop pitched in and bought a goat and slaughtered it in the shop yard. Momodou, the night guard, hung the bloody hide on the inside white wall. Bruce was flabbergasted, even though he thought nothing more could bring him to that point. Forevermore there would be a bloody stain on that wall.

Father Fagan told us that a priest friend of his, a man who had served in The Gambia for fifty years, said that he understood the Gambians even less after all that time than he did when he first arrived in-country.

* * *

Our Peace Corps Director, George, sent word through Nathaniel that we should take some R&R before our time was up. "He worries that you guys work too hard," Nathaniel said. "You guys do work hard, more than anyone I know."

Bruce shrugged. "I wish I felt that all this work amounted to something. I have absolutely no feeling of satisfaction."

"Still, Bruce," I countered, "your team has put in, what, one hundred seventy-five wells? Those wells affect a lot of lives."

"In this length of time, we should have put in twice that many."

I did feel a sense of satisfaction with my work. Just this past week, my replacement had been assigned to Basse. The young Gambian woman brought enthusiasm for the project. Nyanjo seemed eager for me to teach her my system. She was even willing to tally by fives! We had taken two treks together where she had observed my nutrition counseling. As far as I was concerned, this was the way it should be, being replaced by a Gambian.

Another wonderful plus: Nyanjo brought with her a Health Department typewriter and she was a good typist. The use of a typewriter made such a big difference in keeping orderly records.

Just that day we'd had a Senior Staff meeting and I took notes, as usual, and would type them on our new typewriter, rather than take them home to type. Nyanjo was too overwhelmed at this first meeting to understand what was going on. I could see how much I had learned when I watched Nyanjo's perplexed expressions. Of course, some of my savvy came from being on the ground floor formulating many of these routines. Finally, I understood some of the subtle jokes that at first completely missed me. I had come a long way toward understanding my co-workers. Sometimes I wondered how my experience in Africa would affect our lives when we resumed life in the United States.

One incident at the meeting left me chuckling. The senior staff discussed the behavior of one of the auxiliary nurses, one that caused trouble from time to time. Dr. Ceesay said, "I guess there's a black sheep in every family." It was an expression I didn't think I'd ever hear in Africa.

Because of my three weeks in the States, I'd had some real time off, but Bruce had only taken a two or three days here and there. We decided to go downriver for a ten-day stay, the longest ever. Of course, for both of us, some of that would be taking care of business. The Bakau apartment would not be in use, according to Nathaniel. I hadn't been downriver for three months. Bruce had been, but only on quick business trips.

We had received permission to leave The Gambia a month early, September 1st, so that I could start college in the fall. I worried that my brain had long since shriveled up with all the heat and with the effort of African survival. Would I be able to wrap my brain around computer concepts?

It was strange to think that our term of service was so close to the end. Peggy's group had left in April and since then we'd been the "upper classmen." One of the things George suggested (through Nathaniel) was for us to join him in greeting the incoming volunteers at the airport. That would be fun. New arrivals always looked so stunned, just as we no doubt did when we first arrived.

We rode downriver in a project vehicle with Bubacar at the wheel. The word had gotten around that we would be leaving in only two months. "Mistah Bruce, take me home with you. I will be your driver."

"Bubacar, in America we drive ourselves."

"Well, then, I could drive for Mariama. She will need a driver."

"No, Bubacar, I drive myself, too."

He looked shocked. "You can drive a car?"

"Oh, yes, in America most women do."

He merely shook his head.

Bubacar dropped us off at the apartment and we breathed a sigh of relief. It was always so good to be there. We pitched in and straightened up the two rooms, took running water showers to wash off the road dust, and headed out to dinner.

The next morning, when I called on Sister M'Boge, she gave me a rare smile. "How do you like Nyanjo, your replacement?"

"She's going to work out very well, Sister."

"It will be hard to replace you, Mariama, but I think she will do a good job."

At the Peace Corps office, we received a package from Bruce's folks that they had mailed in July,1980, a whole year before. No hint of where it had been all this time, but the contents were intact, though the package itself looked well traveled. Bruce's mom, knowing how starved we were for chocolate, had sent M&M's, but this time put them in a tin container. She'd sent M&M's before, but rats had gotten into the package and eaten every single one, just leaving the empty bag. This time, we were able to enjoy this rare treat. Besides the candy, she'd sent Jello and a book Bruce had asked for.

Charlie, our British friend, left a note in our Peace Corps mailbox asking that we call him the next time we were in Banjul. I used the Peace Corp's office phone and spoke to Charlie's wife, who invited us to tea the next day.

Having tea with Brits was always a special treat. We had learned from Peter Moore that when you call on a Brit at four o'clock tea-time you can expect a nice beverage and sweet biscuits, at least. Charlie's wife, Ruth, whom we hadn't met before, had made a delicious cake loaded with fruit. Charlie had been to our home many times and now seemed pleased to entertain us in his home. Ruth mentioned that Charlie raved about the Christmas party we'd had. That party had certainly struck a chord with him.

The next day we joined George to greet the new arrivals at the airport. George's enthusiasm always seemed to be in high gear, as it was this day. He truly loved Africa and loved to share his love with others.

One of the first things one of the recruits asked me was, "Is it always this hot?" I didn't have the heart to say that it would be even hotter upriver.

This group would spend much of their training in Jenoi as the seminary was being used for another project. George invited us to visit them in Jenoi, and have a meal or two. Among the new recruits was a married couple and they seemed eager to talk with us.

We rode to Jenoi with George two days later. The married couple, Bill and JoAnn, were so delighted to see us and plied us with lots of questions. They were both teachers and would be staying in or near Banjul. We didn't let on that we would have considered that a nightmare, but were able to share some ideas they might use. Their situation would be different from ours, but Bruce suggested they think ahead how they wanted to handle company, and told them our experience.

Lynn, the musicologist from our group, put on an excellent slide show for the group, together with wonderful taped African music. Lynn, a real professional, left her mark on The Gambia with her outstanding work. Very little had been previously done toward recording and preservation of Gambian music and her impressive project would be a lasting asset to the country.

* * *

We stopped at the Peace Corps office to pick up a new supply of chloroquine pills, which we would continue to take for a few weeks after we returned home. While visiting with Ann Saar she mentioned that her part-time assistant, Mary Heaney and her family were at their home in Ireland. Mary had specifically mentioned to Ann that Bruce and I were welcome to stay in their home when we were in the area.

"What a nice offer," I said.

"Yes and not one that she offered to anyone else." Ann said she had the key if we wanted to go there now for the rest of our stay.

That very day, we moved from the apartment to the Heaney's. Right on the beach, the house was next door to the Ambassador's, though we couldn't see into their yard because of a high fence and thick vegetation.

We only knew Mary Heaney slightly and had never met her husband, but they had been in The Gambia for several years. Mr. Heaney was the Director of Education at Yundum College, which was out for summer session and would not resume until September. They had three children, ten and twelve year-olds, and a little two year-old. The older children likely attended school in Ireland, since expatriate children rarely attended The Gambia's woefully inadequate schools.

We relished having this grand home to ourselves. To us, the concrete structure of about twenty-five hundred square feet was a palace. The large rooms were cool with constant sea breezes circulated by large fans hanging from twelve-foot ceilings. The wonderful kitchen had modern appliances with both electric and gas refrigerators and stoves, and a walk-in pantry. The large dining room contained a beautiful mahogany table with twelve chairs and a lovely matching china hutch. Their living room furniture was plush and comfortable. We enjoyed their extensive library. Although the Heaneys had a maid, she had been dismissed for the time they would be gone. A night guard continued to protect the property.

With the sea just down the bluff, in minutes we could get to the beach to swim and to take long uninterrupted walks. We did have an interrupted swim though. We had been in the water for only a few minutes when I noticed some beautiful blue, almost transparent, jelly-fish. "Bruce, look at the beautiful...."

"Mary, get away from them. Those are man-o-wars!"

Too late. One had already stung my thigh. Wow, what a sting. It just wouldn't stop. Returning to the house, I washed it thoroughly, but then had to wait it out. The intensity of the sting was amazing. That sting raised an impressive welt and hurt for days.

The Heaneys would be gone three months, not untypical for Europeans. Our British friends were aghast when we told them that Americans often worked fifty-two weeks on a new job before they got one week of vacation, then another year before they got two weeks. And a two-week vacation is normal until one had been on the job for several years. In Europe, they got at least one month off from the onset. Expatriates often had three months, plus their employer paid travel expenses.

Although we enjoyed the luxury of the Heaney house, we both felt a need to return to Mansajang. American work ethic does get in the way of fun.

Upon returning home, we found we had no electricity. The next morning Bruce discovered it was only our house, not the UN shop. He called on the Gambian Utility Company and, much to our amazement, they came right out. The repair man calmly took a wooden stick, climbed up on a barrel and commenced poking at the wire connection until the electricity came on. That style of repair is probably the most common method in the country. Poke it until it's fixed...or not.

Young woman at her compound preparing dinner

Chapter 23

We'd planted lemon and mango tree saplings a few weeks earlier and just before we left for Banjul, Bruce made a mixture of chicken manure and kitchen scraps and piled it round the trees. Upon our return, we couldn't believe the difference. Because of the rainy season, they'd gotten plenty of water, but it was the added nourishment that made a difference. The trees were bright green and stood strong and healthy. We would never see the lemons and mangoes from these trees, but people would enjoy the fruit in years to come.

Peter Moore invited us to go with him and Keith, his live-in work partner, to look for the locally famous Stone Circles in the Mid-River Division in what is called the North Bank area. Peter insisted on preparing our picnic lunch, which was a treat for me. We crossed the river at

Georgetown, riding on an "arm-strong" ferry, meaning we pulled ourselves across, vehicles and all. The men pitched in, pulling on the cable hand-over-hand. It was actually quite efficient.

Traveling northwest into the bush in Peter's Land Rover for about twenty miles, we found the Stone Circles near the village of Wassu. These impressive remains are a group of cut laterite, a cementation of sandstone in the shape of posts, arranged in a partial circle. The Stone Circles are believed to have been protection for ancient burial grounds and are reminiscent of Stonehenge in England. Afterwards, we explored the area further, enjoying the luxury of having a vehicle to get around.

We spread a cloth on the ground in the shade of a baobob tree and enjoyed the lunch Peter and Keith had prepared, with pâté on good French bread, pickles, canned artichokes and chilled beer. The British do a good job of making meals such as this special. Keith had even made a fruit pudding for dessert.

We found a monument to Mungo Park, not a place but a man, an explorer who searched for the mouth of the Niger River in 1797 and 1805. A plaque commemorates his efforts.

Since we had arrived in The Gambia, the main highway had been under construction and now, nearly two years later, was paved from Banjul to just a few miles from Basse. What used to take seven or eight hours (not counting break-downs) now took about five and a half. As we again crossed the river to return home, we marveled how much faster and more comfortable our trip to Basse was compared to even a few months before.

Peter offered to stop at the market before driving us home, so we could shop. What a treat! We hadn't bought meat for five months now. Meat was too tough and stringy, but fresh fish was available and we bought lady fish for dinner, just minutes off the canoe, lovely half-inch thick steaks for about seventy-five cents per steak. We replenished our supply of fresh vegetables, including okra, now that Peter had shown me how to fix it.

Keith sidled up to me, trying to look nonchalant. "There's a woman over there really staring at you."

"That's my peanut butter lady. We play this game."

Keith shrugged and shook his head.

I turned suddenly and caught her staring. She giggled and I made my way to her. I wasn't prepared with a jar, but she wrapped four balls of peanut butter in a scrap of paper, the usual way it's sold.

We bought two porta, tomato paste cans, of rice. The bread vendor briskly brushed a scrap of paper torn from an empty cement bag against his thigh and wrapped it around a loaf of fresh French bread. Finished with shopping, we climbed back into Peter's Land Rover and were home in minutes. What a priceless friend we had in Peter Moore.

I think one of our important lessons in The Gambia was reaching out to others, particularly those outside Peace Corps. We found such good friends among the expatriates. I'd observed so many volunteers only clinging to one another. They missed so much.

At work I found things in good order. Nyanjo seemed to have a good grasp of record keeping. She felt inadequate about nutrition counseling and I gave her literature that had been given to me. We went on trek together to Manneh-Kunda to follow up with two children who had been hospitalized. I knew Nyanjo would gain confidence in time.

After only a few days home, we received word that our group needed to go downriver for our exit physical examinations. The Peace Corps doctor would be in-country only for a few days and would not return before the end of our tour of duty. It was imperative that we have the various health-screening tests before we could be officially released. We had no choice but to go.

Fortunately, we had the Heaney house to stay in, since Nathaniel and Norman were in our group, too, and would need the apartment

Mr. Lopi had business in Yundum, so we could ride down with him. Our preferred departure time was early morning so that we would arrive in Bakau in time to settle in. But Mr. Lopi said we'd leave at noon, and he was driving.

Noon became one o'clock, waiting, waiting. We would have
thought we'd be used to delays by this time, but it still grated
on us. Finally, we left at four.

By the time we got to Banjul, it was too late to pick up
the Heaney house key from Ann Saar, so Mr. Lopi took us to
the apartment. Nathaniel and Norman, who arrived a couple
of days earlier, were not expecting us. The place was a
mess with dirty dishes in the dishpan, the table so full of junk
there wasn't room for an elbow. But after all, they weren't
expecting us and were good sports about our joining them.
We all went to LaPizza for a cold beer and then Bruce and I
brought the double mattress into the kitchen and slept there.
The guys tried to talk us into sleeping in the bedroom and
they would take the kitchen, but their stuff was strewn
around and they were already settled in on their single
mattresses. Besides, we were much earlier risers than they.

The first thing the next morning, we walked the mile to
Ann Sarr's home, picked up the key, walked back to the
apartment, and moved our stuff into Heaney's, about a mile
away, all before eight in the morning. We settled in and
again absorbed the luxury of this wonderful home.

Catching a bus into Banjul in the morning, we checked
in with the doctor, then to Queen Victoria hospital for chest
x-rays, stool and blood tests. Returning to the Peace Corps
office, we talked with Ann Saar further about our
money/check exchange with her. The doctor passed through
and invited us to lunch.

At lunch, Curt, the doctor, asked us about our stay in
The Gambia and we briefly told him the good and the bad. I
remembered the bat hitting my head during the school play
and told him about that.

"So where did you go?" he asked, aghast.

"Go? After the play we went home so Bruce could clean
it up."

He turned pale, then red. "Do you know why that bat hit
you? He was sick! Bats don't just fly into things, they have
very good sonar. He might have had rabies! You two should
have come to Banjul immediately. I would have ordered the
rabies treatment on the spot."

In those days, treatment for rabies was very painful. Secretly, I was glad we hadn't done that. Of course, we were very lucky that the bat didn't give me rabies.

"The frothing at her mouth was very slight," Bruce remarked.

"Not funny," Curt responded.

"Curt curtly responded," Bruce would say later.

A little neighborhood store carried what we needed for dinner and the next morning's breakfast. The ocean beckoned and we enjoyed a long, refreshing swim, sans man-o-wars. That evening we curled up with Heaney reading material, and then slept in their luxurious bed, lulled by the sound of the surf, with an overhead fan gently stirring Atlantic sea breezes.

Nathaniel would pick us up at ten with his project vehicle, a small Peugeot truck, and we were ready to go back to Mansajang. We'd packed very light since we would only be gone two nights.

By noon Nathaniel still wasn't there. It was unusual for him to be late. With no working telephones, it was hard to know what was happening. There was a telephone at the residence, but it had apparently been disconnected while Heaneys were gone.

"We don't have enough food here for lunch or dinner," I said. "Why don't I walk down to Bakau and stop at the apartment to see what's going on? If Nathaniel can't leave today, I'll go to the Bakau market and pick up some things. In the meantime, if he comes, you guys can come get me."

I set out for the walk, just slightly over a mile. Two loaded trucks of uniformed soldiers passed. I figured they must be going on a drill. The Field Force, the Gambian equivalent of National Guard had their headquarters and training camp in Bakau. I walked on, somehow feeling conspicuous. A man and woman stood in front of the British High Commissioner's residence. They looked at me and then urgently talked together. The man ran up the walkway and into the house and the woman rushed into the street toward me.

"Wherever are you going?" she asked me.

How strange. I didn't feel like going into the whole story, so simply said, "To the market."

The road curved right there. The woman gestured. "My dear, they'll never let you through."

I looked where she pointed and couldn't believe my eyes. A large tank blocked the street. In front of the tank another vehicle stood, full of soldiers.

When I recovered from my shock, I said, "What's going on?"

"They're having a coup! Come, my husband said to get you inside with us."

"What? Inside?" I realized later that this was the British Commissioner's wife and that had been the Commissioner standing outside with her.

A black sedan slowed and a man leaned over to roll down his window. "You women!" he yelled. "Get off the street! Stay inside!" He sped on.

"Come," she pulled on my arm.

I broke away. "No, I can't. I must get back to my husband. He won't know where I am."

She pulled on my arm again. "But you must. There isn't time. Come on."

The black car screeched a U-turn, and sped back to us. "Get in this car!" the man ordered.

I turned to the woman. "I'll be fine. We're staying at the Heaney house." They probably knew the Heaneys and she dropped her hand from my arm.

I climbed into the car, hoping I was doing the right thing. This guy, a Brit, was a total stranger.

"Where to?"

"The Heaney house. My husband is there."

He, too, knew where Heaneys lived. He turned his car around again and within minutes we arrived at Heaneys. He pulled into the driveway and skidded to a stop. "Okay, now stay inside. Listen to your radio!"

I thanked him and ran inside. Bruce met me at the door, his face a question mark.

"We're in a coup," I said. "Do Heaneys have a radio?"

"I've seen one in the pantry." He brought it out to the kitchen counter and we found a radio station, Radio Gambia, repeatedly broadcasting the loud proclamation "Long live the revolution!"

We sat at the kitchen table and listened to revolution talk in English, Wolof, Mandinka and Fula. What we gathered was that the Field Force had by now taken over the airport and radio station. Telephone service had been disconnected. All the main roads were blocked. We couldn't leave to go upriver.

"I wonder why those guys always have to shout," I said. "Why can't they just talk in a normal voice? If I hear them shrieking 'Long live the revolution' one more time, I'm going to scream."

"Well, no matter how they're saying it, what are we supposed to do?"

Up to that moment, we hadn't realized we had no instructions about what to do in the event of a coup. In Africa, of all places. I think The Gambia was considered so peaceful, no one expected it. Bruce's theory was that no one could stay awake long enough to pull off a coup d'état.

"Let's go to the Ambassador's and see what's going on there." With the fence between the houses, we couldn't just cut across the back yards. We had to go down the long Heaney driveway, pass a guard's station, and up the long driveway at the Ambassador's.

It occurred to us that we really couldn't tell the bad guys from the good guys. The Gambian guards were all huddled around the radio by the little watchman's shed at the street end of the driveway. In any event, we knew the Peace Corps would remain neutral.

"Muni kaata?" What's happening? I asked after brief greetings.

They invited us to listen to the radio with them and we again went through the revolutionary shrieking. Bruce asked if the Ambassador was home and learned that he was at the Embassy in Banjul.

Well, no guidance there. "Let's go to Tom Mosier's," Bruce suggested. Tom, the head man with USAID lived

within a block or two. Besides the Ambassador, Tom
probably was the highest ranking American in-country. He'd
know what to do. George Scharffenberger, as The Gambia's
Peace Corps Director, would have been our logical choice,
but he lived too far away for us to walk.

We'd been to the Mosier's home before. They had a
standing invitation to anyone to watch videos at their home
on Friday evenings. They had a video player, very rare in
those days, perhaps the only one in The Gambia, and
generously shared it.

As we approached the Mosier home, Tom came out, his
normally cheerful face a worried frown. I'd never seen
anyone actually wring his hands, but that's exactly what Tom
was doing. Now we were worried.

"Tom, what is it?" Bruce asked.

"We're in a lot of trouble here. The Ambassador's been
'detained' at the Embassy. The Embassy radio is out for
repair so we don't have contact with Washington. We don't
even have contact with the Ambassador."

Bruce looked surprised. "I can't imagine the
Ambassador doesn't have a radio at his house."

"Oh, he does. But it's not assembled and no one knows
how to put it together."

"Tom, I can put a damn radio together. I'm a licensed
radio operator."

Tom's eyes lit up. "Come with me, both of you."

We were led into the Ambassador's house and then into
his bedroom, a place I never thought I'd see. It was large
with a walk-in closet and a private bathroom.

The Ambassador, Larry Piper, was a HAM operator and
that radio was on a small desk. Although Bruce was a HAM
operator, that radio wouldn't have access to State
Department frequencies, so it did us no good at the time.

Among boxes in the closet, Bruce found a short range
radio, the kind of radio ships use, which could be used for
short distances; for instance, to the American and other
embassies in Banjul, and between the various high-ranking
residencies, or between agencies. It was similar to the radio
Bruce briefly used at the shop before it was destroyed.

There were probably only three or four of them in the entire country. Bruce assembled it and made quick contact with Ambassador Piper at the Embassy.

Larry Piper was relieved to hear Bruce's voice and to have communication with someone outside of Banjul now that it was sealed off. The Ambassador seemed calm and in good spirits. Just hearing his voice, it was immediately clear he was a pro.

Ambassador Piper told Bruce he'd find the medium range radio in the closet. This was the type of radio the Embassy usually had, but which was out for repairs. Although it wouldn't reach America, it was the contact used between The Gambia and Washington via Dakar, Senegal. Bruce assembled it and from that moment on, was the voice between Ambassador Piper and the U.S. Embassy in Dakar, which was then relayed to Washington, D.C.

I hurried back to the Heaney house to collect our clothes and the little food we had, lock up the house, and join the others at the Ambassador's.

People began to arrive in their cars, or by foot. One fellow even rode his horse. Both loyalists and rebels brought expatriates to the Ambassador's front gate, not wanting any civilians caught in cross-fire. Everybody needed to be off the streets. Germans, Swedes, Canadians, Indians, tourists (very few), all those who didn't have an embassy or safe place to go, came or were brought to the American Ambassador's. Most of the 80 Americans were those attached to either Peace Corps or USAID. Among the 52 in-country Peace Corps, 17 happened to be downriver and ended up at the Ambassador's.

Larry Piper's basset hound, Bonnie, a friendly dog used to guests, calmly greeted people as they arrived. She kept looking around, probably expecting her "dad."

East Indians were among the more successful businessmen in The Gambia. Their stores, mostly in Banjul, were large by local standards and efficiently run. Visibly upset when they arrived, their young English-speaking spokesman said rebels had burned their compound, stores, living quarters, everything. They escaped with little more than the clothing they wore. All of them, about a dozen people, set up in one of the bedrooms.

Why is it that revolutionaries need to burn things, even when it makes no sense? The other puzzling thing that often happens in a coup, including this one, is that they let prisoners out of jail. What were they thinking? In The Gambia no political prisoners were in jail, just criminals, some of them violent.

Rebels handed out guns to anyone who would fight, which meant many untrained people were armed. Looting in Banjul was rampant, not particularly by rebels but by unleashed tensions of Banjul's marginal society who took advantage of the confusion. So much of what was happening didn't have anything to do with government policies or the welfare of Gambians.

Soon the U.S. Embassy in Dakar radioed questions about how many Germans, Swedes, etc. we had at the residence. It became clear we needed to keep track of everyone who sought refuge at the Ambassador's. It kept me busy, getting everyone's information: names (in some cases families with children), agency, and nationality.

Soon George Scharffenberger came, with his new wife Chris, the rest of Tom's family came, his wife and four children. Many of the early arrivals settled into the Ambassador's bedroom with us. We found the Ambassador's bed could accommodate ten people, by separating the extra-large king size two top mattresses and the spring mattress, plus the bed frame itself which had a pad on a sheet of plywood. I staked out a "single" mattress, about the width of a double bed, for the two of us.

Meri Aimes arrived and gathered a few Peace Corps people to help put together a dinner. From that moment on, that group took care of meals.

Bruce found that he couldn't operate the radios with so much noise and confusion, so the bedroom was set up as a restricted area. Only Tom and Ann (their children were old enough to stay in another part of the house), George and his wife, Chris, Tony, a USAID advisor, Bruce and I, slept in that room. The noise level toned down considerably so that Bruce could manage the radios.

That first night we wondered what was in store for us. We began to hear distant shooting. By nightfall we had more than ninety people registered at the Ambassador's. It wasn't a large house. The concrete single-story structure was only about four thousand square feet, not nearly large enough to accommodate that many people.

Our world became uncertain, even unsafe. Did our families know about this?

Woman drawing water from traditional well

Chapter 24

$\mathcal{A}$ s people began stirring the next morning, reality set in. We were not in an enviable position. At first light, more people arrived, swelling our ranks at the Ambassador's residence to more than one hundred.

Many who sought shelter were with USAID since most of them lived in the Bakau area. Thankfully, our good friends Harry and Suzi were in the States getting Suzi settled in preparation for the birth of their first baby. Most expatriates didn't take the risk of having a baby in The Gambia. Harry would be returning soon to finish his tour of duty.

Soon after breakfast Tom and George called a meeting asking, everyone to attend. Good old American organization. A meeting. Just the thought of it calmed me. We would meet as a group twice a day, 8:00 a.m. and 8:00 p.m. and more if necessary. George and Tom made it clear that they would make every effort to keep us informed. We were encouraged to ask questions or express concerns. People introduced themselves and indicated the agency they represented, or why they were in The Gambia.

Bruce popped in for just a second, long enough for Tom to introduce him, and then he dashed back to his radios. Tom identified me to the group, asking anyone who had not registered with me to do so.

Meri Aimes was called upon to talk about food. A few people had brought food with them, unfortunately, very few. The food supply at the Ambassador's was better than many private homes, but, not knowing how long we would be detained, it had to be rationed. We agreed as a group that adults would have two small meals a day at 10:00 a.m. and 5:00 p.m., but that the seventeen children would eat three times a day. No one wanted to listen to whiny, hungry kids.

Water was a huge consideration. At the moment, we had running water, but as soon as the Bakau generator ran out of fuel, we would no longer have a source of electricity or water.

Dr. Tom Wochjakowski, the Polish doctor with whom I had worked in Basse, offered to take charge of the water. After the meeting he immediately filled all available containers with water and added a bit of bleach to each. He sanitized, then filled the bathtub. But that night, an American tourist drained it all because she wanted to take a hot bath. Livid, Dr. Wochjakowski ordered people to leave that water in the tub and to take brief showers in the separate shower stall.

At a meeting Dr. Wochjakowski said it probably wouldn't be long before we'd be lucky to get a bucket bath.

"A bucket bath? several asked. "What's that?"

Kevin, the fisheries volunteer who frequently came to our home, happened to be in the Banjul area for the same reason we were, for our exit physicals, and, therefore, was at the Ambassador's as well. Kevin offered to show people how to take a bucket bath. After the meeting he demonstrated and it was fascinating watching people's reaction. The majority had a look of disbelief. Kevin, in his walking shorts, made a comical show of it. Leave it to a Peace Corps volunteer to give a positive spin to our situation.

Kevin also helped keep the kids occupied with organized games. Bless him. Noisy kids grated on everyone's nerves.

Norman had returned to his home on the other side of the river before he even knew of the coup, but Nathaniel was with us. He and another fellow offered to dig latrines if we lost our water and could no longer flush toilets. George suggested they go ahead and dig them, so it wouldn't suddenly be a problem. Thus, the Ambassador's residence now had two latrines in the back yard, partitioned by plastic tarps. The majority of people shuddered at the thought of using a hole in the ground to do their business. To Peace Corps volunteers it was business as usual.

Later, in a radio conversation with the Ambassador, Bruce said, "You'll be pleased to know you now have two latrines in your back yard."

Ambassador Piper laughed. "Well, that makes me feel a lot better!"

Our group swelled to one hundred eighteen. We wondered what we would do if more arrived. Sleep in shifts, probably. The one hundred eighteen sleeping people filled every available space in the house.

Bonnie, the Ambassador's basset hound, grew weary of greeting people and hung out on her pillow in the kitchen, expressing her concern at not seeing her "dad" with long sighs and droopy, sad eyes.

People staked out their spots and, for the most part, the crowded conditions were tolerated quite well. Thankful that we could use the Ambassador's bedroom, our nights were peaceful with only seven to share the space. Bruce operated the radio for eighteen hours a day, so by the time he finished for the day, he only had six hours sleep. He needed peace and quiet.

Ann Saar's husband, Mohammed and their four daughters were among our later arrivals. Ann had gone to the U.S. to take a sick volunteer home. Mohammed had at first planned to stay home with his daughters, but decided to join us for his family's safety.

In the main part of the house, Radio Gambia was on much of the time and Mohammed interpreted announcements differently than we, noting subtle inferences that we didn't pick up. We learned that the rebels had timed the coup to coincide with the royal wedding of Prince Charles and Diana. Since The Gambia had been a British colony, there were still strong affiliations between the countries, and The Gambia's President, Sir Dawda Jawara, was in England to attend the event.

We also learned that one of President Jawara's wives, Lady Chilel (after whom the river boat was named), seven of their children, and Mrs. Jawara's father, were being held hostage at a compound in Bakau.

I was so proud of the various roles Peace Corps played at the Ambassador's: George co-chairing the responsibility of the international group with Tom, Meri in charge of the kitchen, Bruce at the radio, I was in charge of registration. Kevin helped with the kids, Nathaniel and Kevin dug latrines—we all played significant roles.

USAID took responsibility for keeping watch. At all times two people stood watch at the bottom of the driveway to keep an eye out on the street, literally running up the long driveway to the house with any significant news. Watches around the house and yard were conducted night and day.

Soon after Bruce established radio contact, they implemented pre-arranged code names, not knowing who else might be listening. The Ambassador's house was "Candyland," The Embassy "Sugarland," the United States Embassy in Dakar "Lollypop," British Commissioner's residence "Sugarshop." The Ambassador's personal handle was "Gumdrop."

Meeting regularly, having a voice in the decisions, and knowing others were aware of our position helped our peace of mind. But that peace shattered every time we heard a round of firing or artillery. One of the USAID fellows, Tony, had served in Viet Nam and he spent much of the daytime hours with us. I considered him a valuable asset because he knew war strategies and could describe various weapons we heard, taking the mystery out of it.

Each day we covered the bedroom windows with mattresses from the beds for protection against flying glass. Occasionally, I would stand on a stool in our headquarters and look out through a small space where the mattress didn't cover the window. At one point I saw three ships on the horizon. Tony thought they were a navy escort and two PT boats, but he couldn't be sure. We assumed they were from Senegal as The Gambia had no navy.

For a while both power and water were shut off, which caused some anxious moments. After about forty-five minutes, both services resumed. Occasionally one or the other went out; the longest period without power was fourteen hours.

Once, around noon, everything turned quiet. "I wonder what's happening?" I said.

"They've stopped to eat lunch," Tony guessed. Sure enough, we found out through an informant at the front gate that the loyalists had gone to one of the tourist hotels for lunch; the rebels had gone to another. It was like when as kids used to play tag: "Time out! Mom's calling me for lunch!"

We took advantage of their lunch hour by stepping outside for fresh air and to mingle with other people. Kevin organized a rough, rowdy game for the kids to play outside so they could blow off steam. That Kevin, what a gem.

Not Bruce, of course, he simply didn't leave the radios. When he had to relieve himself, George took over for those two or three minutes, then gladly turned it over to Bruce when he returned.

Radio traffic at times was frantic. Bruce manned both radios, talking to the British High Commissioner and U.S. Embassy in Banjul on the short-range radio, while relaying messages and questions on the medium-range radio between Ambassador Piper at the American Embassy in Banjul and the Embassy in Dakar, which were then relayed to Washington, D.C. Many of the questions had to do with locating people, Americans, German, Swedish, and others who were known to be in The Gambia.

At this point, the rebels had taken over the public radio station and the airport, and had detained people at various

Embassies. Close combat spread from the capital city Banjul area and now seemed to be concentrated right where we were, in Bakau.

We were told via the radio operator in Dakar that Washington wanted to pinpoint exactly where we were. It's always important for them to keep tabs on Americans abroad when things were going badly. They also needed to know where the fighting was at the moment.

Bruce answered Dakar on the radio, describing where we were. Word came back that Washington verified we were about a block away from the Fajara Hotel.

"No," Bruce said, "it's probably closer to a mile."

"According to the map Washington has, the Ambassador's is just down the street."

"I don't know what map they're using," Bruce responded, "but that is NOT accurate."

Come to find out, they were using a tourist map, intended to draw interest to hotels and points of interest by huge symbols. Washington apparently didn't have a regular map of The Gambia. We found it disconcerting that the U.S. State Department was using tourist maps to evaluate emergencies for American citizens.

Armed skirmishes crept closer and we took cover under tables. Bruce left the radio on the desk, but brought the medium-range mic underneath with him. The house shuddered under a nearby explosion. We all held our breath. We heard a muffled "Candyland, Candyland, Lollypop. Come in. You guys okay? Come in! Over." Then, again.

It became quiet enough for Bruce to be heard. "Lollypop, Candyland."

"Candyland, don't let that long a time go by again. We need to know how you are every minute. Do you read me? What's happening? Over."

"Lollypop, Candyland. We read you. We're all under tables or whatever. The fighting is close. We'll reply when we can. Over."

Another loud explosion shook the house. Bruce left the mic on and talked, but knew he wouldn't be heard.

The British High Commissioner called on the short distance radio. "Candyland, Sugarshop. That was a close one, wasn't it?" His very proper British clip echoed, telling us he was under a table, too.

Bruce chuckled and reached up to retrieve the short-range radio mic. "Sugarshop, Candyland. Yes, sir, it was. Too close. It must have landed somewhere between us."

Among the USAID married couples, one spouse had stayed at the High Commissioner's while the other was with us. They had been caught in a similar position as we, but just ran out of time to make it that extra mile to be together. I was so thankful I'd managed to get back to Bruce.

One day it was absolutely quiet and we became restless. Meri reported a low food supply. Although we had orders from both sides not to leave the residence, we made a plan.

Since there was never fighting at night, a team of men drove a Land Cruiser in the dark of night, using no headlights, to the Martin's, a Mormon family of six who were with us at the Ambassador's but lived nearby. Typical of Mormons they had two years' food supply on shelves and in their freezer. The men formed a human chain, passing food from the house to the vehicle. They returned triumphant and we again were in good supply, though not knowing how much longer the coup would go on, we continued with our two small meals a day for adults, three for children.

Interestingly, Ambassador Piper asked that next day, "How are you doing on the food supply there? It must be getting pretty slim."

Bruce told him what they'd done.

"It's a good thing I didn't know that. I would never have given permission for you guys to take that kind of chance."

Just another case of knowing that, "It's easier to ask forgiveness than it is to get permission."

Water usually continued to be available, though we voluntarily reduced our usage. Since the majority of fighting now seemed to be taking place in Bakau, we figured special effort was being made to keep that generator operating.

The English-speaking spokesman for the East Indians announced at our morning meeting that they would like to be responsible for that evening's dinner. Among the few things they had grabbed as rebels forced them from their compound were some of their special spices. What a dinner! Although our portions were small, the zesty flavor of that dinner lingered for days. The Indians insisted on doing it all: the preparation, the cooking, serving, clean-up. I thought it was wonderful of them to share what little they had with us. They dismissed that praise, however, and said we were the ones to be thanked, for sharing with them.

Two days went by with little fighting. Why were we just sitting here? The silence somehow seemed more nerve-wracking than the fighting. At one of our meetings we discussed simply leaving. Why not? We could slip into Senegal, thirty miles away, by driving south along the beach at low tide under cover of darkness.

Leaving was the main topic of discussion at our twice-daily meetings. An evacuation committee was formed.

Many cars were parked around the compound. Men siphoned gas from smaller vehicles into the larger ones with four-wheel drive, bringing the larger vehicles in position to leave. This brought up more complicated problems. Who would leave; who would stay? Bruce felt he had to stay to operate the radio. If he stayed, I stayed, I claimed, but he looked doubtful. Many families were faced with this decision. Those with children felt the greater need to get their families to safety. Men with government responsibilities felt obligated to stay. Wives, especially those without children, didn't want to leave without their husbands.

That evening, with Tom and George sitting with him at the radio, Bruce told Ambassador Piper our plans.

The Ambassador listened to all that Bruce had to say. In a somber tone Ambassador Piper said, "Wait until you hear from me before taking any action on this."

In a very short while the Ambassador radioed back. "None of you are to leave. You will all remain at the residence. This is a direct order. Is that clear?"

"Yes sir. That is clear." We looked at one another in dread.

We were shocked. For me, it was the worst moment of the entire coup. I wondered if we might actually be hostages. The Iranian hostage situation was still fresh in our minds. Just that past January, after 444 days, 52 U.S. citizens who had been held hostage in Iran were released. Were we hostages but just didn't know it? Would the Ambassador keep that information from us, possibly to avoid panic? Not having a choice to leave was to be a prisoner.

Mosalif and Binta's children, Jariettu and Kujah

Chapter 25

*O*n the morning of day seven, we had just been served our small portions of oatmeal in the radio room when BOOM! BOOM! BOOM!

It was deafening and so close, I couldn't believe the house wasn't demolished. We all hit the deck, scrambling under whatever protection we could find. Meri Ames had brought our oatmeal to us and she and I happened to dive under the same table.

We heard bullets whizz by through trees. People shouted. The war was close and upon us. I had never known such fear.

A little earlier in the day, Bruce had received a message from Washington but had not yet had an opportunity to deliver it to our leader, Tom Mosier. During all the noise and confusion, he passed the note to Tom.

"Folks," Tom said. "Here's a nice note from Secretary of State Alexander Haig." He read, shouting to be heard, as crashing, zinging, window rattling explosions happened around us.

I am personally following your situation and am acutely aware of your difficulties. I send my sincere congratulations to you and your staff on your handling of the situation. Our first priority and concern is American citizens in The Gambia.

The note was just what we needed to break the tension. We laughed like fools until tears came to our eyes. Oh, good! Al Haig will save us! He'll follow his tourist map and come to our rescue.

Once things calmed down, I took advantage of sharing the underside of a table with Meri to express my concern about getting back to our village. Although we had agreed to tell no one about our money stash, I felt it right to share it with Meri now. Who knew what was in store for us? Our situation could drastically change at any moment.

Although wide-eyed at my news about our stash of $2,500 in our chicken coop, Meri felt that even though we no doubt would not be returning to our village any time soon, if at all, both she and George would remain in-country for a while, at least. She asked for a map showing exactly where we'd buried the money.

The day dragged on. Some of us took advantage of the warriors' lunch break to venture outside for fresh air.

We soon had to retreat under tables again. Each time a rebel or loyalist inspector entered the Ambassador's house, I was terrified that one of them would say we were hostages, but, although they often looked sinister, they actually never threatened us.

Both sides, however, firmly instructed that we not make radio contact with anyone. It wasn't clear if they knew we were and just chose to ignore it, or if they really didn't know we were in touch with the Embassy in Banjul and with Washington via Dakar. In any event, every time we were warned by our sentries that we were about to be visited, Bruce dismantled the radios and stashed them under his desk, then he either lay in front of them or placed the chair on which he sat in front of them.

The day slogged along with frequent bursts of mortar and small arms fire, often sounding very close.

Sleep that night came in spurts, even though there was no fighting, only occasional loud voices.

Early morning on the eighth day, we heard helicopters approaching, the whump, whump coming from the beach. I stood on a stool at the window and peaked over the mattress through the small space of unprotected glass that allowed me to see outside. I couldn't believe my eyes! Emerging from the helicopter and climbing up the hill toward us was a column of African soldiers dressed in camouflage fatigues, all heavily armed with every kind of weapon imaginable. As they came up to the house, they surrounded it and began setting up various guns on short tripods.

I relayed everything I saw to the others in the radio room. As the soldiers surrounded the house, I felt panic. Oh, God, now what? What's happening? Tony, our military expert asked me whether the soldiers were facing the house, or facing away.

"Away from the house."

Tony nodded. "Well, then, they're protecting us."

Wonderful! We let out a collective sigh.

With the group were two white men in street clothes, men we later learned were British SAS (Special Air Service), sent by Her Majesty Queen Elizabeth to liberate the President's wife and children. The African soldiers were Senegalese commandoes. They certainly seemed to know what they were doing. We felt like celebrating. What a relief!

The two SAS men, looking like the James Bond character 007, carried guns at their waist, under their arms, on their legs. Efficient and very British, they entered the house, asked to use the radio and accepted a drink of water, "If you can spare it." Their clothes were sweat soaked after climbing the hill on this hot day, plus being weighed down with all that hardware.

They used the radio to call the British High Commissioner which happened to be between us and the Field Force Headquarters where the President's family was being held.

The man who spoke on the radio, who appeared to be of higher rank, turned to us. "Just stay low now. You'll hear a lot of firing soon. We're here to free President Jawara's family." He nodded. "You've done a splendid job here. Good luck."

Then they were gone.

Just as they set out to do, within a few hours after a lot of noise and gunfire, the President's family was released.

Everything quieted down then. The coup appeared to be over. We later learned that we had been in rebel controlled territory for a full week. The Ambassador's residence did not sustain any hits; not a bullet hole could be found. Both rebels and nationalists kept their word to keep us safe.

Ambassador Piper called on the radio and asked how things were. We learned that when Bruce announced to him our plans to leave, he couldn't divulge what he'd learned from his contacts with the Senegalese military, already in The Gambia. A big offensive was planned for the morning we had planned to evacuate. He wanted us all to be safe and out of the way. Not knowing who might be aware of our radio contacts, he couldn't warn us over the air.

The Ambassador apologized to Bruce. "After all that you've done, I hated to give you an order like that, but I had no choice."

We learned that at the beginning of the coup, President Jawara, while still in England, called upon neighboring Senegal to assist in quelling the rebellion under the terms of a defense agreement between the two countries. Within days the Senegalese armed forces had recaptured the airport and had moved into the capital city to restore order.

We could relax, even wander around the back yard for fresh air and exercise.

Later, in the early evening, Meri Aimes approached me. "Do you know if there is cinnamon at the Heaney house?"

"If the Irish use cinnamon, it would be there. I saw lots of spices."

Meri wanted to make a special treat, cinnamon rolls, to celebrate our "liberation."

"Okay, I'll ask one of the soldiers if we can leave for a few minutes and go into the Heaney house."

Although the situation was not officially over, we felt more relaxed than we had in days. In fact, I hadn't realized how tense I'd been until now. I didn't mention my plan to go to Heaney's to Bruce. Radio traffic was crazy with health and welfare messages going back and forth. Sometimes he had both radios going at once. In any event, I knew he wouldn't approve. I didn't want to worry him.

Meri and I ventured out into the back yard together. I approached a soldier to ask permission to go next door before I remembered they were Senegalese. I spoke neither French nor Wolof. I turned back to find someone who could interpret for me. Then, I heard a surprising voice.

"What can I do for you, ma'am?" The soldier spoke in a perfect southern drawl.

"Where are you from? I asked.

"Senegal, but I got my special training at Fort Benning, Georgia. That's where I learned English."

I explained my "need" to get something from the house next door. As a sergeant and in charge of operations at the moment, he hesitated. "Do you have to do it now? It's almost dark."

I knew Meri, who hovered just behind me, had her heart set on making the cinnamon rolls that evening so they could rise during the night and she could serve them at breakfast. And I knew this tough commando wouldn't appreciate the importance of cinnamon rolls. My only chance, I figured, was to make it seem like something personal, a feminine urgency perhaps. "Yes, I really do need to get it tonight," I said, with a tinge of anxiety in my voice.

He used his hand-held radio and spoke in Wolof. Two soldiers trotted over to where we stood. One of them signaled us to follow them. I had supposed we would use the driveways, but apparently they felt the streets were not yet safe. Armed with machine guns, our little group looked as though we were going on a pretty serious mission. I didn't even dare look at Meri.

We set off to the property line. They radioed ahead. We four climbed over the wire fence as one of the soldiers held it down. We made our way through brush, then climbed under a second fence while the soldier held it up for us. We arrived at the back door of the house and one of the soldiers called his check point on the radio. I produced the key to the house which one of the soldiers took and unlocked and opened the door. He signaled us to wait while he did a quick house surveillance. The other soldier stood with us, machine gun at the ready. The first soldier returned, nodded, and they posted themselves at the door and signaled us to go ahead.

We felt really silly going into the kitchen pantry and getting a can of cinnamon, the small size at that. We put the spice in an over-sized paper bag to increase its significance and went back outside to do the whole procedure in reverse.

When we returned, both George Scharffenberger and Bruce were waiting, neither pleased nor impressed with "our mission." But the cinnamon rolls were a big hit the next morning.

Bruce remained busy at the radios. Now much of the radio traffic was inquiries of families abroad seeking word about those who took refuge at the Ambassador's. My lists came in handy as Bruce could refer to them and verify whether specific people were with us.

Bruce then set up the Ambassador's Ham radio and, through the kindness of other Ham operators in the States, patched phone calls through to the U.S. for people so they could call home. We were up until late at night with this project.

Finally, the attempted coup was officially put down. But the mess remained and many people still carried guns, including the "freed" prisoners. The country was still considered unsafe for expatriates. The only expatriates to remain would be those who held key positions. As Meri had predicted, both she and George would remain but all other Peace Corps volunteers who had been with us at the Ambassador's were to be evacuated.

The Ambassador was able to return to his home the next morning, the ninth day after the coup began. What normally would have taken a half hour from Banjul to Bakau took nearly three hours by the time he went through the various check points. Upon entering the house, the first thing he asked was, "Where's Bonnie?"

The touching reunion between the Ambassador and his basset hound brought tears to my eyes. What devotion they had!

We left soon after Ambassador Piper reclaimed his house. We formed a caravan to the airport, protected by armored personnel carriers. It saddened us to see Gambians lining the streets, waving to us. On the way we saw many gutted and damaged buildings.

Tom Mosier's house had several gaping holes. That morning, the family had briefly returned home to pick up clothes. Their teenage daughter found clothes hanging in her closet severed at the waist from machine gun fire.

Ann Saar's housekeeper lost an eye from flying glass. Their house had serious damage and Mohammed's car was a burned shell. It was a good thing Mohammed and their daughters had stayed with us.

We didn't drive through Banjul, but we understood that fires had raged, destroying an entire block, plus other isolated buildings. The airport was a mess with bombed out brick walls but the lone runway was undamaged.

For a relatively small coup, the death toll was high, about 1,000, we were told. In that heat, disposing of the bodies proved to be an astronomical task. Bodies had been dumped at the morgue and had to be removed with a front-loader. Other bodies were stacked in the market place of a neighboring village near the Ambassador's. Doctors worked around the clock to attend the many injuries sustained.

The Military Airlift Command Group sent a C-130 troop transport from Germany and another from the U.S. to fly all expatriates to Dakar, Senegal. To board, we walked up a ramp designed to load vehicles. Inside the cavernous plane, we sat in webbed seats along the sides, facing inward. Before takeoff, a military official asked us not to discuss our experience with anyone who might ask, such as newspaper reporters. We were not to become involved or express an opinion of the incident.

Landing at the Dakar airport and walking across the tarmac, we saw a familiar face walking toward us–Harry. He had been returning to The Gambia after getting Suzi situated, but then couldn't get back into the country because of the coup.

Harry gave us a warm welcome and made a dinner date with us, saying he'd pick us up at our hotel.

As a consideration of our ordeal, Peace Corps treated us to three days in a hotel, two to a room, to rest and relax. We also received walk-around money for meals and to replace items left behind.

At the very nice hotel, I was so keyed up, I couldn't lie down. We had so few clothes with us, which had been the case all week at the Ambassador's, that I decided to hand wash some items. Calmed by that domestic chore, I lay down with Bruce and took a long, welcomed nap. We marveled at the stillness of the room, at the coolness of air conditioning, at the lack of threats.

Harry treated us to dinner. It was so comforting seeing our good friend. He surprised us by becoming very serious. "I need to talk to you guys about something. Are you familiar with post traumatic stress disorder? Sometimes it's called PTSD. In World War II they called it 'shell shock'. Anyway, you guys need to know about it."

We scoffed. "Harry," Bruce chuckled, "we haven't been through anything that serious."

"I don't agree. What you guys went through was significant. I've talked to Tom Mosier. I want you to listen to what I have to say."

Harry explained that we would likely experience traumatic dreams, or at least interrupted sleep, feelings of disorientation, changes in appetite, maybe depression. By the end of dinner and a glass of wine, we could barely keep our eyes open. Harry took us back to the hotel and we dropped into bed, exhausted.

I awoke, startled. Bruce was already awake. "What is it?" I whispered.

"I don't know. I just feel uneasy."

"Me, too."

"I'm hungry," Bruce said. "Could you eat?"

"Sure. Let's go."

We quickly dressed and made our way to a nearby restaurant, apparently open all night since we were fairly close to the airport. At the buffet, we each selected a pastry. Bruce picked up juice and I got a demitasse coffee. It seemed so good to have all we wanted to eat among these safe, quiet surroundings. Lynn, the musicologist from our group, walked in and grinned at us and sat at the table. "I'm so glad you're here," she said. "I was feeling uneasy." We shared with her what Harry had told us.

Satisfied, we returned to our room, but I awoke with a screaming nightmare. Bruce immediately calmed me.

"I'm glad Harry warned us," I said. "Otherwise, I'd think I was going bonkers."

Within the next day or so, we felt perfectly normal. Three days at the hotel and Peace Corps "pulled the plug," as Bruce said. We Peace Corps volunteers were all transported to the University of Dakar where we stayed in a dorm.

Far from luxurious, the dorms were two-story structures, no glass or screens on the windows, nothing but concrete walls, ceilings and floors. The single beds consisted of metal legs and frame with a foam mattress on springs. Some beds had mosquito netting; ours did not. The mosquitoes were a problem until we bought some mosquito coils, repelling incense. Not to be used indoors, we felt the coils safe with the open windows. It seemed to keep the mosquitoes at bay but we could hear their persistent high-pitched whining.

The dorm was quite satisfactory, however, and certainly more typical of Peace Corps accommodations. Our instructions were to stay there until we received further notice from George, but we were free to move about during the day.

We marveled that two years ago we had found Dakar threatening. It now seemed lovely. A few people approached us with something to sell, but we just waved them away and went about our business.

One day we boarded a passenger ferry for a thirty minute ride to Gorée, an island just off Dakar that serves as a memorial to those lost to the slave trade. It was a sobering sight. I can't imagine the terror those people felt being brutally taken from their homeland.

Another day we visited the outdoor silver market and marveled at the long tables laden with silver in every form possible: jewelry, dishes, candlesticks. We bought a necklace for Bruce's mother and a set of earrings for me.

We managed to keep ourselves occupied for the two weeks we were in Dakar, even if it was just reading outside on a bench. Word came via a member of Senegal Peace Corp staff that we were to be ready to leave in a van the next morning. We would enter The Gambia mid-country so that we could avoid the still unsafe Banjul area.

Volunteers formerly assigned to jobs in Banjul were temporarily reassigned to mid- or upper river-divisions until things calmed down. Those of us who were scheduled to leave in ninety days or less would be permitted to leave whenever we could get our affairs in order.

A Senegalese Peace Corps driver picked us up and we made the short trip, crossing the river at Jenoi. He dropped people off at their villages.

I couldn't wait to tell our Gambian friends where we'd been all this time. After all, we had been gone more than three weeks.

Binta and Mosalif greeted us as we opened the gate to the compound. Tombomg arrived within minutes. We greeted one another and then I began to tell them our story."Mariama, we all know where you've been," Tombong said. " At the American Ambassador's. We knew you and Mistah Bruce were safe. Then you went to Senegal."

That took the wind out of my sail. You can't keep anything from these people. Those darn drums. Even Alieu, when he stopped by after school, knew where we'd been.

Binta mimed that we looked thin and she fixed our first meal home. It was so good to see our own place and feel safe among our friends. When we discreetly could, we found our stash of money, intact, in the chicken coop.

Women selling groundnut paste (peanut butter) at market

Chapter 26

Seeing our places of work was a sobering sight. Although people had been safe, both the UN shop and the Health Centre were missing essential vehicles which had been confiscated at the beginning of the coup. We knew many vehicles were ruined, because we'd seen abandoned wrecks along roads. Having no vehicles would put a serious halt on project activity. At the hospital, there was no Land Rover to go to outlying villages or even to use as an ambulance.

Both of us could see that we might as well return to the U.S. a bit earlier than we had planned. We set a date to leave within two weeks. Amazingly, phone service from the hospital worked and I called Peace Corps and talked to Meri Aimes, telling her our plan and receiving her official permission to close down our positions.

A couple of months earlier, about the time we exchanged our money, I had announced to the Health Centre staff that we would be selling many household items when we left. Although Peace Corps had tried to obtain a volunteer to replace Bruce, one had not been found. The UN house and hut we occupied would soon be vacant.

Several of the nurses showed an interest in our goods and had come to our home to claim items with the agreement we would use them until we left.

We purposelessly didn't mention our actual departure date to our friends and work associates. We just didn't want a big fanfare or parties. For one thing, the local people were already under a financial strain with uncertainties caused by the coup.

As for our Peace Corps friends, we had a quiet get-together at Jobot's All Necessary Foods and topped it off at Pa Peacock's White House Fuladu East Bar

I mentioned our departure to Doctor Ceesay and he wanted to have a party, but I told him I preferred not to. We had a satisfying, long talk about our Gambian experience. I was able to thank him for all he had done for me; and he acknowledged how much I had contributed to the Health Centre. It was a wonderful farewell and I felt very gratified.

After talking with Doctor Ceesay, I went to the market one last time. Spotting my favorite peanut-butter lady, I stepped behind a post a distance away and watched as she waited on another customer. Then, as we had done so many times, she looked around, feeling my eyes and knowing I was there. I popped out, and we laughed. I bought three balls of peanut-butter, knowing we couldn't use it all, but I could give what remained to Binta. I gave her five dalasi, more than four dalasi too much. She glanced around, looking for someone who might have change.

I wrapped my hands around her small ones, "No, no change is necessary. This is for you, my good friend. M'bita. I am going."

"Going? But you'll be back." Tears sprang to her eyes. She knew my answer.

"No. We will go to our home in the United States now." Tearfully, I thanked her for her good service, for her generosity, for the great laughs we'd had.

She called out to the other vendors. "Mariama Manneh is leaving!" and there was a chorus of farewells. I waved to them all, tears streaming down my face.

Mr. Lopi returned home several days after we did and we told him we were leaving, but it was only three days before we were to leave. He apologized, saying if he'd known he would have given us a party, but we assured him we wanted it this way.

Alieu's mother came to our home for the first time, with a tiny baby on her back and carrying a live chicken in the crook of her arm. She thanked us for our kindness to Alieu, her oldest child, and gave me the chicken. I knew this family had very limited funds, and I gently returned the chicken to her, thanking her, and telling her that we would be returning to the United States in an airplane and that we couldn't carry a chicken. She probably couldn't even imagine, but nodded. I prepared tea and served it with lots of sugar, as Gambians like it.

The transition was easy in terms of our household goods. Sister Ruth somehow came up with a car and driver and offered to deliver items to various people. She herself bought our stove and butane tanks. The stove, the size of a camping stove, fit easily in the back seat of the car. We gave her the little table the stove had sat on. She was the perfect one to use it because she was quite progressive and would be a good example to the others. Wood and charcoal were becoming scarce, plus cooking with butane would save so much time.

Another nurse bought our small refrigerator, which fit into the trunk of Ruth's car. Mara wanted one of our beds and a nurse wanted the other two. The beds were delivered to their new owners via donkey cart from Mara's compound.

A Peace Corps married couple bought the table and chairs we'd had in the hut, and we gave them some bowls, our meat grinder and my old rickety typewriter.

We gave many things to Binta and Mosalif: our chickens, our sheets, my favorite chair, containers, canned food. We gave Tombong tools, two padlocks, the machete and a nice enamel bowl for his wife.

The day of departure came and I had dread in my heart. We lined up our luggage and backpacks by the road, awaiting the Peace Corp driver who had arrived the night before and stayed with friends. Tombong, Binta, Mosalif and the girls came over to say good-bye. We all had tears in our eyes. I thought my heart would break. I wanted to go home and see my own family, but saying good-bye to these people was even harder than I had imagined. I knew we had made a difference in their lives, but I also knew that my life was forever enriched because of them. They would forever remain in my heart.

* * *

Nathaniel and Norman had closed down our jointly-rented apartment since they were also leaving. They had sold the few items we'd bought and gave us half the money.

George invited us to stay at his home in Bakau since only authorized personnel were allowed in Banjul. Ann Saar had returned to The Gambia and she and her family were living at the Heaney house until they could repair their damaged home. She stopped by George's to settle up our cash and check exchange, and buy our radio. We gave her our cassettes which thrilled her since very little American music could be bought in The Gambia.

United States bound flights left Dakar only twice a week, so we timed our departure for the Monday flight out. On Sunday, George arranged a ride for us to a hotel in Dakar.

As it happened, we stayed at the same hotel where we initially began our African experience. What a difference in our outlook!

On our way to catch a taxi early Monday morning, I gave a bundle of my African clothes to a blind woman I had seen whose begging spot was always by a certain store. I greeted her and placed the package by her and said it was from me, a Peace Corps volunteer, and that we were going home. I spoke in Mandinka and she understood and thanked us, wishing us well.

At the airport we were faced with the same inefficiency we'd encountered for two years. Airlines shared counter space and we were so early Pan American still hadn't displayed their "shingle."

Crowds of people milled around. We happened to be the only Peace Corps people leaving that day. Our luggage of two trunks, a backpack and a smaller day pack, took a fair amount of space. We piled it together and one of us always stayed with it.

Once Pan American hung their shingle, the crowd surged. As planned, I stayed back with the luggage and Bruce fought to get to the counter. To miss this plane would mean to stay in Dakar until Thursday to get the next flight out. That would be expensive and besides, we really wanted to get home.

Bruce came back, triumphant, but with only boarding passes, not seat assignments. The airline's procedure was to issue more boarding passes than there were seats on the plane. The procedure was first come, first served. It was sort of like musical chairs. When the seats on the plane filled up, those not sitting were told to leave the plane and they would have priority on the next flight.

At another counter, we checked in our trunks. We could then move about more easily.

We still had a long wait, nearly two hours. While Bruce stayed with our carry-on luggage, I scoped out the boarding area and made a great discovery. On this late August flight about twenty American school children waited, accompanied by a Pan American escort. Most of these kids would be seasoned travelers. Hardly any expatriate children went to school in either The Gambia or Senegal. These kids had probably been with their parents for summer vacation and were now returning to U.S. boarding schools.

I hung around while the escort instructed the children. "When we receive the signal, I want you to fall quietly in line behind me. Walk two by two. I'll stand by the airplane stairs until you're all on board. The flight attendant will tell you where to sit. Go straight to your seats and stay there."

I beat it back to Bruce and explained the routine. We gathered our backpacks and sat as close to those children as possible.

Sure enough, at the signal the escort indicated to the children to follow her. We gave the group a small space, then followed along behind. The children were the first to board; we were next.

Aboard, we grabbed the first seats available. The plane filled quickly. I noticed a family of three tubobs, parents and what looked like a two-year old girl. They sat three abreast. A flight attendant asked to see their tickets. They produced two. "You'll have to hold that child. You only have two tickets."

The woman loudly complained. "Hold her! For the whole ten hours?"

The flight attendant nodded. "If you didn't want to do that, you should have bought a ticket for her."

What were those parents thinking? I'm sure that was a long flight for them, holding a wiggly two-year old.

The 747 had two aisles with seats three-abreast on the sides and rows of five seats in the middle. People circulated, searching for seats. Soon, the announcement came over the loud-speaker. "Will all those who do not have seats, please leave the plane."

We were so thankful to have gotten seats. I didn't breathe easily until we actually took off. The flight seemed even longer going home than coming, we were so anxious to see our families.

Upon arrival in New York, we had a three hour wait for the flight to Seattle. We enjoyed a quiet American meal of hamburgers and French fries with milkshakes. What a treat! We marveled at the airport restaurant's clean, smooth, orange plastic tables and chairs. Such a treat compared to gritty concrete or sticky tables we encountered in The Gambia. Despite the crowds of people, the airport was so quiet—no shouting!

While walking around the airport, we were amazed at the out-of-shape and overweight Americans we encountered. What a difference between what we were seeing and the fit Gambians we were used to. It seemed everyone was in a hurry—we weren't used to the fast pace.

Another long flight to Seattle and we'd done it. My dream of going to Africa had been fulfilled. For the rest of our lives we would carry the rich memories of Africa. We would marvel at large supermarkets stocked with goods unimaginable in The Gambia. When we saw fat cows in lush pastures, we remembered the skin-and-bones of the scrawny long-horned cattle in Africa. We continue to use many of the Mandinka expressions in our day-to-day conversations. On hot days, we compare our discomfort with that of the heat of Africa.

Everything looks different after Africa.

We are indebted to the Peace Corps for giving us the opportunity to experience life in a third-world country. Established by President Kennedy in 1961, the Peace Corps has made a significant difference in 139 countries and in so doing, has changed the way those who served view the world.

There is no doubt that we made a contribution to our host country. However, in our hearts we know that *we* reaped the benefits of the experience. We were the recipients of kindness and friendships, and sometimes a little more excitement than we bargained for, that few have experienced. We've been asked if we would do it again. No. But we'll never regret the time we spent as Peace Corps volunteers in The Gambia. For us, it was an experience of a lifetime.

Foo watido, mteerimaalu. Abaraka. Farewell, my friends. Thank you.

Sun setting behind our hut in Mansajang

Epilog

Soon after arriving home, Bruce received a Special Achievement Award recommended by Ambassador Larry G. Piper. In the accompanying letter, Ambassador Piper said, in part, "I would like to add my personal thanks to both you and Mary for what you did in maintaining the high morale at the Residence during the difficult period."

The Special Achievement Award to Bruce stated

In appreciation and recognition of your Superior Achievement, Leadership, and Courage in providing for the safety of over 120 persons during the rebellion in The Gambia.

It is the practice of Peace Corps to furnish letters of recommendation to help pave the way for Peace Corps Volunteers in their endeavors after service. George

Scharffenberger's letter included these words of praise of Bruce:

>...During the recent coup attempt in The Gambia, Bruce found himself at the residence of the U.S. Ambassador. Using his radio operation skills he maintained a direct link between the U.S. Embassy in Banjul and that in Dakar. He himself manned the radio for up to 18 hours a day for eight consecutive days. Throughout he remained calm and professional. His actions contributed directly to the safe release of the 118 foreigners seeking refuge at the Ambassador's residence. His courage and humor, even with firing going on around the Residence compound, won him the deep respect and admiration of all those present.

Bruce resumed his vocation working in the marine electronics industry.

As planned, I began my college career, graduating with an associate degree in computer science. Afterward I worked for a large insurance company at their corporate headquarters in Seattle as a programmer analyst.

Ten years after our Peace Corps experience, we followed Bruce's dream of sailing throughout the South Pacific. But that's another story....

Other Books by Mary E. Trimble

Tenderfoot

A romantic suspense novel, *Tenderfoot* takes place on a working cattle ranch in 1980, the year the world remembers for the catastrophic eruption of Mount St. Helens. The story is fiction though incidents relating to the mountain are true and accurately portrayed. *Tenderfoot* won a Silver Spur (Finalist) with Western Writers of America, Best Western Long Novel category. Available in print and e-book formats.

—"A page turner and a delight." Jane Kirkpatrick, Award-winning author of *Where Lilacs Bloom*

McClellan's Bluff

Leslie Cahill, 17, falls in love with a 28 year-old cowboy. Flattered by the attention of this "older" man, she's swept along by her strong emotions, but danger lurks. Follow Leslie's rise to womanhood in this suspenseful story set in the Northwest high desert country. A sequel to *Rosemount, McClellan's Bluff* was the recipient of the EPIC Award, Best Young Adult novel. Available in print and e-book formats.

—"An impressive example of the complications of teen years...very highly recommended." Cindy Penn, Word Weaving

Rosemount

Sixteen year-old Leslie Cahill learns the hard way how tough life can be when on her own. Modern ranch scenes, wilderness adventures and family dynamics make *Rosemount* a memorable coming-of-age tale. Available in print and e-book formats.

—"The characters are as varied as the route Leslie follows on her trek for independence – old, young, generous, selfish, nurturing, threatening." Gloria MacKay, author of *Chalk Dustings.*

About the Author

Award-winning author Mary E. Trimble was born into a camping family and went on her first camping trip when only two-weeks old.

The mother of four grown children, all living in the Northwest, Mary loves family get-togethers. Camping with her husband Bruce is also high on her list of favorite activities. Nowadays they travel with a truck and camper, seeking out-of-the-way places to explore.

Married for only a year before they embarked on their African adventure with the Peace Corps, Mary and Bruce found their greatest joy was experiencing new adventures together. When asked if they would do it again, the answer is, "No, but we're so glad we took the opportunity to have the African experience and to fulfill this lifelong dream."

When they sailed the South Pacific, Bruce and Mary rejoiced in being together—days on end! But being at sea with only two people on a 40-foot sailboat means a strict watch system of four hours on duty, four hours off. That means during passages someone is on deck at all times. After their longest passage of 35 days, they had the routine down pat, but were glad to reach landfall. There again, they rejoiced in the experience of being on their own. While in the South Pacific they often anchored off various islands for weeks, including Nuku Hiva, Tahiti, Bora Bora, Samoa and The Kingdom of Tonga.

Mary's other experiences include serving as purser and ship's diver aboard the tall ship Explorer, and as Admissions Director for a professional deep-sea diving school. After obtaining a degree in Computer Science, Mary worked at a large insurance company as computer programmer/analyst.

As an author, in addition to writing four books, she's had more than 400 articles published in magazines and newspapers on subjects that include travel and items of interest to homeowners.

Mary and Bruce live on Camano Island, Washington.
Visit Mary's website: *www.MaryTrimbleBooks.com*